❧ Personalist Papers

Personalist Papers
John F. Crosby

The Catholic University of America Press
Washington, D.C.

Copyright © 2004
The Catholic University of America Press
All rights reserved

LIBRARY OF CONGRESS CATALOGING-IN-PUBLICATION DATA

Crosby, John F.

   Personalist papers / John F. Crosby.

     p. cm.

   Includes bibliographical references and index.

   ISBN 0-8132-1317-7

   1. Man (Christian theology)   2. Personalism.   I. Title.

BT 701.3.C76 2004

126—dc21

                                        2002155213

Dedicated to Karol Wojtyla,

profound personalist thinker and teacher,

who as John Paul II has for 25 years born witness, as no one else,

to the dignity and the mystery of human persons

Contents

Preface, ix

STUDIES ON THE HUMAN PERSON

1. *A Neglected Source of the Dignity of Persons* 3
2. *The Empathetic Understanding of Other Persons* 33
3. *The Personal Encounter with God in Moral Obligation* 64
4. *Conscience and Superego* 93
5. *The Estrangement of Persons from Their Bodies* 113
6. *Person and Consciousness* 128

SOURCES OF PERSONALIST THOUGHT

7. *Max Scheler on Personal Individuality* 145
8. *Max Scheler on the Moral and Religious Solidarity of Persons* 174
9. *Dietrich von Hildebrand on the Fundamental Freedom of Persons* 194
10. *John Henry Newman on Personal Influence* 221
11. *Karol Wojtyla's Personalist Understanding of Man and Woman* 243

Bibliography, 265
Index, 271

Preface

In my book *The Selfhood of the Human Person* (Catholic University of America Press, 1996), I began work towards a personalist understanding of human beings: in the papers collected in the following pages I continue this project. Though they were not written as one book, and though they were published at different times in recent years and for different audiences, they are all sprung from the same personalist inspiration—from my fascination with the fact that each person is unrepeatably and incommunicably himself or herself, that each is not only an objective but also a subjective being, that each lives out of his or her interiority, that each is a being of surpassing, indeed infinite worth and dignity, that each can live and thrive only by existing with and for other persons. Most of these papers have been extensively revised and rewritten for this collection, and they have thereby come to hold together much more than they would have if they were merely being reprinted.

I have divided these papers into two main groups, the first called Studies on the Human Person, where I offer my own investigations of certain aspects of the human person, and the second called Sources of Personalist Thought, where I try to appropriate the work of those thinkers—Scheler, von Hildebrand, Newman, and Wojtyla—who more than any others have given the impetus for my own work on the human person.

As for the term "personalism," it comes naturally to an author who is above all else concerned with the mystery of human persons. Of course historically the term has expressed something rather more specific than this concern. It has expressed not one unified philosophy, but rather a movement in philosophy that comprises philosophers as disparate as the American Personalists, Max Scheler, and Jacques Maritain. Sometimes the different personalists are sharply at odds with each other, as when they discuss the theological foundations of their understanding of persons. On the other hand, there is a common denominator to the various personalisms, which Maritain has well expressed by saying that they are all united in opposing both liberal individualism and collectivism. In other words, all the personalist thinkers resist turning persons into autonomous selves and then detaching them from all bonds of solidarity, and they resist no less the opposite error of absorbing the individual person into the social whole, as if the individual were nothing but a part of the community to which it belongs. I too understand myself as trying to vindicate the incommunicability and dignity of persons against both individualism and collectivism, and so it seems natural for me to appropriate the term personalism for my own purposes in these papers.

The friends and colleagues who have aided me with their advice and criticism are mentioned at the end of each of the papers. I also thank my assistant, Joshua Miller, for his help in preparing the text for publication, and Elizabeth Kerr, of the CUA Press, for her thoroughness as copyeditor. And a special thanks to my son John Henry Crosby for his careful work of proofreading and for creating the index.

Studies on the Human Person

CHAPTER 1

A Neglected Source of the Dignity of Persons

Christians claim that persons have an incomparable worth, or dignity, because persons are created and redeemed by God. Paul Ramsey once forcefully asserted this theonomy of human persons by saying that our dignity as persons is extrinsic; it is rooted not in what we intrinsically are but rather in how God relates to us. He was making the point that Christians need not be too fastidious about the exact moment of the beginning of each new human person; since persons have their dignity not just from what they are in their own right but much more from what they are to God, we should look beyond the immanent makeup of the zygote to the intentions of God the creator.[1] While I admire the deep theocentric spirit out of which Ramsey speaks in that article,[2] I also think

---

* This essay was first published in *Faith and Philosophy* 18.3 (2001), 292–306, under the title "The Twofold Source of the Dignity of Persons." It has been considerably revised and enlarged for its publication in this collection.

1. "One grasps the religious outlook upon the sanctity of human life only if he sees that this life is asserted to be *surrounded* by sanctity that need not be in a man; that the most dignity a man ever possesses is a dignity that is alien to him. From this point of view it becomes relatively unimportant to say exactly when among the products of human generation we are dealing with an organism that is human. . . . His [man's] dignity is 'an *alien* dignity,' an evaluation that is not of him but placed upon him by the divine decree." Paul Ramsey, "The Morality of Abortion," in *The Ethics of Abortion*, Baird and Rosenbaum (eds.) (Buffalo: Prometheus Books, 1989) 66, 67.

2. What Ramsey wants to say was already said by Anders Nygren: "God does not love that which is already in itself worthy of love, but on the contrary, that which in itself has no worth acquires worth just by becoming the object of God's love. Agape has nothing to do with the kind of love that depends on the recognition of a valuable quality in its object; Agape does not recognise value, but creates it. . . . The man who is loved by God

that the dignity of persons is in part grounded in their immanent makeup. It is not conferred by God in a purely extrinsic way. After all, God creates plants and animals and provides for them, but this relation of Him to them does not invest them with anything like the dignity proper to human persons. If we persons were in our immanent makeup indistinguishable from plants and animals, on the level of dignity, then no conceivable divine attention could invest us with that dignity that we in fact have. In this paper I propose to examine dignity insofar as it is intrinsic to human persons and so to examine it without any direct reference to God. But I will return at the end to the question of how this dignity is related to God.

1. *Some preliminaries*

An important preliminary remark concerns the way I distinguish between personal dignity and the basic rights of the person. We frequently hear these concepts used interchangeably, but I propose to distinguish them in two ways. First, the rights of a person have a social dimension that is foreign to dignity. Only another person can respect or violate my rights. If I commit suicide, one cannot explain the wrong I undeniably do by saying that I violate my own right to life; it takes a person other than myself to be capable of violating my rights. Just as I cannot steal my own property or commit adultery with my own wife, so I cannot violate my own right to life. But my dignity as a person is there for me no less than for others; I can act against my own dignity no less than others can act against it, as when I throw myself away in despair over myself. Secondly, my basic human rights, as they are called today, are not as strictly inalienable as my personal dignity. If I ask another to take my life, then, though I act wrongly, I remove my right as a moral obstacle for the other, and the wrong he does has to be explained in terms other than the violation of my right to life. If I tell someone to help himself to my property, I thereby prevent him from being a thief and violating my property rights, even if I act irresponsibly in offering him my property. Thus I can suspend or block my rights as a morally relevant factor in a given situation. But I cannot remove my dignity from a moral situation in this

---

has no value in himself; what gives him value is precisely the fact that God loves him." *Agape and Eros* (New York: Harper and Row, 1969), 78.

way. A prostitute may try ever so hard to make herself mere flesh for sale, but despite herself she forever retains her personal dignity, which is inevitably violated by her customers. Since, then, my personal dignity is not just there for others but also for me in relation to myself, and since it is absolutely incapable of being suspended or in any way alienated by me, it shows itself to be something distinct from and deeper than the basic human rights of persons. My concern in this paper is with this dignity rather than with rights.

Another preliminary. One commonly speaks of depriving a person of dignity by some unworthy or humiliating treatment of that person. But as I will speak here of dignity, unworthy treatment of another is absolutely powerless to abrogate the other's dignity. The dignity I am searching for is, as I said, intrinsic to being a person, and you would have to abrogate the other as person before abrogating his or her dignity. Besides, unworthy treatment *presupposes* dignity; a given treatment of another is qualified as unworthy just because it fails to give the other what is due to him or her as a person having dignity. If dignity in my sense were stripped away from a person, then so would be the reason for calling the treatment of that person unworthy. So by "dignity" I do not mean that treatment of a person which is appropriate to him or her as person, but rather that in a person in virtue of which some treatment is appropriate and other treatment is inappropriate.

A somewhat different sense of dignity is at stake when we speak of a person's consciousness and affirmation of his or her own personal dignity. We say that someone bore himself with dignity under very trying circumstances, say in the face of unjust accusations. We mean that the person did not buckle under in a servile way, or lose his head in panic, but remained throughout mindful of his dignity as person. Though the self-consciousness that makes for this new sense of dignity is internal to the person, being born of the person's self-possession, and so is the very opposite of all that befalls a person from without, it is still not exactly the dignity that I aim to bring to light in thus study. For I am concerned not with this consciousness of one's dignity but with the dignity of which one is conscious.

2. Not one but two sources of the dignity of persons[3]

I begin with the traditional account of human dignity given by the Greek philosophers, who saw the unique dignity of man in his reason; man is a rational animal and in this he is superior to all subhuman animals. The Greek philosophers saw reason as the divine element in man; for Aristotle man never lives in a more godlike way than when he exercises his reason in the way of philosophical understanding. Of course, Plato and Aristotle saw reason at work in nature and in the cosmos, but here creatures only passively undergo reason, being ordered according to a rational plan; man by contrast has an essentially more intimate relation to reason, in that he understands the meaning of things with his own reason. Reason is internalized in man as it is in no subhuman being, so that he is not just governed by reason but governs himself with his own reason.[4] The point for us in the setting of this study is that human beings, through their more intimate relation to reason, have a greater share in the dignity of reason; since reason enters into their essential definition, they surpass all sub-rational beings in dignity. Here we have a timelessly valid element of the philosophical heritage of the West.

The rationality of man is so rich and deep an idea that one might wonder whether anything more is needed for a full account of the dignity of persons. In explaining the ethics of the respect we owe each other, in explaining the inviolability that others should recognize in us, do we need to do more than affirm the dignity flowing from the rationality of each human being? I think that we need to do vastly more, and I will now try to explain what this more is.

Notice that rationality is something common to all human beings; it belongs to human nature, in which we all share. Reason is not my exclusive possession, for you too have it. This commonness of reason shows itself in a certain way in and through the universal validity of rational

---

3. Cf. the rich discussion of personal dignity by Josef Seifert, who distinguishes four sources of it: Seifert, *What Is Life?* (Amsterdam/Atlanta: Rodopi, 1997), ch. iv. But none of his four sources coincides with the one source that I am above all concerned with in this paper.

4. One sees from this that reason is understood in such a way as to comprise what we call freedom, even though the Greeks did only partial justice to freedom. In any case, Greek reason far exceeds the degenerate residue of reason that today goes by the name of instrumental reason.

activity; whatever I rightly understand as rationally necessary must also be understood by you as rationally necessary. The work of reason is supposed to be impersonal, the same for all, valid for all possible beings endowed with reason. You cannot say that some essentially necessary relation is valid for you but not for me, as if rationality itself varied from one rational being to the next. This commonness goes so far that the idea has crept into Western philosophy more than once that human beings are plural only through their bodies, as if the rational spirit in them were literally one, so that each human being does not have his or her own reason in the same way that each has his or her own body. As against this view we have of course to say that each human being has his or her own intellect and rational powers, no less than each has his or her own body. And yet true it is that the rational activities of each converge with those of all other human beings in the sense explained. Individual though reason be in each human being, it is also in some strong sense common to all; and so the dignity of rationality is a dignity common to all.

But you will ask, why does this commonness of dignity represent a problem for a philosophy of human dignity? I answer that it represents a problem only if it is taken to be the sole source of dignity. You will counter asking what else there is in a human being that is dignity-grounding besides the rational nature common to all human beings. I answer as follows.

Each human being, besides sharing in this common nature, also has something of his own—something his own and not another's—incommunicably his own. Obviously a human being would not amount to an individual being if he were not, over and above all that he has in common with others, also incommunicably his own. And so we find that each of us is a certain composition of what we have in common with others, and what we do not have in common with others. Now notice that the dignity of human beings, as we have so far discussed it, is tied only to our common rational nature and has as yet no connection with that which is incommunicably each person's own. It is not because I am *this incommunicable* human being that I have dignity, but because I am *a human being* endowed with reason. What gives me dignity is not incommunicably my own but is found in every other human being. One may still see no problem for the philosophy of human dignity, and in fact readers following closely will be quick to point out an advantage that seems to be gained by deriving dignity from our common human nature. They will say that the much-celebrated equality of human beings as to dignity is secured, for if that which endows me with dignity also endows you with it, then we are equal in dignity, a conclusion that seems to be of the first importance for the organization of the political community. And one may discern yet another advantage to be gained from this derivation of human dignity. By deriving it from that which is common to all human beings we can readily show how to reach out to other persons so as to acknowledge their dignity. I have only to start with the dignity that I know in myself, and thence to proceed to the other, seeing in the other an *alter ego*, a being in whom the same rational nature that I have exists as it were a second time. In other words, my task is to love my neighbor as myself; and it is our common human nature that makes possible this transition from self to other.

And yet there is a problem here if the account of dignity so far proposed is meant as a complete account. Notice that the incommunicable element in man belongs to man *as person*. One of the best-known utterances of the Roman jurists about the person connects being a person with being incommunicable: *persona est sui iuris et alteri incommunicabilis*. It is precisely as person that I am myself *(sui iuris)* and no other *(alteri incommunicabilis)*. St. Thomas Aquinas clearly teaches that being a person is not a common nature like human nature that can be shared in by many;[5] being a person is rather a matter of being an incommunicable individual within some common rational nature.[6] This means that the account we have so far given of human dignity does not ground dignity in man as person; it is not because I am this incommunicable person that I have dignity, but because I share in the rational nature common to me and many others. This raises the question whether we have yet really taken the full measure of dignity. Is it really true that personhood has

---

5. Cf. *Summa Theologiae* I, q. 30, a. 4, especially the second objection and the response to it.

6. This important truth finds expression in a certain linguistic usage: philosophers are liable to speak not of "the human person" but of "human persons." See, for example, Derek Parfit's title, *Persons and Reasons*, (Oxford: Clarendon Press, 1987) or Robert Spaemann's *Personen* (Stuttgart: Klett-Cotta, 1996) or, in various encyclopedias, entries with the title "persons." The reason seems to be that "the human person" suggests a common nature shared in by all human persons, whereas "a person" or "persons" expresses precisely the individual of some nature. I must admit that my book *The Selfhood of the Human Person*, (Washington, D.C.: The Catholic University of America Press, 1996), would have been more correctly called *The Selfhood of Human Persons*.

Neglected Source of the Dignity of Persons

nothing to contribute to dignity, that our dignity does not also belong to us in virtue of our being persons?

These doubts grow on us if we consider how difficult we would find it to encounter a notorious proposal of Peter Singer using only the account of dignity given in terms of our common rational nature. Here is the much-discussed passage in Singer's *Practical Ethics* defending a certain kind of infanticide:

> ... suppose that a newborn baby is diagnosed as a haemophiliac. The parents, daunted by the prospect of bringing up a child with this condition, are not anxious for him to live. Could euthanasia be defended here? Our first reaction may well be a firm 'no,' for the infant can be expected to have a life that is worth living, even if not quite as good as that of a normal baby.... His life can be expected to contain a positive balance of happiness over misery. To kill him ... would be wrong.

Singer proceeds to say that there is a somewhat different utilitarian perspective in which the killing of this infant turns out to be the right thing to do after all.

> Suppose a woman planning to have two children has one normal child, and then gives birth to a haemophiliac child. The burden of caring for that child may make it impossible for her to cope with a third child; but if the defective child were to die, she would have another.... When the death of a defective infant will lead to the birth of another infant with better prospects of a happy life, the total amount of happiness will be greater if the defective infant is killed. The loss of happy life for the first infant is outweighed by the gain of a happier life for the second. Therefore ... it would ... be right to kill him.

Singer concludes this passage with the significant statement that his view "treats infants as replaceable."[7] Our question is whether we can take a principled stand against Singer on the basis of the dignity born of our common rational nature. Suppose that we object to him like this: "the hemophiliac infant has human and hence also rational nature. The infant, having all the dignity that comes from this nature, stands before me as inviolable; no one may directly kill him for the utilitarian reason given by Singer or for any other reason." Is this a decisive response to Singer? Not really; he can grant everything we say about the rational human nature of the impaired newborn, and still hold his ground on infanticide. He has

---

7. Peter Singer, *Practical Ethics* (Cambridge, UK: Cambridge University Press, 1993), 185–86.

only to exploit the fact that the dignity of persons depends on their common human nature, saying that all that is lost when the hemophiliac infant is killed, exists again in the healthier infant that he wants to make room for. For this new infant also shares in rational nature and so has dignity from exactly the same source and in exactly the same measure as the hemophiliac infant had it. One instance of rational nature succeeds the other; the first is replaced by the second. The loss in terms of dignity that comes from the infanticide is perfectly and exactly annulled by the gain in terms of dignity that comes from the new child who takes the place of the first child. But in addition to this "wash" of gain and loss there is also a gain not annulled by any loss, an absolute gain, namely the gain of full health in the new child. People like Singer might even make bold to say that we are in fact *required* by our respect for human dignity to carry out this replacement, for we show respect for human dignity by seeing to it that human beings live in the greatest possible state of flourishing. And so I say that if we cannot enlarge our account of human dignity, if we cannot find some way to let the incommunicable personhood of each human being play a role in the grounding of dignity, then we are left with no good answer to Singer. As long as the dignity of human beings is entirely and exclusively tied to that which is common to them all, they are replaceable one by another, and Singer has the last word.

Let me try to bring out a little more this replaceability by means of an extreme example of it. Take any copy of today's *New York Times*. Everything of interest in any one copy can be found in any other copy; no one copy has any point of interest that would distinguish it from the others. In fact, each copy exists simply for the sake of that which is common to all the copies of today's paper; each copy is well made just to the extent that it contains neither more nor less than the other copies. Of course, each copy is an incommunicable individual; one copy of the paper is not another. And yet that which is common to all the copies in some sense dominates each individual; the individuals exist simply for the sake of multiplying the common content. This is why any one copy is so easily replaceable by any other copy. If you lose the copy that you first bought, your loss is completely replaced by the purchase of another. In fact, the replaceability of one by another goes so far that under certain circumstances the difference between one and another is indiscernible. If I step away from my desk leaving a copy of today's *Times* on it, I cannot tell when I return whether it is the same copy or a replacement copy that someone has secretly supplied. What is common to the individual copies is so strongly present in each copy that it may be impossible to tell one individual copy from another.

Clearly it is along just these lines that Singer is thinking when he proposes replacing one human infant with another. Killing the hemophiliac infant so as to make room for a perfectly healthy one is just like turning in a frayed copy of today's *Times* for a perfectly clean one. Even if that which is common to many individuals is not just the content of today's news but is the much grander thing of human nature with its power of rationality, the individuals that are taken to be mere instances in relation to the common nature will still be subject to the same law of replaceability that we see with the newspapers.

Let us then turn our attention to human beings not insofar as they share in the same nature but insofar as each is himself and no other. If we continue the old tradition of using Socrates as a kind of logical dummy, then we can say that we are now turning our attention to Socrates not as a human being but as Socrates, and ask whether Socrates does not have some dignity just by being the person Socrates.

Let us consult those who knew and loved Socrates and ask them whether all that they knew and loved in Socrates could be repeated in some other human being. The human nature of Socrates is in a sense repeated in all other human beings; his being a Greek is in a sense repeated in all other Greeks; his being a philosopher is repeated in all other philosophers; even his famous irony was practiced by at least a few disciples who might have been called specifically "Socratic" thinkers. But those who knew and loved Socrates will not grant that everything that they knew and loved in him can be repeated in others; they will insist that there was in Socrates something absolutely unrepeatable, they will say that there was a mystery of the man and that Socrates was not a mere instance or specimen of this mystery but that he *was* this mystery, so that a second Socrates is strictly, absolutely impossible.[8] When Socrates died, a hole was left in the world, such that no subsequent person could possibly fill it. It was not just that a great philosopher died, the likes of whom were not likely to be seen again; with this one would push the incommu-

---

8. I suppose it goes without saying that a clone of Socrates would not be a second Socrates, any more than identical twins are two copies of the same person.

nicable personhood of Socrates into the realm of unusual achievements[9] and would miss the mystery of it. The incommunicable Socrates was something ineffable, something too concrete for the general concepts of human language;[10] something knowable through love but not utterable in concepts.[11]

Now I want to say that those who knew Socrates in all that made him unrepeatable were in fact finding worth, dignity, value in him, otherwise they would not have revered and loved him as they did. I also want to say that what we see in Socrates holds universally. It is not only because I share in the rational nature common to us all that I have dignity, but also because I am the unrepeatable person I am. Whoever gets acquainted with me in all my unrepeatable selfhood, gets acquainted with a dimension of my dignity that would otherwise escape him. Each person is, over and above all the qualities and kinds that he has in common with others, unrepeatably himself or herself, and each has dignity just by being the unrepeatable one that he is. We have here that aspect of dignity that we can with all precision call the dignity of human persons.[12]

---

9. This is just what Alcibiades tends to do in his speech about Socrates in the *Symposium:* " . . . but personally I think the most amazing thing about him is the fact that he is absolutely unique; there's no one like him, and I don't believe there ever was. You could point to some likeness to Achilles in Brasidas and the rest of them; you might compare Nestor and Antenor, and so on, with Pericles. There are plenty of such parallels in history, but you'll never find anyone like Socrates, or any ideas like his ideas, in our own times or in the past . . ." In *Symposium,* 221c, Joyce translation. *Collected Dialogues of Plato,* Hamilton and Cairns (eds.) (New York: Bollingen Foundation, 1964), 572.

10. It is just this ineffability that lets us distinguish the unrepeatability of persons from another kind of unrepeatability. If we consider the concept "even prime number" it is clear that it can be instantiated in one and only one number, namely the number 2. It seems to be like a person in that, just as there can be only one Socrates, so there can be only one even prime number. But there is this difference, that "even prime number" is entirely effable; it is uttered with all precision in the concept "even prime number." But that in Socrates which can exist only once, and never be repeated, is simply unutterable, ineffable. Socrates is not an unrepeatable person in virtue of clearly defined notes of his being that intersect in such a way as to allow of only one Socrates.

11. I develop this unrepeatability, or incommunicability, of persons at some length in my book, *The Selfhood of the Human Person,* especially in ch. 2, "Incommunicability."

12. I find a remarkable convergence with my result in the Swiss theologian Hans Urs von Balthasar, who writes in one place: " . . . if one distinguishes between *individual* and *person* (and we should for the sake of clarity), then a special dignity is ascribed to the person, which the individual as such does not possess. We see this in the animal kingdom where there are many individuals but no persons. Carrying the distinction over to the realm of human beings, we will speak in the same sense of 'individuals' when primarily

And it is only when our understanding of the sources of dignity has been expanded to encompass the incommunicable personhood of each human being that we are in a position to defend hemophiliac infants against the infanticide proposed by Peter Singer. For now, and only now, can we say that this infant has dignity, not just as the bearer of rational human nature, but as this infant, as this incommunicable newborn person. The hemophiliac infant cannot be replaced, because as person it is absolutely unreplaceable and is invested with dignity in its very unreplaceability. Only now does human dignity bring with it moral protection for the individual person. Only now can the invocation of dignity do the work in moral analysis that we expect it to do. Singer actually agrees with this. However much he may grant us, for the sake of argument, concerning the common rational nature of human beings, he will never grant that the hemophiliac newborn is a person; he realizes that so much dignity would then flow back into the newborn infant taken as *this individual* that the proposed infanticide would present itself to most people as morally intolerable.

We may come to understand better this specifically personal dignity if we notice the "intimation of immortality" that it contains for individual persons. Let us assume that human beings really were mere instances of human nature. In that case an endless succession of human beings would provide all the immortality that anyone could wish. Their ability to replace each other would allow for an immortality accomplished through mortal individuals continually reproducing themselves. The immortality of man need not bring with it the immortality of any individual human being. But since human persons are not mere instances of human nature, since the final destruction of any one of them would tear open a hole in being that could never be filled by any subsequent human being, there is a deep point to the immortality of individual persons. This is of course not a finished proof but only, as I put it, an "intimation of immortality" for persons. But it does add something to our understanding of personal dignity. The inviolability of individual persons known to us from our

---

concerned with the identity of human nature, to which, of course, a certain dignity cannot be denied insofar as all human beings are spiritual subjects. We will speak of a 'person,' however, when considering the uniqueness, the incomparability, and therefore irreplaceability of the individual." Hans Urs von Balthasar, "On the concept of person," *Communio* 13 (Spring 1986), 18.

moral dealings with them, becomes an intimation of immortality when persons are considered in relation to death.

It follows from our argument that those contemporary philosophers who, in speaking of personal dignity, stress the *otherness* of other human beings (for example, Levinas) find dignity precisely in the personal incommunicability to which I have been calling attention. They form a certain contrast to those who speak of the other as a *fellow* human being and who approach others in terms of our common humanity.[13] I have in effect argued that both groups of thinkers have a part of the truth; they have divided up between themselves the twofold source of the dignity of persons.[14]

I conclude with an historical observation. The same Greek philosophers who understood so deeply the excellence of the rational nature in which all human beings participate, did not equally well understand the dignity that goes with being this or that incommunicable person, or rather they did not understand it all. Though Plato in a sense "discovered the soul" and brought its immortality to light for the first time, he does not yet really have the idea of man as unrepeatable person. One has only to recall the passages in Book IV of the *Republic* where he proposes abortion and infanticide for children conceived unlawfully in the ideal city he is constructing. Perhaps Plato is so taken with his Forms or Ideas that he sees in individuals only instances of the Forms; this would have interfered with him grasping each human being as unrepeatable person. Or perhaps he goes so far in situating each human being in the city-state that he ends up making them mere parts of it; this would have produced the same interference in his intellectual vision. However one explains it, human beings do not yet stand forth in Plato, or in Aristotle for that matter, with that mystery of concrete individuality that makes them persons endowed with immeasurable worth.[15]

---

13. Cf. Alain Finkielkraut, *In the Name of Humanity* (New York: Columbia University Press, 2000), especially the rich and suggestive ch. 1.

14. In no way do I claim to have given in this section a complete account of the sources of personal dignity. I wanted to call attention to the two sources that have been discussed, especially to the second, but without in any way impeding the search for further sources. For example, if we were to explore the deeper forms of interpersonal solidarity we would find that the very great value they embody is a source of dignity for the individual persons who are called to live in such solidarity with one another.

15. Linda Zagzebski seems to want to make the same historical observation when she writes in her "The Uniqueness of Persons," *Journal of Religious Ethics* 29.3 (2001): "We get

3. On the unity of common human nature and incommunicable person

Some readers of earlier drafts of this paper have objected that they find something suspicious about the dualism of common nature and incommunicable person that seems to result from my analysis of the sources of personal dignity. They find something unreal about the idea of human beings functioning only as bearers of human nature and hence as interchangeable instances of it, and they say that no serious thinker ever thought of human beings in this way. They think that they could disagree with me about the neglected source of dignity and could acknowledge only the long-recognized *universal* source of dignity, and yet do this without holding that human beings are degraded to the status of replaceable instances of human nature. Perhaps these critics will be reconciled to my analysis if I now add something about my understanding of the unity of the two aspects of human beings that I have distinguished.

First of all, it is evident that the very idea of a *mere specimen of rational nature* is absurd; that rational nature cannot be multiplied in interchangeable individuals in the way today's newspaper can be multiplied; that rational nature is such that it can exist only in incommunicable persons. This is why St. Thomas Aquinas teaches that the subsistent individual within rational nature can only be a person (*Summa Theologiae*, I, 29, 1). One could even pick out certain elements of rational nature, above all the freedom proper to it, and show how they imply an incommunicable person as the only possible bearer of it. A being that in a sense creates itself in freedom cannot exist as a mere instance of any kind. This would mean that the Greek idea of man as having a rational nature already contains in a way the idea of man as person, and that the Christian idea of man as person does not overthrow but completes the Greek idea of man as sharing in a rational nature.[16]

---

from the ancient Greeks the idea that particular being needs to be explained. It is not fundamental. A *what*—a kind or quality something can be—comes first; a particular thing is just an instance of a what. Philosophers think exactly the same way today. To be is to instantiate qualities" (415).

16. We have here the basis of Scheler's thesis (see *The Nature of Sympathy* [Hamden CT: Archon Books, 1973], 99–102) that love for persons is based on the love that he called *Menschenliebe*, which is a love for a human being insofar as he or she is the bearer of human nature. This is obviously not yet a love for the unrepeatable person, but it stands in the service of personal love in this way: if we fail to notice the humanity of human

But the unity of common nature and incommunicable person goes much farther. That which a human being has in common with other human beings does not remain outside of himself as incommunicable person but it is in different ways *absorbed* by his incommunicability. Consider the hands of a person whom I know in a personal way. All human beings have hands; one shares in the common human nature by having hands. And yet the hands of this person present themselves to me as belonging to him or her, as being his or her own hands. They may or may not seem to me to be particularly expressive of that person, but they have the character of being his or hers. They are thus to some extent withdrawn from what is common to him and other human beings and become rooted in what is incommunicably that person's own. I hardly encounter another as person if I do not detect this *ownness* in the other; on the other hand, it is a sure sign of encountering another as person that I begin to experience the entire bodily being of the other, indeed all that the person has in virtue of being a human being, as not just common to that person and others but as also being incommunicably that person's own.

But the absorption of the common nature in the incommunicable person can go farther still. The common nature can enter so intimately into an incommunicable person as almost to seem to be an element of the incommunicable person. I experience this whenever a human being seems to me to exist *as if the only human being*. What I mean is this. When a single human being is considered in relation to the six billion humans now alive on earth, he may at first seem to become a negligible quantity, one among innumerably many. But if we hold fast to the fact that he is an incommunicable person and if we *realize* his incommunicability, then he does not become a mere one six-billionth of the human race, nor is he relativized into insignificance. On the contrary, there is something about him that makes us say that the laws of finite numerical quantity are suspended; even when you surround him with billions of other humans, he

---

beings, we are sure to overlook them as persons. For example, if black slaves seem to us sub-human, then they are lost to us as persons. We are as it were alerted to the presence of a person in those whom we recognize as human beings; we are ready to encounter a person in them. We begin to love with a love that can give rise to a love for the incommunicable person. One readily sees that this fact about the foundation of our knowledge of persons and of their worth as unrepeatable persons presupposes the just-mentioned ontological connection between having rational human nature and existing as a person.

remains undiminished in the minds of those who really apprehend him as person, existing as if the only human being. This is why the news of just a single human person whose plane crashes, or who is killed by terrorists, can catch the attention of the whole world, why it can stun all who hear of it, and why we are not reconciled to the loss by the thought that the one who perished was after all just one six-billionth of the human race.

There is an interesting analogy to the curious behavior of mathematical infinities. Take the infinitely many positive numbers; they can, it seems at first, be added to, as when you add to them some negative numbers; but they cannot really be added to, since the infinitely many positive numbers cannot become more by any adding to them; they cannot even become more by adding the infinitely many negative numbers to them. In an analogous way, you cannot really add to a given human being by bringing in other human beings; you do not really enlarge what is already given with just the one human. Perhaps another way of saying it is that each human person mysteriously comprises within himself or herself all the others. Hence the Jewish saying that the one who saves a single human being saves the whole of humanity. It follows that the common and the incommunicable are not different parts of a human being that fall outside of each other; rather, each incommunicable person modifies the human nature he shares with others, not just instantiating it but almost taking it over as his own, so that each exists, not as one among many, but as if the only human being.

Of course I say *as if;* no individual person ever completely absorbs human nature, for otherwise there could not exist more than one person. Thus the distinction between common human nature and incommunicable person remains even when they seem to interpenetrate; and so the sources of personal dignity remain distinct.

We see the same interpenetration at work not only with human nature but also with certain instantiable *modes* of being a human being that some have and others lack. Take for instance being a woman. The womanhood of a woman can, in the eyes of the man who loves her, form such a unity with her personal incommunicability that she stands before him as if she were the only woman: "che sola a me par donna" ("who is for me the only woman"), says Petrarch referring to Laura de Noves, his beloved. A similar merging of the incommunicable individual with a universal aspect of human nature occurs when a child wants to say of his or her mother: "mamma è una sola," as one says in many Romance languages. The woman does not just instantiate the feminine, the mother does not just instantiate the motherly; they rather incorporate these types so strongly into themselves as to make the idea of other women and other mothers seem almost bewildering.

We might also express it like this: the incommunicable person seems to function as a kind of *principle of individuation* with respect to the human nature that he or she shares with all other human beings, or with respect to the modes or qualities that he or she shares with certain others.

It follows that if we speak of a human nature that is the same in every person, we produce an abstraction and run the risk of letting this abstraction obscure the way in which human nature is incorporated into each incommunicable human person. Perhaps the reader felt that I was resorting to some such abstraction when I spoke above of the difficulty of engaging and defeating the position of Singer. But what I wanted to say is that *this abstraction results only if we omit the incommunicable person from our account of human beings*. In order to show this it was only natural for me to think through what human beings would be if completely stripped of personal incommunicability. It is just because they then become unrecognizable in being reduced to interchangeable instances that we must, in our philosophical reflection on them, restore personal incommunicability to them. But it is not enough just to restore it. We must also understand that the incommunicable person in each human being does not just stand juxtaposed to an abstract human nature that is the same in all human beings, but rather *acts on* the common human nature so as to individuate it and to impregnate it, so to say, with his or her incommunicability. Thus to avoid thinking of the common human nature of human beings as an unreal abstraction, my critics have to agree with me about the neglected source of personal dignity.

I hasten to add that the incommunicable selfhood of a human person does not function as a source of personal dignity *only* by its work of individuating the common human nature. Whoever deeply experiences the mystery of a person's unrepeatable self experiences something more than a thoroughly individuated and owned human nature. We will try to approach this *more* as we proceed to work through the following objections.

4. Objections

1. One way of objecting to my claim about the neglected source of personal dignity is by producing counter-examples. One reader objected that if we take away a child's favorite doll and try to replace it with another, the child may insist that the first is irreplaceable and unrepeatable. Here we have unrepeatability yet no dignity of the magnitude of personal dignity; thus when we find unrepeatability and dignity in persons, they may not be connected in the intimate way that I have claimed they are connected. An obvious response to the objection is that the child is very likely personifying her favorite doll, that is, projecting personal life into it; and then it is only in accordance with my account of personal dignity that the child would find both unrepeatability and incomparable value in her doll. But let us suppose that the child is old enough to avoid such personification. If the child is thirteen or fourteen years old and has had the doll for as long as she can remember, then of course she will not want to hear of a replacement doll. The reason is that the doll has become as if a part or extension of the child, who thus feels she is losing something of her very self in losing the doll. It is as if the embodiment of the child extends beyond the limits of her body and encompasses things that she has grown up with and grown in to. So the doll is irreplaceable, not in its own right as doll, but in its relation to the child, as a result of the way it has been incorporated into her life. One sees the very great difference between this case and the case of a person who is irreplaceable in his or her own right without having to be incorporated into some other. Perhaps we can say that the doll has a derived irreplaceability, whereas a person has a primary, originary irreplaceability.

2. Some might think that in my argument I mean to *infer* from the unrepeatability of persons to their dignity. And they may object that it is after all possible that something could be uniquely, unrepeatably bad; the formal fact of unrepeatability or incommunicability does not seem to imply value or dignity. But I do not mean to propose any such inference. What I mean instead is that this unrepeatable person has value, and the person has it, not as just being unrepeatable, but as being this unrepeatable person. Thus you can discover and experience this value, *not by picking out unrepeatability as an abstract moment, but by getting acquainted with the individual person who is unrepeatable*. In fact, once acquainted

with some unrepeatable person, it is hardly possible for anyone to fail to experience the dignity of which I speak. This experience of personal dignity through acquaintance with an unrepeatable person has, then, nothing to do with an inference: there is not enough universality in an incommunicable person to support any inference.

3. A keen-thinking logician might say that what I have called the incommunicable in persons resolves itself in the end into something communicable; for *all persons* have this incommunicability, which seems therefore to be common to all of them. The attempt to secure personal incommunicability or unrepeatability seems to destroy itself dialectically, with the result that my two sources of dignity resolve themselves into one. But it must be remembered that what all persons have in common as persons is not some common nature, such as human nature, but rather the fact that each is unrepeatable and cannot exist in duplicate or triplicate. Thus the sense in which human nature is common to all human beings is fundamentally different from the sense in which personhood is common to all persons. St. Thomas Aquinas teaches this with all clarity when he says that the personhood of several individuals is not a matter of them sharing in a common *essentia* but rather a matter of them being alike in that each has the same *modus existendi incommunicabiliter*.[17] As long as I hold fast to this difference I can continue speaking of the twofold source of dignity in persons.

4. Another objection says that my view exaggerates the importance of that which is incommunicably each person's own. What distinguishes one person from another is in reality peripheral to the person. Put together such things as the place of one's upbringing, the year of one's birth, one's IQ, and you will soon have a set of properties that serves to distinguish one person from all others. But these individuating factors are not central to a person; what is central is his having a soul, having free will, being made for God, and the like. These central determinants of a person are common to him and all other persons, whereas the determinants of him being himself and no other are relatively peripheral. But that which is relatively peripheral to a person can play no very large role in establishing the dignity of the person; if dignity is to depend on what belongs most centrally to a person, it will have to depend on what is common to him

---

17. *Summa Theologiae* I, q. 30, a. 4, especially the ad 2.

Neglected Source of the Dignity of Persons

and all persons. Hence the attempt to include incommunicable personhood in the ground of human dignity is misguided.[18]

This objection trivializes what I mean by personal incommunicability. I do not mean merely a bundle of traits which serves to identify a being as this one and no other (even though each separate trait in the bundle is common to that being and to many others). Such a bundle just provides a device for picking out one individual among other individuals and for referring to it with precision; it does not capture that ineffable mystery of a person of which I spoke above, since such a bundle is entirely effable, entirely utterable. Besides, most bundles of traits that happen to pick out one individual could in principle be instantiated by more than one individual; however unlikely it is to be repeated in others, this could in principle happen, and hence the bundle falls short of the unrepeatable person.[19] It follows from my discussion above that the whole conception of personal incommunicability as peripheral is fundamentally flawed; it is simply not true that the deeper we go into the center of a person the more we find that which is common to all persons. Just the contrary is true: we arrive at the center of a person, at the mystery of this individual person, at that which above all engenders love for the person, only when we encounter the person as unrepeatable.[20] It is, then, quite in order to let personal incommunicability play a large role in our account of human dignity.

5. According to another objection, my view compromises the unity of the human species. One may suspect that I am saying of human persons what St. Thomas Aquinas said of the angels, namely that each is its own species, and that human persons are therefore not gathered together in

---

18. Here is a specimen of this line of argument: "Even if people are all unique, it seems impossible that we could value them infinitely for their unique characteristics, primarily because their differences are just not so important. I do not care about a stranger in her uniqueness (her never-to-be-repeated fingerprints or her possibly unusual facial appearance or odd sense of humor), but in her humanity." Richard Stith, "On Death and Dworkin," *Maryland Law Review* 56.2 (1997), 344.

19. For penetrating criticism of this bundle theory of individuality, see Jorge Gracia, *Individuality* (Albany: State University of New York Press, 1988), 64–69, to mention just one relevant passage in his book.

20. Max Scheler argues for just this thesis and in fact regards it as central to his ethical personalism; see my discussion of this Schelerian theme in ch. 7 of the present volume, "Max Scheler on Personal Individuality."

the unity of one human species. And there are indeed weighty reasons, including weighty Christian reasons, for wanting to preserve the unity of the human species. But the unrepeatability of human persons does not prevent them from sharing a common nature, any more than sharing a common nature prevents them from being persons. I have acknowledged this common nature throughout this paper, and have made a point of all that it contributes to the dignity of persons. We can in fact express the unrepeatability of persons in terms that *presuppose* a common nature, as when I say that each human person has human nature *in his or her incommunicable, unrepeatable way*. This "adverbial" way of expressing personal incommunicability inserts it from the beginning within our common human nature and avoids even the appearance of annulling this common nature.

6. A particularly interesting objection, in my opinion, is the one that says that the equality of persons is jeopardized by letting dignity be based in part on persons as incommunicable. As we remarked above, we seem to secure this equality by letting dignity flow from our common human nature, for then dignity arises in each person from the same source. But if we let it also flow from the unrepeatable personhood of each human being, then this dignity is no longer the same in each person; it is rather one thing in one person and another thing in another. This might seem to open the door to persons differing in dignity, some having more of it and some having less. In this case the appeal to personal dignity could function in moral discussions in "elitist" ways that would yield some suspicious moral and political conclusions.

To this objection I would first respond that the equality of human dignity is by no means secured by deriving dignity from our common rational nature. For one could still say with Aristotle that man realizes this rational nature more perfectly than woman, that masters realize it more perfectly than natural slaves, and that Greeks realize it more perfectly than barbarians. One can thus still posit large differences in dignity among human beings. The equality of dignity can in fact be better preserved by letting dignity also derive from personal unrepeatability. For you cannot say that one incommunicable person has more dignity and another has less, since you would then be positing some common dignity-grounding quality possessed to different degrees by the two persons. With such a common quality, however, you abandon the incommunicability of the persons who are being compared. *The fact is that by being incommunicable and unrepeatable, persons are incommensurable with each other, they cannot be compared with each other, and because of this a certain equality is established among them.* They are alike in that each is incommunicable and unrepeatable, but more importantly, the comparisons that give rise to more and less dignity are blocked by the incommensurability of persons with each other.

Let us sum up our response to this objection. Dignity belongs to persons both because of their sameness in a common nature and because of their personal differences one from another; as for the equality of dignity in persons, we get the surprising result that the differences among unrepeatable persons lend more support to this equality than the sameness does.

We can also put this result to the test of history; let us just ask whether the equality of men and women has made its way into consciences because women are now regarded as sharing in human nature no less than men, or because women are now regarded as being persons just like men are persons.

7. Another objection says that my position would make it possible to recognize only in relatively few people this second source of personal dignity, for, as the example of Socrates shows, it is not easy to get as closely acquainted with a person as the friends of Socrates were acquainted with him. It is not easy to know a person so as to love that person, as Socrates' friends loved him. It seems that in the absence of this intimate experience of another we could only recognize that dignity in him that flows from his rational human nature. Since this human nature has a certain universality and hence is common to all human beings, it is easy to recognize in all of them, but the unrepeatable identity of this or that person has to be sought out separately in this or that person; it does not in any way follow from what we know about other persons, nor does it disclose anything to us about what other persons, not yet known to us, unrepeatably are. Hence we will really experience this personal identity, and the dignity that goes with it, only in the case of those few persons whom we have time and opportunity really to get to know.

The objection is right in this, that only in the case of these few persons can we experience the unrepeatable person in such a way that this person engenders in us love for him or her. But the objection works with a false alternative to the extent that it implies that we either love a human being as unrepeatable person, or else only appreciate a human being as an instance of human nature. It seems that a third way of apprehending human beings is possible; we can know that a human being must be an unrepeatable person even though we do not experience the particular identity of that person, and knowing this we can show respect for the human being as unrepeatable person. Though the personal love of which we have spoken cannot be shown to all persons, there is a personal respect that can be shown to all of them. Human beings can be apprehended as persons but without being given to us in all their concrete personal particularity. One might think here of Husserl's analysis of sense perception, according to which the back side of the moon is given in our perception of the moon—not inferred but immediately given—even though it does not present itself to our intuition like the side facing the earth presents itself. Our apprehension of another person usually has this element of blindness as to the particular identity of the person. But such deficient apprehension suffices to let us show personal respect for the other; it is very different from the apprehension of the other as a mere instance of human nature.

This way of responding to the objection admittedly leads to the paradoxical result that, from the point of view of this respect, personal unrepeatability seems to become something common to all human beings just like human nature is common to them all. But as I said in response to the third objection, and as is obvious, personal unrepeatability is not common to all in the same sense in which human nature is common to all.

5. *Concluding remarks on personal dignity and God*

One now sees what I meant at the outset in saying that I was looking for a personal dignity that is immanent in, or intrinsic to human beings, and so is understandable without reference to God. For what is more a person's own than his existing as this unrepeatable person? How can that which is supremely each person's own be entirely extrinsic to the person in the sense of arising only in relation to God and making no sense apart from that relation? How can that which we love in another be extrinsic to the beloved person? For in loving the other our intention does not bypass the other, or pass through the other to God, but aims precisely at the other person himself or herself. If it is the other as unrepeatable person that especially engenders our love, then this unrepeatable element is nothing extrinsic to the beloved person but must be entirely intrinsic to him or her. And is it not undeniable that all my claims about the neglected source of personal dignity are indeed intelligible to believer and non-believer alike?

What then could Paul Ramsey, to whom we referred at the beginning, have meant in affirming the extrinsic or alien character of the dignity of human persons? What is the truth in his position? Perhaps this, that the dignity of persons of which we have been speaking is nowhere so deeply experienced as in the setting of Christian existence. If I ask what it is in Christian existence that supports believers in those convictions about personal dignity that I have defended in this essay, then I would say that it is the experience of the living God of Israel and of Jesus Christ, calling me by name, creating me when He could have as well not created me, giving me particular tasks for my life, waiting for my consent before entering my life in a more intimate manner, calling me to account for my life at the end of it, letting me stand before Him face to face, letting His counsels be changed by my petition. All of this cannot fail to awaken and deepen and confirm in me the conviction that I am not just a specimen of rational nature, that I am not replaceable by subsequent persons, that I exist as if the only person, that I have an incomparable worth *as this person*. And we might mention here something else, namely the faithfulness of the Christian God; He does not abandon His creatures when they go astray but He acts to redeem them. If He just wanted them to instantiate divine qualities that are rooted in Himself, He might lose interest in them when they fail to have these qualities; but the faithfulness that He practices to them in their misery suggests that He is committed to them as incommunicable individuals and not just as bearers of divine qualities. And there is still something else. We should not limit ourselves to the encounter with God which unfolds face to face but should also recall the very different encounter with Him in and through His indwelling in each believer; this indwelling, far from being an immersion in a divine *concursus*, belongs to me as incommunicable person and so also awakens in me a sense of my dignity *as this person*. If I were to lose this faith in being personally called by the living God and in being personally inhabited by Him, then my sense of myself would be shaken and my experience of myself as unrepeatable person would receive a severe blow. Other human beings might still take me seriously as person and so preserve in me some sense of my dignity as person, but the loss of the divine partner would greatly weaken my hold on this dignity. It is along these lines that one might unfold the important theocentric truth affirmed by Paul Ramsey.

But perhaps Ramsey wanted to go farther; perhaps he wanted to say that just as calling a thing "desired" means nothing more than that the thing stands in a relation to one who desires it, so calling a person unrepeatable means nothing more than that this person stands in a relation to a God who calls him or her irrevocably. Perhaps he wanted to say that the difference between being a mere specimen and existing as an unrepeatable individual, as if the only one, is a difference entirely constituted by the presence (in the latter case) and the absence (in the former) of a relation to a personal God. Then we would have to disagree, for then Ramsey would be denying the immanence in persons of unrepeatability, which he would be resolving into a relation between God and human persons. Then he would render personal unrepeatability unintelligible to all but believers. But to the extent that he says that no one experiences personal unrepeatability like those who live their Christian existence radically, to that extent I agree with him. I just insist that the unrepeatability that is thus brought to light in radically lived Christian existence is not just the term in man of a relation to God but is also something immanent in man as person, something eminently belonging to his *Eigensein* and thus something in some way knowable to non-believers. This is why unbelievers can be enriched by the encounter with Christian existence and Christian thought; even without becoming believers they can be sensitized to something in their self-experience that they had previously been unable to thematize. But on Ramsey's radically relational view of personal dignity this process of enrichment and sensitization does not make any sense and should not be possible at all.

Needless to say, I would acknowledge a dignity all its own in the fact that human persons are willed by God, called by God, redeemed by God. Here the dignity is indeed unintelligible without considering the relation to God. But I say that there is also an unrepeatability of persons where the role of God is different—where the dignity is not in the same way constituted by a relation to God. This is not to say that persons as unrepeatable are not connected to God, as if they ceased to be creatures and became absolutely autonomous. No; religious men and women will say that human persons in some way show forth God through the unrepeatable mystery that each embodies.[21] But this relation to God entirely coheres with my thesis about the immanence of personal unrepeatability, for a person can show forth God through his or her unrepeatable being only if this being, and its dignity, is in some way intelligible even before being set in relation to God.[22]

APPENDIX. *Some Recent Work on the Neglected Source of Personal Dignity*

I am aware of two recent studies that so converge with my argument in this paper that I want now to give them more attention than I could in the main text.

1. In her paper, "The Uniqueness of Persons," Linda Zagzebski distinguishes two aspects of the dignity of persons, the infinite value of persons and the irreplaceable value of each of them.[23] The former she traces back to certain shareable qualities or characteristics, such as rational nature, and the latter she traces back to the incommunicable or unrepeatable character of a given person. These two sources of dignity correspond closely to the two sources that I have been distinguishing. Here she wants to call attention to what I have called the neglected source of personal dignity and in doing so she stresses its irreducibility to shareable characteristics:

Each definition [of a person] identifies a shareable property, a property that all persons have in common and that all nonpersons lack. Each person is equivalent to another in having such a property. That property could be rationality, self-consciousness, or the capacity to set ends, but in each case it is the same in all persons, and, in fact, the discovery of such a property was the point of our

---

21. One notices here that the personalism being explored in this essay requires us to re-examine the notion of the "image of God" in man. One traditionally thought all persons show forth the same image of the divine nature; now we have to add that each human being as unrepeatable person also shows forth something in the divine Personality that only he or she can show and that no one else can show.

22. Thanks to Linda Zagzebski, Norris Clarke, S.J., Louis Dupré, Josef Seifert, and two reviewers at *Faith and Philosophy* for their critical reactions to earlier versions of this paper.

23. Linda Zagzebski, "The Uniqueness of Persons," 401–23.

original question, What makes a person different from everything else? Now we find ourselves with a new question: How can *any* shareable property make each individual that has that property irreplaceable in value? The answer is, I think, that it cannot. (412)

A little later she go farther and says, agreeing entirely with the argument of this paper: "Persons have irreplaceable value because of their incommunicable subjectivity" (418).

She notices that the doctrine of the equality of persons has to be rethought on the basis of this irreplaceable value:

Human dignity is often expressed by the platitude that all persons are equal. I find the word "equality" misleading because it implies that persons are being compared with each other and that they all come out the same on some scale of comparison. I think the point of asserting the distinctive value of persons is to establish that persons cannot be compared. There is a space around all the qualities a person has that constitutes the domain of her selfhood and may also be the domain of her freedom. It is the area in which persons are separated from their nature and the qualities that they share with others. (421)

But she does not take the further step that I took above, namely the step of recognizing a new kind of equality that emerges among incommunicable persons, the equality that comes precisely from the incomparability of persons one with another.

I also find noteworthy her brief reference to the theological implications of these two sources of dignity:

Philosophers of religion have traditionally thought that everything interesting to be said about God philosophically pertains to the divine nature. I propose that the distinctiveness and uniqueness of persons is of great importance in talk about God. We cannot begin to resolve philosophical problems about God without understanding God as a person, not just an instance, even the only possible instance, of a divine nature. (421)

This would seem to imply that we can get to know God as person only on the basis of revelation, which is the source of our knowledge of those words and deeds of God that reveal Him as incommunicable person. But she does not explore this implication, nor will I explore it here.[24]

---

24. But Max Scheler explores it in his treatise on philosophy of religion, *Vom Ewigen im Menschen* (Bern: Francke Verlag, 1968), in which he argues that while the divine nature is always available to the rational investigation of the metaphysician (as far as it is available at all), the divine personality is known only when God reveals Himself to religious men and women.

Neglected Source of the Dignity of Persons

The one claim of Zagzebski that I cannot make friends with is the claim that what she calls the infinity of personal dignity is foreign to persons considered as irreplaceable and is proper only to (certain aspects of) the common rational nature of persons (402–3; 418–19). By the infinity of personal dignity she seems simply to mean that essential superiority of persons over nonpersons whereby the value of nonpersons, however much you augment it quantitatively, never approximates to the value of a single person. The value of persons seems in this sense to surpass infinitely the value of nonpersons. Notice that the adverb, "infinitely," used to modify "surpass," seems to work better in expressing what Zagzebski wants to say than does the substantive, "infinity." But I cannot understand why she would want to exclude personal unrepeatability from that in human beings which essentially surpasses all non-persons and hence gives rise to what she calls the infinity of personal dignity. The fact that human beings are not replaceable instances of human nature but rather unreplaceable, unrepeatable persons certainly has to do with the fundamental difference in kind between persons and non-persons and in fact it helps to explain why persons "infinitely" surpass non-persons. She herself says as much when she writes: "What makes human persons more valuable than . . . other animals is not simply that a human person is an instance of a more valuable nature, but that a human person is more than an instance of a nature. Persons . . . are irreplaceable" (419).

At one point (418) she says that if persons have infinity, then they become comparable with other beings (for example, by being greater than merely finite beings) and that this is inconsistent with the incomparability of unrepeatable persons. But this thought is far too abstractly conceived to be convincing. As we saw, she does not really affirm an infinity that persons "have;" she asserts only a modal infinity, characteristic of the way in which persons surpass non-persons. Besides, unrepeatable persons can perfectly well be compared with each other in ways that do not interfere with their unrepeatability, as when we say that all persons are alike as to unrepeatability, or when we say that all persons are alike in surpassing non-persons as to dignity. Only if "infinity" had been a type or kind that was variously instantiated by different human persons would the comparison of persons as to infinity have tended to obscure the unrepeatability of persons.

2. Richard Stith has written a significant monograph, "On Death and Dworkin: a Critique of His Theory of Inviolability."[25] He engages Ronald

---

25. Richard Stith, "On Death and Dworkin," 289–383.

Dworkin in debate in something like the way I engage Singer in debate, and he tries to bring out against him the same truth about personal incommunicability that I try to bring out against Singer.

When Dworkin explains in his book *Life's Dominion* our sense of the sanctity or inviolability of a human life, he seems to be speaking about the same thing that has engaged me in this study, namely the dignity of a person. The novelty of his position is that it is an "investment theory" of inviolability.[26] He thinks that a human life is sacred or inviolable to the extent that nature and/or people have invested time and care in bringing forth and cultivating that life. "[T]he nerve of the sacred lies in the value we attach to a process or enterprise or project rather than to its results. . . ."[27] A sign of this investment for him is the frustration, the sense of waste that is felt at the death of a human being. This sense of waste does not come just from future possibilities being cut off but also from some investment having been made in the past and then prevented from bearing any fruit. Thus for Dworkin the death of a child is worse than the death of a newborn infant, because the parents have put more into the child than they could have put into the infant, and the child too has begun to put something into herself, beginning a work of self-creation that has as yet no place in the infant. The greater sanctity, or inviolability of the child is reflected in the greater sense of waste that we have in contemplating the death of the child. Using the same logic Dworkin argues that an intended pregnancy gives rise to more inviolability in the embryo than does an accidental pregnancy.

One wonders why Dworkin is driven to a theory that is open to such obvious and weighty difficulties (such as the fact that sanctity will vary greatly from one human person to another). One needs to know that he is trying to explain what he takes to be a paradoxical fact about inviolability. With some intrinsic values, he says, our interest in the value is shown in our desire to bring into existence always more of the value; thus when we fall under the influence of the value of knowledge we are always striving to enlarge our knowledge. Bentham must be thinking of values of this kind in putting forth his celebrated imperative that morally responsible people should aim at producing as many benefits as possible for the greatest possible number of people. Such values are governed by the principle that more is always better. But it is otherwise with those intrinsic values that Dworkin calls the values of the sacred and the inviolable.

26. Ronald Dworkin, *Life's Dominion: An Argument about Abortion, Euthanasia, and Individual Freedom* (New York: Alfred Knopf, 1993), ch. 3, "What Is Sacred?"
27. Ibid., 78.

Consider the inviolability of human beings; we find that we can show respect for existing human beings without feeling any imperative to bring as many human beings as possible into existence. Indeed, a man and a woman may fully acknowledge the inviolability of their children without intending to have any more children. Dworkin tries to explain this puzzle by means of his investment theory, that is, by saying that possible children have no claim on us since no investment has been made in them, whereas already existing children are always the beneficiary of some investment in them; thus no investment is wasted when a woman declines to conceive a child she might have had, whereas some investment is always wasted when an already existing child dies or is destroyed.

With this presentation of Dworkin we may seem to have drifted away from the issue of personal unrepeatability that has been occupying us in this study; but let us look more closely at the study of Stith, who takes personal unrepeatability to be the main thing that is missing in Dworkin, the capital truth that undermines Dworkin's whole theory of inviolability.

Stith detects an attitude of "valuing" in Dworkin's approach to personal dignity. This attitude is clearly the opposite of the attitude that sensitizes us to the unrepeatable person, as we see as soon as Stith explains that "the attitude of valuing can have no objection to destruction accompanied by the substitution of more of the . . . valued type. In other words, valuing is inherently indifferent as between particular instances of that which is valued. Thus, no amount of valuing . . . can make individual persons . . . inviolable" (342). He adds that ". . . all valuing . . . is and must be for *types* (or essences), rather than for particular examples of these types." One might think that we break out of valuing when we have to do with infinite value, but Stith rightly challenges this, saying, "Even if all lives had infinite value, we would have no rational objection to killing whenever an equal *substitute* were available" (343). Finally, Stith develops a contrast between loving and valuing that converges with what was said above about the love that the friends of Socrates had for him:

> . . . some lovers care about the beloved as a *particular* individual, whereas valuing regards only types. Valuing is willing to *exchange*, to accept substitutes of at least equal value. This willingness is quite appropriate for value because valuing proceeds from a value judgment, an evaluation, and it would be silly not to value two entities equally if both were judged to have the same valued characteristics—to be the same valued type. Love, by contrast, is often not willing to accept substitutes, even identical ones. Even if God were to promise me that he would immediately substitute an identical person . . . for my wife if I would let

him take her away, I would refuse. I do not want someone *like* her; I want *her*. (345; cf. 344)

In these last sentences we see Stith inclined to the view that the focal point of personal dignity is not *definite characteristics* of a person but rather the *existence* of a person: "one might say that 'existence' is part of the essence of an individual [person]. In searching for a way of thinking that can respect the individuality of people, we are thus looking for a mode of thought that can take existence seriously" (346).

Now it may at first not be entirely clear why Stith detects in Dworkin the attitude of what he calls valuing, but perhaps the reason is this: the investment of nature and of parents in a child can be repeated in a second child; a wasted investment can be compensated for by a second investment of exactly the same kind; there is nothing in the natural or parental investment that can happen only once. This is why Stith argues that there must be vastly more to a person and to a person's dignity than Dworkin allows; the unrepeatable individual person must be vastly more than an expression of repeatable processes of production. Hence he says, "Dworkin's first fundamental error is simply his denial that human beings themselves matter, not just the creative effort going into them" (330). And: "it is the human being that we care about, not what went into making that being" (333). And better still:

If Dworkin were ever to seek to console a parent who had lost a child . . . he would do well to avoid speaking of a tragic "waste of human investment" and concentrate instead on the loss of that child herself. It is not the bricks but the building that matters, not the human input (nor the natural or divine input) but the human being that has dignity and inviolability. (334)

Persons, being unrepeatable, are vastly more than the repeatable investment that nature and parents have made in them.

CHAPTER 2

The Empathetic Understanding of Other Persons

I propose to study some aspects of empathy in dialogue and debate with Max Scheler's great book, *Wesen und Formen der Sympathie*.[1] In particular I want to show the role of our own experiencing in coming to understand another person empathetically. Even though I depart from Scheler in developing a position on the role of our own experiencing in empathy, this paper is hardly imaginable apart from my encounter with his seminal thought on empathy and sympathy. In the last part of this paper I move beyond Scheler to consider the solidarity that is presupposed for empathy. In doing this I will be led to complete in an important respect the image of the human person that emerged in the previous paper on personal dignity.

1. The need for empathy

Insofar as we live as incommunicable persons, we live in a way hidden from others. I live in my interiority, or subjectivity, to which others do not have access as I do. I am present to myself at the center of my subjectivity in a way in which no other person can be present to me, just as any

---

* This paper was originally published as "On Empathy" in *Fides Quaerens Intellectum* vol. 2, no. 1 (2002).
 1. The work was originally published in 1913 under the title, *Zur Phänomenologie und Theorie der Sympathiegefühle und von Liebe und Hass*. Scheler revised and enlarged the original book in 1923, putting this work in its final and definitive form. I have used the 1923 version as it appears in vol. VII of Scheler's *Gesammelte Werke* (Bern: Francke Verlag, 1973). The work has been translated by Peter Heath as *The Nature of Sympathy* (Hamden, CT: Archon Books, 1973).

other person is present to himself in a way in which I can never be present to him. Another person would have to be me if he were to stand in that place where I stand in experiencing myself. We could appropriate the language of some analytic philosophers and say that as conscious person I have first-person being, which forms a sharp contrast with the third-person being of things in the world. The idea is that things in the world lie in a kind of public space and are open to the inspection of anyone who wants to inspect them. In fact, this is their only relation to personal consciousness: to be objects of the consciousness of anyone who wants to inspect them from the outside. But a personal consciousness does not lie open in this public space; it is turned within, being fully accessible only to the person whose consciousness it is, and hidden from everyone else. "Nur eine Person kann schweigen,"[2] says Scheler, meaning that only a person can remain hidden from others and hence remain inaccessible to their cognition.

This hiddenness of their subjectivity makes for a unique kind of obstacle for our knowledge of other persons, an obstacle in a way more formidable than any of the obstacles that we face in knowing non-personal beings. For the obstacle is not a temporary, contingent thing, like the limit on our knowledge of something that is too far away to be seen by any presently available instrument of magnification. We will eventually perfect instruments of magnification to the point of being able to see the distant thing, but there is no eventual perfection of our powers of cognition that will let us know the subjectivity of another like we know our own subjectivity. The subjectivity of the other is always, necessarily, turned towards the other and away from us. Even if the other is not trying to keep silent but freely expresses himself, we can still not get inside the other as he is inside himself.

But this hiddenness of each person from others should not be exaggerated. It does not mean that others can form no judgment about my inner life, nor does it even mean that my judgment about my inner life is always better than theirs. I can fall prey to all manner of self-deception and need the help of others in coming to acknowledge the truth about myself. This is especially clear with my morally dubious motives; I have an interest in repressing the consciousness of my avarice, or envy, where-

---

2. Scheler, *Vom Ewigen im Menschen* (Bern: Francke Verlag, 1968), 331. "Only a person can keep silent."

as others, lacking this interest in repressing *their* consciousness of *my* avarice and envy, see them clearly and are thus in a position to help me towards self-knowledge. One has only to recall the memorable encounter of King David and the prophet Nathan (2 *Kings*, 12). While David was in denial about his murder and adultery, Nathan found a way to make him acknowledge these crimes. But none of this is inconsistent with what I just said about the hiddenness of a person's interiority from others. For when I stop repressing my bad motives and face up to them, I experience them "from within" in a way in which those others who see them from without can never experience them. When David came to his moral senses he had an experience of his sins that the prophet Nathan could not have. It was an experience that Nathan could only have of his own sins.

The hiddenness of persons from each other is also not inconsistent with what has been called collective subjectivity. Consider the children of a father as they grieve together, one with another, at the death of the father. The sons and daughters form in their grieving a kind of collective familial subjectivity in which they all share, which is why we might well speak of the whole family as grieving at the funeral, as if they formed a kind of collective subject. As Scheler pointed out, they do not just share a common motivating object, the death of their father, but they also share something subjective, namely the very experience of grieving; they experience their grieving as a co-grieving.[3] It may seem strange that persons, each hidden from all others in his or her subjectivity, should be able to constitute a collective subjectivity to which each of them has the same access. They would seem thereby to be taken out of their solitude in a way that is not possible to personal subjectivity, in virtue of which each person, as we just said, is hidden from all others. But we should not think of collective subjectivity as if it were individual subjectivity expanded to encompass several persons, all of whom now have equal access to it: no, it is rather another level of subjective life, one that builds on the individual subjectivity but is a mode of subjective life all its own. Collective subjectivity shows in fact the same hiddenness that we just noticed in individual subjectivity; someone who did not know the deceased cannot join in the collective grieving but remains outside of it. Just as you cannot experience another exactly as he experiences himself unless you are that

---

3. See Scheler's discussion of Miteinandererleben in *The Nature of Sympathy*, as at 12–13. I translate Miteinandererleben as co-experiencing.

other person, so you cannot experience a community exactly as it experiences itself in its collective grieving and rejoicing unless you are a member of the community. These concepts of co-experiencing and collective subjectivity will also be important for us at the end of this paper when we explore the solidarity on which empathy is based.

There arises now the question whether we always know the experiencing of others only from without, or whether we can in some way enter into the subjectivity of other persons or of other collective subjectivities. It would seem that, though we can never experience them exactly as they experience themselves, we can nevertheless understand what it is like for them to experience what they experience and in this way we can achieve a certain solidarity with them. I refer to the act of empathetically understanding others; this act lets us get beyond the external view of the others and, at least in some way, enter into their subjectivity and share in the first-person perspective that each person or community has. This is why many personalist philosophers have explored empathy; they are driven to it as soon as they go deeply into the subjectivity of persons; they are driven to it as a way out of a certain solipsism that threatens them.

Notice that the need for empathy diminishes with respect to certain acts. Purely cognitive acts, such as those in which we understand the elementary equations of arithmetic, do not keep people hidden from each other and hence in need of some way of reaching each other. This is perhaps because the whole reason-for-being of the cognitive act is to apprehend some object on its own terms, an object that, in the case of a mathematical object, is identically the same for all who cognize it. The experience of something common is so strong that none of those who cognize the equation is liable to feel hidden from the others who cognize it. It is of course true that each has his own experience of understanding the equation, and that you cannot be inside my experience as I am inside it. But since the act of understanding lives from the object understood and since this object is so strongly experienced as the same for all who understand it, those who share this understanding have the strong sense of being one in sharing it. Each understands effortlessly what it is like for the others to grasp some mathematical equation. It is well known how the Averroists tried to interpret experiences such as this; they were led to the teaching that there is really only one mind that thinks in all human beings. Though this interpretation is indefensible, its plausibility is in-

Empathetic Understanding

structive; Averroism expresses the strong sense of oneness that is sometimes possible among cognizers of the same fact. The real work of empathy does not lie here, but rather in acts and experiences with a larger subjective dimension than is found is such purely cognitive acts.

2. The structure of empathy

By empathy I do not mean just any apprehension of "other minds," or of the experiencing of other people. When Nathan confronted King David, he had evidently already apprehended something of David's motives, but he was not empathizing with him. Nathan was not trying to understand David "from within," nor was he trying to realize his own vulnerability to committing the same kinds of wrong that David had committed; he was instead giving full rein to his indignation and trying to shock David out of the denial he was in. I can apprehend the murderous rage out of which some teenage boys start shooting at their classmates and killing them, but as long as I find such rage incomprehensible I do not have empathy with them. Or I can apprehend the sexual desire that one man has for another man, but empathy with him I lack entirely as long as I do not know what it is like to feel homosexual desire. And so my question in this paper is not how I come to experience conscious life in others; I assume such experience and I ask about a particular perfection that it sometimes has, namely the perfection whereby one understands another from within, so that one can understand, in the felicitous expression of Thomas Nagel, "what it is like" to experience what the other experiences. In German one calls this act of understanding the other from within *nachfühlen*. If I say to someone, "ich kann dir das sehr gut nachfühlen," I say in effect, "I understand well what it is like for you to experience that." In other words, I am looking for a certain "subjective" experience of others in contrast to the "objective" experience of others that comes from seeing them "from without." For it is through such subjective experience that I overcome as far as possible the hiddenness of others in their subjectivity.

This understanding does not seem to be a mode of knowing that has a content all its own. The sense of sight has color for its object, or one of its objects; whoever lacks sight has no contact with color qualities. The intellect has necessary truths as its object; whoever does not know these through the intellect does not know them at all. It is not clear that empathetic understanding has in the same way some object of its own. Suppose I first consider David's lust from without, as Nathan does, and then move towards some empathetic understanding of David by considering my own vulnerability to lust. I do not seem to be getting an entirely new object, as when a person born blind recovers his sight. The third-person perspective gives way to a sharing in the first-person perspective; I see David's lust now in such a way that it presents itself as more grounded in him as person. What I knew to be hidden in the subjectivity of David emerges now partially into view. But it is not as if some fact about David's lust is now clarified. It is rather the case that I now understand "what it is like" to be subject to such lust. This "what it is like" expresses a new kind of subjective familiarity with what was already known in a more objective way.

I follow Scheler in distinguishing empathy from sympathy like this: empathy is primarily a mode of experiencing another (hence our frequent expression, the empathetic understanding of another), whereas sympathy contains a moment of love for the other. It presupposes empathy, but surpasses it by the gesture of love proper to it. Scheler thinks that one can see the difference in this way: a sadist may have, indeed may need to have, a certain empathetic understanding of his victim; he needs to know what it will be like for the victim to suffer this or that, so as to choose the suffering that best satisfies his sadism. In this case we have empathy in the service of the very opposite of love.[4] But sympathy by its nature includes a gesture of love based on empathetic understanding of the other. Our interest in the present study is turned primarily to empathetic understanding but sometimes also extends to include sympathy.

I also follow Scheler in distinguishing both empathy and sympathy, on the one hand, from what he calls identification *(Einsfühlung)* with another, on the other hand.[5] Let us consider the flood of patriotic feeling that breaks out in a nation when the nation goes to war to defend itself. This patriotic feeling may be lived in the form of co-experiencing, mentioned above, but it may also be lived in the spiritually more primitive form of identification, where all those clamoring for war dissolve into the flood of

---

4. *The Nature of Sympathy*, 13–14. Though the translator never uses "empathy" here and sometimes uses instead the misleading expressions, "vicarious feeling" and "reproduction of feeling," I think that the underlying German, "nachfühlen," is best rendered as "empathetic understanding," for reasons just given above in the text.

5. Ibid., 18–36.

patriotic feeling. With the co-experiencing, each person remains intact as distinct person, but with identification the distinctness of persons breaks down. If you are suffering from the burden of existing as a distinct person, the situation created by the impending war is highly desired, for it provides an escape from this burden. Now Scheler wants to say that the empathetic understanding of another, as well as the loving sympathy for another, is not a turning to the other by way of identification; you do not lose yourself in the person with whom you empathize, or feel that you and the other are one; no, it is essential to empathy and sympathy that you experience yourself as a distinct person, irreducible to the one for whom you have empathy and sympathy. Thus empathy finds a way into the subjectivity of another without creating the illusion that the other and I are really one. The other remains other and yet is subjectively approached by me through my empathy. Scheler thinks that identification is situated at the level of *psychic* life in human beings, where experiences of amalgamation are possible, whereas empathy and sympathy are situated at the level of properly *personal* life, where persons remain intact as distinct persons even in the closest forms of union and communion.[6]

And in yet another point I follow Scheler, namely in his claim that empathy is uniquely suited to apprehending another as person.[7] Scheler understands that the first-person perspective of a person is not just a perspective that he or she happens to have; it coincides with the first-person being that makes him or her be a person. Thus by entering into a person subjectively, or in others words, into a person as the person experiences himself, we really come to know the other as person. Or as we put it above, a person ceases to be hidden from us as person when we come to know him or her subjectively. But we do not have to reason to the con-

6. Schopenhauer thought that the achievement of sympathy consisted in tearing down the walls of individuality that separate one person from another and in coming to realize that I and the other are not two but one, literally one. Scheler rightly objected that with this Schopenhauer destroyed the very possibility of sympathy. The whole genius of sympathy, and of empathy as well, lies in the way one person transcends himself so as to participate in the subjectivity of another person. See Scheler, *The Nature of Sympathy*, 51–68.

7. Cf. Scheler, *Der Formalismus in der Ethik und die materiale Wertethik* (Bern: Francke Verlag, 1966), 386, where the German words that might be rendered as empathy are Mitvollzug, Nachvollzug, Vorvollzug. He says here and in the following pages (especially 389) that it takes empathy to apprehend the other as person because a person is essentially no object; any non-empathetic apprehension, he thinks, inevitably objectifies that which is apprehended and so loses the person.

clusion that in apprehending another subjectively we apprehend the other as person; we can also "feel" it in a most experiential way. There is a memorable passage in Newman where he is considering how we apprehend other people when we see them in the swarming crowds of a large city. He says that others are hidden from us as persons insofar as they are apprehended as making up a crowd. "But what is the truth? why, that every being in that great concourse is his own centre, and all things about him are but shades, but a 'vain shadow,' in which he 'walketh and disquieteth himself in vain.'" But how do we take people out of the crowd and reveal each as being his or her own center? Newman does it by looking for the conscious experiencing of each of them: "He has his own hopes and fears, desires, judgments, and aims; he is everything to himself, and no one else is really any thing."[8] With this Newman turns from apprehending the other objectively to apprehending him subjectively; as a result the other is taken out of the objectivity of the crowd and is revealed as person. "No one outside of him can really touch him, can touch his soul. . . . He has a depth within him unfathomable, an infinite abyss of existence; and the scene in which he bears part for the moment is but like a gleam of sunshine upon its surface."[9] Now this act of apprehending the other subjectively and hence as person is an achievement of empathy.

Notice, then, that empathy does not just let us into some particular experiencing of the other, as when we empathize with the rejoicing or the suffering of another; it also lets us into the other as person, and in some cases this encounter with the other as person is the whole achievement of empathy.

But there is a part of Scheler's teaching on the empathetic apprehension of persons that I cannot accept. He thinks that this apprehension is *the* way of knowing a human being as person. I can indeed know a human being in ways other than empathetic understanding, Scheler acknowledges, I can even get to know something of the conscious experiencing of a human being without recourse to empathy, but to know him or her precisely as person is for Scheler impossible apart from empathy. As we saw, Scheler makes this claim because a person lives as person in and through his subjectivity. And yet I see at least two cases of knowing other per-

---

8. Newman, "The Individuality of the Soul," *Parochial and Plain Sermons* IV (London: Rivingtons, 1870), 82.
9. Ibid., 82–83.

sons—and really knowing them precisely as persons—where the knowing is not specifically empathetic.

The first of these showed itself in the example of Nathan confronting David with the wrong he had done: Nathan is not interested in empathizing with David but in awakening his conscience. It is not at all important for Nathan's task as prophet that he feels keenly "what it is like" to be tempted as David was tempted, in fact it would be almost comical if Nathan in this encounter with David made a great point of his own vulnerability to adultery and murder. Perhaps David, if he were in despair over his wrongdoing, might need the support of someone who understands him empathetically; but he is in a moral condition the very opposite of despair when Nathan comes to him, his conscience is asleep and he has not yet acknowledged doing any wrong. And yet Nathan takes David entirely as person; only persons can be guilty in the way in which Nathan declares David to be guilty, only persons can repent in the way Nathan leads David to repent. I conclude that you can encounter someone as person without having any empathetic understanding for that person.

We can go farther in the analysis of this first case and can state the principle of it. Other persons can mediate self-knowledge to me by seeing me from their point of view; I overcome illusions about myself and gain new self-knowledge by seeing myself with the eyes of others. Now while my act of understanding how the other sees me requires empathy by me, the act of the other seeing me from his point of view is precisely not an act of empathy by him. For here the other is seeing me from *his* point of view and not from mine. If he does not look at me in this non-empathetic way, then he loses the capacity to challenge me to grow in self-knowledge. If the other only understands me empathetically, as I understand myself, then when I see myself with his eyes I will only find again in the other what I already know in myself. The other can challenge me to critical self-examination only if he knows how to see me in a way that is precisely not the way of empathetic understanding. Since in this self-examination I come to know myself as person better, as we can see from the example of David, it follows that the view that the other has of me is a view of me as person; otherwise my sharing in that view would not contribute to my own self-knowledge as person.[10]

10. Cf. my critical discussion of this Schelerian teaching in *The Selfhood of the Human Person* (Washington, D.C.: The Catholic University of America Press, 1996), ch. 5.2.

The other case of non-empathetically understanding a person is given when your sense of the otherness of the other person is strong. I am thinking of what in other writings I have called the incommunicability, or unrepeatability of a person.[11] When I strongly experience that a person is unrepeatable, that nothing I know in myself or in other persons "prepares" me for what I find in this person, that I am emphatically not the other and the other is emphatically not I; when this sense of otherness prevails over the sense of the other as a fellow human being, over all sense of solidarity with the other; when it tends to block all sense of deep kinship with the other, then the other is too "far away" in his otherness to be encompassed by my empathy. And yet I eminently experience the other as person. Thus we have here a second kind of non-empathetic experience of another as person (which apparently plays a large role in the thought of Levinas).

It follows that there is a difference between experiencing another as subject, as personal center, as an I, which is the achievement of empathy, and experiencing another as unrepeatable, as radically other than myself, which is not a possible achievement of empathy. We will return to this distinction below and try to explain it.

Though Scheler is, as I say, wrong to take empathy as the only way of apprehending another as person, the truth in his teaching is this, that empathy is *one* way of doing this and in fact a particularly excellent way. As we have seen, we have a unique experience of another as person when we enter into the first-person perspective of the other and share through empathy in his or her subjectivity.

3. *The basis of my empathy with others in my own experiencing*

We cannot help wondering how empathy is possible. For as we have seen, an immediate apprehension of the other as he experiences himself is impossible: I would have to be the other in order to experience him in this way. I can indeed immediately experience the anger in the red face and in the clenched fists of the other, but if I try to understand the other subjectively, as he experiences himself in his anger, then he slips away

---

11. Above all in *Selfhood*, ch. 2, but also in my "A Neglected Source of the Dignity of Human Persons," in this volume.

from me into the hiddenness of which we spoke at the outset. Where then is a basis to be found for my act of empathizing with another?

My central affirmation is this: empathy and sympathy are typically based on my own self-experience; I find a path into the subjectivity of the other, not through the immediate givenness of his or her subjectivity, which is impossible, but through my own subjectivity. The following examples make abundantly clear that it is my own subjectivity that provides me with a path into the subjectivity of others. If the reader wonders why I offer so many examples of what may seem to be such an obvious feature of empathy, I say that I have been made nervous by the fact that Scheler does not acknowledge this feature of empathy, and in fact denies it, and so I feel the need to bring it to evidence as fully and unambiguously as possible.[12]

Suppose I want to extend sympathy to my friend over the untimely death of his child. I need first to stir up empathetic understanding for him, and to do this I have to recur to my own experience of having lost a child. If I can say, "I know what this is like, I have been through it myself," then my friend will feel that I understand him from within and will feel less alone in his suffering. My sympathy will approximate more closely to authentic sympathy than the sympathy of someone who has never had to endure such a loss, for such a person cannot really know what it is like to lose a child; he lacks the experience that he needs for achieving empathy. I may be able to offer some empathy and sympathy if, though I have never lost a child, I have children and so understand in myself the unique kind of bond that ties parents to their children. I am in a better position to imagine the loss of a child than is a childless person. Thus my inner resources for offering empathy and sympathy seem to reach just as far as my personal experience (actual or potential experience, as we will see directly below) resembles that of my suffering friend.

The mention of the child brings to mind another act of empathy, the empathy of an adult with a child. How can one hope to understand empathetically the mentality of a child, the way he likes to play, the way he interacts with his playmates, the way he perceives adults, the way he

---

12. In the next pages I take over, with permission from the editor, Michael Bawr, paragraphs from my "Inference and Intuition in the Understanding of Other Persons," *Proceedings of the American Catholic Philosophical Association* 73 (1999), 141–42.

expresses himself, his relation to time, if one does not go back to one's own experience of childhood and try to understand the child through that experience? If I forget that I was once a child myself then I remain entirely outside of all the conscious life and feeling that I perceive in a child.

Notice that I am not making a claim like this: "if I have not experienced color qualities for myself, I cannot understand what other people are talking about when they talk about color qualities." For in this case the focus is on an objective content; I have to be familiar with it in order to understand other people in their dealings with it. It is identically the same content that I am familiar with and that others are familiar with; and it is given to me and to them as identically the same. But in this whole discussion of empathy the focus is on the subjective dimension of an experience, on living one's own experience, on having it as one's own. This subjective aspect cannot be given to me and to others as identically the same; as we have seen, my experience is given to me in a way that others' experience cannot be given to me. Thus "the delight of a child in play" is not an objective datum that I need to be familiar with before I can understand a group of children at play. "What it is like for a child to take delight in play" is a subjective datum that I need to know first in myself before I can understand empathetically children at play. Let us now continue with the examples of how my own experiencing provides me with a way into the experiencing of others.

Recall the command given to the Jews in *Exodus* and *Leviticus* not to oppress the stranger and foreigner in their midst; the command is repeatedly supported by the reminder that "you were yourselves once foreigners in Egypt." It may seem that Moses is just impressing on the Jews the unfairness of exercising the very oppression that they had wanted not to endure in their days in Egypt. But sometimes his language suggests that he wants the people of Israel to recur to their own experience of being a foreigner in order to gain some empathetic understanding of the foreigners now living in their midst. Thus in *Exodus* 23:9 we read, "You shall not oppress an alien; you well know how it feels to be an alien, since you were once aliens yourselves in the land of Egypt."

Another example. We often look at the bad behavior of another from the outside; we find it to be unreasonable, wrong, and above all incomprehensible. "How could he or she do such things?" If we can only turn back into ourselves and realize that we ourselves have often done things not essentially different from what we so disapprove of in the other, or at least could easily have done them, or might yet do them, then our disapproval will lose a certain hardness. We will still disapprove, but without finding the disapproved behavior to be incomprehensible; our disapproval is now situated within a certain solidarity with the other; we rebuke as a fellow human being, speaking our words of disapproval from within the human condition and not from some elevated point outside of it. The one whom we rebuke will feel himself vastly better understood if we who rebuke have the courage to speak out of our own moral frailty, and as a result he will find it vastly easier to listen to our rebuke and to take it seriously. Here is the point: by understanding the other through ourselves we achieve empathy with the other and perhaps begin to feel sympathy with him or her.

And another example. A person doing wrong to another commonly has no empathetic understanding for the suffering of the one whom he wrongs. We try to awaken such understanding in him by asking him how he would like to have that same wrong done to him that he is inflicting on the other. It is always possible that he will say that he would not like it at all but has no objection to someone else undergoing the wrong. But we think that once he realizes what it would be like for him to suffer the wrong that he inflicts on the other, he will have a hard time resisting a new kind of empathetic understanding of the other.[13]

The fact that empathy and sympathy are grounded in my self-experience can be verified not only among *human* persons. Consider what the Letter to the Hebrews says about the sympathy of Christ, in whom we believers see a divine person: "For we do not have a High Priest who cannot sympathize with our weaknesses, but one who was in all

---

13. One critic of mine objected that in one treatment center for rapists the following therapy was employed with considerable success: the rapists were asked to consider the rape from the point of view of the woman raped. Here one seems to bypass one's own experience of being violated—men cannot be raped—and to move directly to a new empathetic understanding of the woman. My critic wanted to put into question my claim that the recourse to my own experience is really always a necessary basis for achieving empathy. But the question is whether the new understanding that the rapist thereby gains of his victim really qualifies as empathetic understanding if he does not also bring into his deliberation the prospect of undergoing some grievous bodily degradation himself.

points tempted as we are . . ." (*Hebrews* 4:15). This seems to say that it is Christ's own temptations that enable him to understand with sympathy our temptations. A few lines below we read of "every high priest:" "He can have compassion on those who are ignorant and going astray, since he himself is also subject to weakness" (*Hebrews* 5:2). The Son of God puts Himself in the position of practicing empathy and sympathy with us just because He puts Himself in the position of sharing with us experiences of weakness.

We mentioned in the previous section that through empathy we not only enter into the experiencing of another but also into the other as personal subject. It seems that this aspect of empathy also has its basis in my own experience of existing as personal subject. I surely first experience in myself what it is to live one's being from within oneself and so to exist as a personal subject; if I understand this subjectivity in another this is because I first know it in myself. I surely first experience in myself what it is to have experiencing as one's own; if I understand this ownership in another this is again because I first know it in myself. Of course we cannot argue here as in the previous cases, claiming that if I had no subjectivity of my own I could never recognize it in others, for it is impossible to be in the situation of looking for subjectivity in others while having none in myself. And yet it seems certain that my apprehension of subjectivity in others is in some way based on my sense of subjectivity in myself. This is why we typically say that the other is a self no less than I am a self—this expresses the priority of my experience of my own selfhood. When Newman says, in the passage introduced above, that the other has his own hopes and desires and fears and hence must have an "infinite abyss of existence" in himself, he is not directly apprehending this depth of subjectivity in the other but is rather extending or transferring to the other what he first of all knows in himself. I hold, then, that just as the suffering of another is empathetically understood on the basis of my own similar suffering, so another is empathetically apprehended as personal subject on the basis of my own personal subjectivity. This is perhaps a necessary truth about empathy given the way in which each person is, as we said above, turned towards himself and hidden from the view of others.

On the other hand, if I cannot find in myself what the other is experiencing—for example, if I have never experienced strong suicidal tendencies and cannot imagine how a person could possibly want to hurl himself into an oncoming train, or if I have never experienced certain neurotic or psychotic conditions and do not readily understand what these sufferers are talking about, or if I have a normal relation to my bodily size and shape and cannot make sense of the obsession with extreme thinness in the anorexic—then I am in no position to practice empathy with those who experience these things. They will feel that I remain outside of their suffering. Even if they may feel my compassion for them as sufferers, they will feel that I cannot enter into their particular suffering with empathetic understanding.

Sometimes the hindrance to empathy does not lie just in the accidental limitations of my previous experience, but in more fundamental limitations that cannot be transcended. Can I as a man understand empathetically what it is like to exist as a woman? Can I achieve the empathy that women can achieve among themselves? There are undoubtedly certain excellences proper to a man's apprehension of a woman, excellences that are not in the same way possible in a woman's apprehension of a woman, but empathetic understanding is not one of them. Or consider a far more fundamental limitation: can I understand empathetically what it is like to be the incommunicable and unrepeatable person that another is? Nothing that I know in my incommunicable self really prepares me for, or introduces me into, the incommunicable self of another; no self-experience reduces the surprise I feel when I come to know the other person in all of his or her otherness. This encounter with the other as other is a deep and significant knowledge of the other; it is just the knowledge that can engender in me love for the other. It may even let me know the other in ways in which the other cannot know himself. But it is not knowledge distinguished by the particular excellence of empathetic understanding.

Notice that we have to distinguish again, as we did above, between apprehending another as personal subject and apprehending another as this unrepeatable person: the former is an achievement of empathy, but not the latter. Now we have the reason for the difference: whereas I have in myself as personal subject all that I need to apprehend another as personal subject, I have nothing in my own self-experience that provides me with a basis for coming to know the other as the unrepeatable person that he or she is.

We thus see yet again that empathetic understanding is by no means the whole of our knowledge of other persons, or even the deepest part of such knowledge; it is just one particular perfection of it. Scheler overshoots the mark, as we have already seen, when he teaches that empathetic understanding is the only way in which we know others as persons; he overlooks significant non-empathetic ways of knowing other persons. This will be important for our debate with Scheler in the next section.

It is important to add something to all that has been said: I do not have to have *actually experienced* in myself what I empathetically understand in another; it is enough for empathy if I can find the potency or capacity for it in myself. Thus I do not have to have in fact committed adultery in order to feel empathy with David in his adultery. If I exercise a certain moral imagination towards my own moral failings, and in particular towards my own vulnerability to selfish concupiscence, then I will readily discern in myself the potential for such a wrong and will readily understand how great the temptation to it could be for me and I will say, "there but for the grace of God go I." And with this I understand what "it is like" to be tempted as David was tempted. Thus do I come to understand the adulterous David through myself without actually having to be an adulterer.

Or consider a celibate priest who tries to understand married people. At first glance it may seem that his empathetic understanding of them is bound to be limited by the fact that he has never lived in the spousal relation they live in. And this is just what people commonly say when they disparage the observations about marriage made by celibates. But one would think that the celibate has in his human nature all the "materials" he needs for understanding the married love of others. Through his sexuality and his manhood, through that which Wojtyla has called the "nuptial meaning" of the human body, through his human capacity for love and his masculine capacity for the love of woman, he has in him that which, imaginatively put together, can enable him to understand empathetically the married love of others by passing through his own human nature. He has in himself that which will resonate empathetically with all that he hears from married people and observes in them.

Consider the way in which the young typically perceive the elderly. They consider the elderly to be strangely afflicted in all the ailments that go with age; they think of the elderly as simply other than themselves, who by contrast are the healthy, thriving ones and who have nothing to do with the sufferings of age. But as soon as they acknowledge that they too will one day be weighed down with age, that their own mortality, already at work in their flesh, will one day make itself felt as old age, they are beginning to practice empathy with the elderly. They may have as yet little idea what it is like to be sick and debilitated as a result of age, but the mere fact that they see their future in the elderly creates a certain solidarity with them and lets the young begin to approach the elderly empathetically.

Of course, people possess to very different degrees the moral imagination that lets them find others in themselves. The unimaginative can reach others only through that which they have actually experienced in themselves, and in fact some are so unimaginative that they do not even know how to recognize those actual experiences in their lives that would let them understand others through themselves. And then there are highly imaginative ones who know how to read even the tendencies and potencies and aspirations of their human nature and thus to reach many of their fellows with empathetic understanding. These are the ones who are able to say with the Roman poet, "homo sum, humani nihil a me alienum puto" ("I am a man and nothing that is human is foreign to me").

But perhaps there is an even more significant difference among people with regard to the capacity for empathy. I refer to the difference in the *willingness* to understand others through ourselves. We often have to give up, at least in many cases of empathy, a certain proud isolation, a desire to breath a purer air than the rest of humanity; we have to be willing to stand on the same ground with all other human beings. Whenever the other is suffering from some brokenness, we naturally incline to reckon his brokenness to what is incommunicably the other's own, so as to keep clear of it ourselves. We have to own up to a certain solidarity in brokenness if we are really going to achieve empathetic understanding with certain others. Thus the empathetic understanding of others is a kind of understanding that has a clearly defined tie to the freedom and the moral character of one who empathizes. Of course, this tie to freedom is not just given when I imaginatively go beyond my actual experience; it is equally given when I empathize on the basis of my actual experience.

In order to recapitulate much of what I have wanted to say in this section about empathy and sympathy I turn to a striking passage in Newman. In the course of speaking of the exceptional gift of sympathy that he finds in St. Paul, he says, not indeed meaning to speak with the technical precision of a philosopher, but still suggesting something important to the philosopher, as he so often does:

> ... human nature, the common nature of the whole race of Adam, spoke in him (St. Paul), acted in him, with an energetical presence, with a sort of bodily fullness.... And the consequence is, that, having the nature of man so strong within him, he is able to enter into human nature, and to sympathize with it, with a gift peculiarly his own.... St. Paul felt all his neighbors, all the whole race of Adam, to be existing in himself.... He (St. Paul) knew himself to be possessed of a nature ... which was capable of running into all the multiplicity of emotions, of devices, of purposes, and of sins, into which it had actually run in the ... multitude of men; and in that sense he bore the sins of all men, and associated himself with them, and spoke of them and himself as one.[14]

We see here my idea that empathy and sympathy with another is based on what I first experience in myself, for St. Paul understands human things in other persons on the basis of the experience he has of human nature in himself. Particularly striking is this expression: in empathy I feel the other to be as it were "existing in myself." We could say that in empathy I understand the subjectivity of the other through my own; I in a way read the other in myself. Also present in Newman's text is the thought that empathy does not require that I have in fact experienced in myself what I see in the other. St. Paul did not have to have committed all the sins that he could empathetically understand in others; he understood them on the basis of his capacity for sin.

At the end of this section let us try to state as succinctly as possible what it is that the act of empathy accomplishes. I typically begin by apprehending some conscious life or experiencing in another person, such as the love of play felt by a child. At first I do not apprehend it empathetically, which means that I apprehend the child's love of play from without and not from within, or in other words as I experience the child playing and not as the child experiences itself playing, or in still other words, objectively and not subjectively. I want now to understand the playing child subjectively. But the subjectivity of the playing child is hidden from me. So I have recourse to my own childhood experience of taking delight in play, where I experience delight in play from within. The subjective dimension missing in my apprehension of the child playing is found in

---

14. John Henry Newman, "St. Paul's Characteristic Gift," *Sermons Preached on Various Occasions* (London: Longmans, Green, and Co., 1900), 95–96.

Empathetic Understanding

my reliving of my own childhood playing. Then I look back to the playing child and try this time to enter into his subjectivity by thinking that his subjectivity must be like mine; I try to read the child's subjectivity in my own. But I do not conflate the two subjectivities, and in fact I am reminded of their distinctness by the fact that, however deep my empathetic understanding goes, I never get into the subjectivity of the child as I am in my own subjectivity. And yet I gain some subjective understanding of the child; I understand what it is like to take a childlike delight in play and I in some way extend this understanding[15] beyond myself to the child. And if I talk to the child about play I can make him feel understood by me.

4. Scheler's objections

Scheler does not agree that our empathy passes through our own experiencing on its way to the subjectivity of the other. Let me now try to deal with all the objections to my analysis that can be gathered from his work, *Wesen und Formen der Sympathie*. As we will see, the common denominator of the objections is that the transcendence of empathy is jeopardized by my position, which introduces my own experience into the act of empathizing in such a way as to keep me from really attaining the other as a person in his own right.

1. Scheler was a sharp critic of the analogical reasoning theory of how we come to know other minds, and he would certainly say that my discussion in the previous section restores this untenable theory. Let me explain.

That theory was devised to explain how it is that I come to acknowledge conscious life and experiencing in another. The theory assumes that I directly perceive in the other only a body, and that I infer to conscious life in that body on the basis of what I know about my body and its connection with my conscious life. Thus if I see a clenched fist and a tense face in another, I infer anger in the other on the basis of the anger I know in myself when my fist is clenched and my face tense. Scheler made such a devastating criticism of this theory[16] that it is hard to see how anyone

---

15. I grant that this act of "extending" to the child what I experienced in myself is in need of further study.
16. He did this above all in the final chapter of *The Nature of Sympathy*, "The Perception of Other Minds."

could hold it after Scheler. Above all, he argued that we never see expressionless, merely physical bodies in other human beings, but rather always only bodies that embody and express conscious life in such a way as to make it visible to us and available to our direct intuition. We do not need an inference for apprehending that which offers itself to our direct intuition. Now Scheler's critique of the analogical reasoning theory does not challenge my central claim about empathy, because this theory concerns the way in which one first comes to apprehend conscious life in others, whereas my claim concerns the much more specific thing of experiencing others as they experience themselves. I can agree that the conscious life of others is commonly immediately perceptible through its embodiment, and yet still hold that empathetic understanding is not gained by any immediate perception of the other but passes through my own self-experience.

Scheler will respond that I seem to be holding the analogical reasoning theory in a restricted form, that is, limiting it to empathetic understanding, but still that it is an untenable theory even in this restricted form. And indeed I must admit that my position bears a certain resemblance to the theory; the way in which I in some sense start with my own experiencing and then attain to a more subjective perspective of the experiencing of the other bears a certain resemblance to an inference based on analogical reasoning. But this is a misleading resemblance: in reality I do not hold this theory even for the limited purpose of explaining empathetic understanding. And the reason is this: the empathy with which I am concerned in this paper is not something that could be meaningfully achieved by means of an inference. For, an inference establishes a state of affairs, but when I strive for empathetic understanding of another I am not trying to establish some state of affairs about the inner life of the other. I am not trying to establish some "knowledge that" in regard to the other; I am trying to participate more intimately in the subjectivity of the other, as we remarked above (section 2). And even though I typically come to understand through my self-experience what it is like to experience what another experiences, I am not thereby using my self-experience as the premise in an inference, nor am I reaching the inner life of the other as the conclusion of an inference. It is rather the case that my self-experience serves as a *medium* through which I come to *participate* more intimately in the subjectivity of the other. Thus I do not restore the ana-

Empathetic Understanding

logical reasoning theory even in the restricted form just mentioned and so am not vulnerable to any of Scheler's criticism of it.

To sum up: analogical inference, as Scheler says, is superfluous for our first coming to know the experiencing of another, for this we commonly grasp immediately in its embodiment. And analogical inference is inappropriate for coming to know what "it is like" to experience what the other experiences, for this empathetic understanding is not the kind of thing that can be meaningfully achieved by means of an inference.

2. I turn to another objection that Scheler would surely make to my central claim about empathy. In one place he masterfully describes the person to whom you go looking for sympathy and who can respond to you only by relating some pain or suffering of his own that he takes to be similar to yours. Instead of empathetically understanding you in your own pain, he relives some pain of his own that at most runs parallel to your pain. Such a person does not succeed in achieving empathy with you; he rather remains idiopathically stuck in his own experiencing and hence prevented from entering into your pain.[17] Scheler thinks our efforts at empathy are bound to be overtaken by such idiopathic self-absorption if we try to find the subjectivity of the other in our own subjectivity.

I respond that Scheler describes here only a natural danger to which empathetic understanding is exposed; he does not describe a deformity that is intrinsic to it. Someone who says to us at the funeral of our child, "I know what it is like to lose a child, I lost one myself last year, I am with you in your inconsolable grief," may really reach us with empathy and sympathy: it is in no way necessary that he remain idiopathically stuck in himself. Not only that, but the danger envisioned by Scheler is not as great on my view as it is on his, for I acknowledge, as I remarked above, various non-empathetic ways of knowing other persons. To apprehend a person in all the mystery of the incommunicable, unrepeatable being of that person, of his or her radical otherness, is not an achievement of empathy. We also saw that it is not an achievement of empathy to apprehend another person from my own point of view rather than from his point of view. If our attempts at empathetic understanding are coordinated with

---

17. *The Nature of Sympathy*, 46–47. "In so far as our own reproduced experiences may intervene between our fellow-feeling and the other person's state of mind, the genuine and purely positive fellow-feeling is veiled in an obscuring medium originating in the particular state of our psychophysical organization at the time."

such non-empathetic acts, are supported by and anchored in them, then the transcendence of these attempts can be protected against the tendency towards idiopathic self-absorption. But if one holds with Scheler that our entire approach to other persons is by way of empathy, and if one holds with me that empathy involves getting at others through our own experiencing, then it is only natural to fear for the transcendence of empathy. Scheler deals with this fear by denying the path to the other that leads through my own experiencing: I deal with it by denying that our entire approach to others as persons is by way of empathy.

3. There is also a related objection that can be gathered from Scheler; it, too, calls into question the transcendence of the act whereby one gains understanding of others by going through one's own experience. Scheler writes:

> Quite a number of philosophers have alleged that the phenomenological course of fellow-feeling *(Mitgefühl)* largely consists in a kind of *comparison*, which, if put into words, would run as follows: "How would it be if this had happened to *me?*" ... the answer would very often be, "had it happened to *me*, with *my* character and temperament, it would not have been so bad; but being the sort of person he is, it is a serious matter for him." True fellow-feeling reveals itself in the very fact that it includes the existence and character of the other person as an individual, as part of the object of commiseration or rejoicing.[18]

The objection would be that my own experiencing is not a reliable point of departure for attaining to and sharing in the experiencing of some other, because the other, being other, differs from me in his experiencing; if I try to read his inner life in the prism of my own I am liable to misread him. Whereas the previous objection referred to the danger of the self-transcendence of empathy being blocked entirely, the present objection refers to the danger of self-transcendence being skewed as a result of differences between my experiencing and the other's experiencing.

It is once again important to appeal to the non-empathetic ways of knowing other persons. The objection would carry much more weight if my apprehension and understanding of another were entirely and exclusively based on empathy. It is also important to appeal again to the fact that for empathy with another I require not actual experiences like those of the other but the potency for such experiences; this vastly enlarges the points of departure in myself for achieving empathy with the other.

18. Ibid., 39.

Empathetic Understanding 55

But the objection can be encountered best of all by thinking concretely about empathy. While the Jewish experience of being a foreigner among the Egyptians must have differed from the experience of being a foreigner among the Jews, the lot of the foreigner is a fundamental "role" in the human condition, so that Moses was surely right to think that the Jewish experience of being foreigners enabled Jews to have a particular understanding for the foreigners among them. We can find even more for our response to the objection by returning to the example of sympathizing with a friend who has lost a young child. Surely the bond between parent and child is not one thing for me and another for my friend, as if my own grief over losing my child had no kinship with the grief of my friend over his child. Of course, there may have been a special closeness between my friend and his child, a closeness that I did not have with my child, so that his was an even more piercing grief than my own. But even such a difference between us as this one can be best understood on the basis of my own experience; if I can go back to my own experience of special closeness with a child or with a parent, then I can enter with greater understanding into my friend's experience of his relation to his child. And so the fact that I start with my own experience by no means implies that I will take the experience of some other to be just like mine. I am capable of a certain moral imagination whereby I sift the materials of my own experience so that I can not only affirm that the other's experience is like mine, but also negatively state that it is unlike mine.

4. Here is another feature of empathy that was important to Scheler: through empathy I can have the horizon of my experience enlarged in the sense that I can get acquainted in others with feelings and attitudes that I have never known in myself. But on my view it seems that I can empathetically experience in another only that which I already know in myself; thus on my view, Scheler would object, empathy loses its power to expand my understanding of the human heart beyond the limits of what I have in fact hitherto experienced.

I respond that on my view we are entirely capable of experiencing in others all manner of feelings and attitudes that we have never experienced in ourselves; I affirm only that this self-transcending experiencing is not empathetic understanding. Again we see that my analysis of empathy comes out very differently than Scheler would expect because of the fact that I do not let empathetic understanding, as he does, be the only form of our knowledge of others as persons—that I recognize non-empathetic modes of knowing others as persons.

But even if we confine ourselves to empathetic understanding, my position does not have to constrict our ability to learn from the experiencing of others in the way Scheler thinks it has to. For, as we saw, empathy does not require that I have *actually experienced* in myself that which I empathetically understand in another; it suffices that I have the potency for the experience and that I show a certain moral imagination in "reading" this potency. This means that when I encounter in another say a suicidal temptation such as I have never known, I can turn to the potencies of my own human nature as well as to kindred experiences of my own, such as non-suicidal despair, and by an exercise of moral imagination begin to understand the other empathetically. Thus the other can challenge me to a new exercise of empathy, one surpassing all the empathy I have previously experienced. It is just that my relation to the other does not qualify as empathy until I achieve some solidarity with the other on the basis of what I know in myself.

To conclude. While I want no less than Scheler to secure the transcendence of empathy and sympathy—to make sense of the power of these acts really to reach the other and really to participate in the subjectivity of the other—I think he is wrong to say that we have to exclude any mediating role of our own experiencing, as if this could only interfere with the transcendence of empathy and sympathy. The facts of experience seem to show clearly that it is our own experiencing, and nothing but it, that makes this transcendence possible. Even if I do not transcend myself in empathy in such a way as to leave myself behind, even if I understand the other empathetically "in myself," as we have said, I can still reach the other in this way and make the other certain of being taken out of his or her solitude. Self-transcendence is entirely preserved on my view. It is just shown to have a somewhat different structure than other forms of self-transcendence by passing through my subjectivity rather than simply surpassing it.

This is as far as our encounter with Scheler extends. We turn now to a fundamental presupposition of the empathetic act of finding another in ourselves.

5. The solidarity on which empathy is based

Our account of empathy is still incomplete. The mere fact that I experience in myself the same thing that another experiences in himself—that I have the same experience, for example, of being a foreigner that another has—does not by itself guarantee empathy with the other. Let us think of the old contrast between Greeks and barbarians; if I understand myself to be "Greek" and understand the other to be "barbarian," then the experience of being cast as a foreigner in the midst of some nation, though we have both known this experience and know that we have known it, will not necessarily let me achieve empathy with the other. For as a barbarian the other is too "other;" I am blocked by his otherness from passing from my subjectivity to his subjectivity. It is not that I deny the similarity in his and my experiencing; it is rather that as barbarian he is fundamentally inferior to me and for this reason is kept beyond the reach of my empathy.

De Tocqueville says in *Democracy in America* that the nobility in an aristocratic society looks upon commoners as being so different from itself that it "scarcely believes that they belong to the same race."[19] The nobility is thus prevented from empathizing very deeply with them. He offers as evidence the cool detachment with which a French noble woman, writing in 1675, describes the appalling cruelties with which the police enforced a new tax imposed on the common people. Then he says, "It would be a mistake to suppose that Madame de Sevigné, who wrote these lines, was a selfish or cruel person; she was passionately attached to her children and very ready to sympathize in the sorrows of her friends.... But Madame de Sevigné *had no clear notion of suffering in anyone who was not a person of quality*"[20] (my italics). He proceeds to discuss the slaveholders in the United States, and says, "The same man who is full of humanity towards his fellow creatures when they are at the same time his equals becomes insensible to their afflictions as soon as that equality ceases."[21] He did not interpret this insensibility as a willful refusal on the part of white slave holders to extend empathy beyond the circle of

---

19. Alexis de Tocqueville, *Democracy in America*, II, trans. by H. Reeve (New York: Vintage Books, 1954), Book 3, ch. 1, 173.
20. Ibid., 175.
21. Ibid., 176.

their own, but rather as an incapacity for empathy that was inevitable as long as white slave holders saw negro slaves as fundamentally other than themselves. He thought that the "otherness" perceived in the negro slaves blocked the flow of empathy that was possible among those belonging to the slaveholding class. From these sociological factors inhibiting empathy de Tocqueville drew the conclusion that, as the aristocratic classes dissolve with the spread of democracy, the common humanity of the citizens is freed up to serve as the basis for a farther reaching empathy than was possible under the old aristocratic order.

In vain did Shylock appeal to all that the Jew has in common with all other human beings: "Hath not a Jew hands, organs, dimensions, senses, affections, passions, fed with the same food, hurt with the same weapons, subject to the same diseases, healed by the same means, warmed and cooled by the same winter and summer, as a Christian is?" (*Merchant of Venice*, III.1) All these points of sameness have been fully acknowledged by non-Jews; but as long as they think of the Jew as some kind of outcast or accursed being, he is too "far" away from them to be reached by their empathy.

One might think that we have only to secure the fundamental equality of all human beings and that then the parallel experiencing described above will engender empathy and sympathy without encumbrance. I have argued elsewhere that the equality of human beings can best be secured by affirming that each of them is a person; personhood is a great equalizer. And the reason is this. Beings that have their identity by instantiating some type or kind may instantiate the kind more or less, better or worse; the beings that fully instantiate the kind will be excellent ones of their kind, whereas those that poorly instantiate it will be substandard beings of their kind. But this "more or less," this "better or worse" has no place among persons, because a person does not have his or her identity by instantiating some type or kind. A person is incommunicable and unrepeatable; a particular person has an identity that is radically the person's own, that coincides with the individual being of the person; thus the identity cannot be repeated in any other person, and so it cannot exist more in one person and less in another. This equalizing tendency that results from acknowledging human beings to be persons can sometimes be almost felt. If, for example, we ask what it is that has led to our consciousness of women being fundamentally equal to men, we get the

Empathetic Understanding

answer, as we saw already in the previous chapter, that they have been acknowledged to be persons just as men are persons. Now it is certainly true that this acknowledgement of personhood can undermine the distinction between Greek and barbarian along with the many variants and derivatives of this distinction. A human being ceases to be a barbarian, that is, a substandard human being, as soon as he or she is acknowledged to be a person.

But this acknowledgement of personhood, though it does indeed remove one obstacle to empathy, does not suffice to let empathy flow freely among persons. Suppose my sense of the other as person is inserted into a strong individualism of the kind where persons show themselves as persons by asserting their rights and protecting their rights from the intrusions of others; then I live in a social setting that is extremely unfavorable to the exchange of empathy, even if the fundamental equality of persons is acknowledged. It seems that something more is needed for empathy besides the equalization of persons.

Let us stay with the division of human beings into Greek and barbarian, where a little more reflection will readily bring to light the further condition for empathy that we are searching for. What is it that Greeks experience among themselves if not a certain solidarity, a certain belonging together, a deep sense of community to the point of feeling themselves to be members of the same body? Is this not an important condition for the free flow of empathy among Greeks? When one Greek experiences in himself what he knows some other Greek also experiences, he is confident of understanding what it is like for the other to experience what he experiences: does he not have this confidence because he is bound together with the other as in a body? He does not have this confidence about understanding the experience of barbarians: their experience may be ever so like his own, but since they exist outside the solidarity in which he exists with his fellow Greeks, he achieves little empathy with them. If we again look over the examples of empathy given above we will find in each case this factor of solidarity without which the empathy would not have been possible. Take the so significant case of the "softening" of our negative judgment of another as a result of realizing our own vulnerability to the same negative judgment; can we not discern a sense of solidarity with the other in human fallenness, a sense of being together with the other in the same moral brokenness and neediness? If I think that the condemned behavior of the other is altogether the other's fault, and that my similar behavior is altogether my own fault, if in other words I think that his condemned behavior is incommunicably all his own and that mine is incommunicably all my own, so that there is no common human condition of fallenness that we both share in and suffer under, then the recognition of a similar fault in the other and in myself does not give rise to much empathy. Similarity alone does not suffice for empathy; the similarity must be situated in some solidarity.

We will gain a great deal for our investigation if we now bring in co-experiencing for comparison. We spoke of co-experiencing earlier in this study, using the example of the children who grieve together over the death of their father. We said that this co-experiencing must not be confused with the lower thing of identification with others (where the distinctness of persons is effaced), and that it must be distinguished from empathy and sympathy (the grieving children do not empathize with each other, they are too close to each other for empathy). We said that in and through co-experiencing a collective subjectivity is formed, a term that seems especially appropriate when it is many persons who come together in co-experiencing. Now the very affirmation we just made about empathy holds as well—and in fact even more clearly—for co-experiencing: co-experiencing, too, is not merely a matter of parallel experiencing but requires in addition some solidarity among the co-experiencing persons. Two people who grieve over the death of the same person do not necessarily co-grieve; even if each knows of the other's grief, they may still stand next to each other with parallel griefs, with two griefs that do not become one shared grief, as happens with co-grieving. Only if the two persons stand in some solidarity with each other is there a chance for co-grieving. If, for example, they are both children of the deceased, or parents of him, or were both once students of the deceased, or were both citizens of the state of which he was president, then they are in a position to grieve together in the sense of co-grieving. Some kind of solidarity over and above the parallel grieving is required for the parallel grieving to become co-grieving. And so with empathy and sympathy: some kind of solidarity over and above the similar experiencing is required for the similar experiencing to give rise to empathetic understanding. If the person who has lost a child is a member of my extended family, or of my church, or of my nation, I may be sufficiently one with him so as to feel empathy with him over his loss. But some kind of bond with the other—that is, something opposed to casting the other out as a barbarian—is needed if empathy is to be possible.

But there seems to be still more of a connection between co-experiencing and empathy than appears from this comparison. In fact in certain experiences of empathy one can discern a basis of empathy in co-experiencing. When I show empathy and sympathy to the one who has lost a child I seem to co-experience with that person the unique tie that binds children to their parents and the resulting vulnerability of parents. Or if a full co-experiencing has not yet arisen between the other and me, I am at least mindful of the solidarity that comes with sharing the vulnerability of a parent; I am at least mindful of a solidarity that has the full potential for being co-experienced. This mindfulness of solidarity seems to be just the factor that enables me to understand another "in myself"; it lets me experience myself as being in a sense one with the other, so that what I know in my subjectivity serves to introduce me into the other's subjectivity. If I am mindful neither of this nor of any other such solidarity, then I am too "far" from the other to offer empathy and sympathy, however similar our experiences may be, however equal as persons I may understand myself and the other to be.

We want to add just a word on the range of our empathetic capacity. It is well known how difficult it is to break down the division of human beings into Greeks and barbarians so as to achieve an empathetic capacity that encompasses all human beings. And the reason is, in accordance with the main idea of this section of this paper, that it is difficult to achieve a sense of solidarity with all human beings. Our sense of solidarity tends to be limited to our tribal fellows; it does not come naturally to us to feel solidarity with all our fellow humans and to cast no one into the position of barbarian. The French anthropologist Levi-Strauss reminds us in the following of the magnitude of the difficulty of achieving this sense of solidarity:

... the concept of an all-inclusive humanity, which makes no distinction between races and cultures, appeared very late in the history of mankind and did not spread very widely across the globe. What is more, as proved by recent events, even in the one region where it seems most developed, it has not escaped periods of regression and ambiguity. For the majority of the human species, and for tens of thousands of years, the idea that humanity includes every human being on the face of the earth does not exist at all. The designation stops at the border of each tribe, or linguistic group, sometimes even at the edge of a village. So common is the practice that many of the peoples we call primitive call themselves by a name which means 'men'... thus implying that the other tribes, groups, and villages do not partake in human virtues or even human nature, but are, for the most part, 'bad people'... 'land monkeys....' They often go so far as to deprive the stranger of any connection to the real world at all by making him a 'ghost' or an 'apparition.' Thus curious situations arise in which each interlocutor rejects the other as cruelly as he himself is rejected.[22]

The division of people into Greeks and barbarians seems to be almost the natural position of the human mind and heart.

But it is also true that we are capable of a universal human solidarity, such as is celebrated in the last movement of Beethoven's Ninth Symphony. The intuition expressed in the Ode to Joy and the musical expression of it, or the ideas expressed by Dostoevsky when he speaks (through Fr. Zosima) of the responsibility of each human being for all other human beings, resonate profoundly in us and are even more deeply natural to us than is the division of people into Greeks and barbarians. It would exceed the limits of this paper to explore the sources (including the specifically Christian sources) of this sense of universal human solidarity.[23] It is enough for us to observe that this sense is the basis for the capacity to extend empathy and sympathy to all human beings.[24]

In conclusion I observe that the result of this paper in a way completes

---

22. Claude Levi-Strauss, *Structural Anthropology*, II, trans. by Monique Layton (Chicago: University of Chicago Press, 1983), 329.

23. There is in Scheler a rich account of this universal human solidarity; for an introduction to it see my paper in this collection, "Max Scheler on the moral and religious solidarity of persons." But I am not aware of him ever recurring to this solidarity for the sake of completing his account of empathy. He perhaps takes a step in my direction in *Der Formalismus in der Ethik*, 515–18, where he shows that it is difficult to apprehend the conscious experiencing of others in the individualistic setting of the *Gesellschaft* and much easier to apprehend this in the communitarian setting of the *Lebensgemeinschaft*. But he does not seem to be speaking here precisely of the empathetic understanding of others.

24. This human solidarity was present, though not yet thematized, in some of our previous examples of achieving empathy on the basis of our own experience. For example, Moses was assuming that this solidarity exists among Jews and foreigners; he wanted to say that foreigners, too, are fellow human beings. If he had thought of foreigners as barbarians, he could not have been so sensitive to their feelings of vulnerability in the midst of the Jews.

Empathetic Understanding

the result of the previous paper. In that paper I was mainly concerned with human beings as unrepeatable persons, for I claimed to find a neglected source of the dignity of persons in the unrepeatable person that each is. In the present paper on empathy, too, I focused on persons as unrepeatable and incommunicable. It is just because each person is incommunicably himself or herself that something like empathetic understanding is needed. We also saw that entering into the inner life of another incommunicable person by way of empathy involves no illusory amalgamation of persons but preserves the experience of myself as incommunicable person and of the other as incommunicable person. We further saw that one of the achievements of empathy is precisely to apprehend the other as being an incommunicable person no less than I am one. In all of this we continued along the line of the previous essay. But we have also had our attention drawn to what is common to human persons, for empathy is enacted through the medium of this common element. And here in the last section of the present essay I introduced an idea that distinctly completes the work of the previous one: the solidarity of human beings that puts us in a position to give and receive empathy is in a way the very opposite of personal incommunicability. In standing in solidarity with each other, in co-experiencing, we become as it were members of each other, we exist in the same body. We can in fact think of the act of empathetic understanding as involving a dialectic of the incommunicable and the communicable, of what is incommunicably my own and what is common to me and others, of what separates us into irreducibly distinct persons and what binds us into one body.[25]

25. Many thanks to Norris Clarke, S.J., Pia Crosby, and John Henry Crosby, for helpful comments on earlier drafts of this paper.

CHAPTER 3

The Personal Encounter with God in Moral Obligation

In the present paper I try to make a contribution towards a personalist philosophy of religion.

With his "The Natural Law Doctrine of Suarez," William May[1] continues a critique of Suarez which apparently originates in Germain Grisez and which has been recently developed by John Finnis.[2] I propose to take my point of departure from one particular point that is insisted upon by all three of these authors. They all reject the claim of Suarez that the binding force of moral obligation ultimately derives from a divine command. I think that they thereby fail to do justice to something that Suarez must have seen. The moral datum that I think he saw, and that seems to have escaped his critics, is in my opinion of the very first importance for moral philosophy. One cannot really understand rightly the relation of the moral life to God without doing justice to this datum. I am of course far more interested in this datum, and in calling attention to it, than I am in making a contribution to Suarez scholarship, which is in any case beyond my competence. Suarez simply provides me with a point of departure for discussing the relation between moral obligation and God.

---

* This paper originally appeared as "The Encounter of God and Man in Moral Obligation," in *The New Scholasticism* 60.3 (1986), 317–55. It has been considerably reworked for the present publication.

1. *The New Scholasticism* 58.4 (1984), 409–23.

2. Finnis, *Natural Law and Natural Rights* (New York: Oxford University Press, 1980). Since I will usually be quoting from this work of Finnis, which is his major work, I will give the page references directly in the text. Whenever I quote from another work of Finnis I will give the reference in a note.

Encounter with God in Moral Obligation

My contribution means to be phenomenological. I will try to bring to evidence certain aspects of moral obligation, and then to suggest that these almost certainly underlie the controverted thesis of Suarez. It is true that he does not himself offer much of a phenomenological grounding of the thesis. But then his critics, if I understand them correctly, are for their parts not sufficiently attentive to the things themselves, and in their attempt to secure certain important ethical truths they do not attend closely enough to the datum of moral obligation.

It ought to be said right at the beginning that this critical discussion of Grisez and Finnis is offered by one who greatly admires their works and has learned much from them, and who understands himself as living in the same moral universe that they inhabit, and as sharing their most basic intuitions regarding the existence of an objective moral order, and as opposing many of the same ethical errors they oppose, such as consequentialism, proportionalism, relativism, etc. Precisely the fact that I share so much with them leads me to be perplexed at the few areas of disagreement which seem to remain, and at the same time leads me to expect that it will be very fruitful to discuss our disagreements, and that such discussion is undertaken with unusually good chances of ending in agreement.[3]

3. This optimism was confirmed by the paper of Olaf Tollefsen, who is close to Grisez, "Crosby on the Prescriptive Force of Moral Obligation," *The New Scholasticism* 61.4 (1987), 462–76. He raised some very intelligent and challenging objections to the original version of this paper, of which the main objection was the following. He thinks that in this paper I undermine a certain moral autonomy that is proper to human persons: "human moral agents are fully able to direct their own behavior according to the moral judgment they reach by way of practical reason." But "Crosby implicitly denies this, for in the final analysis, his human moral agents cannot will what they are to do solely because it is reasonable to do so; they must have the added causality of a divine command" (470–71). Tollefsen thinks that this loss of autonomy comes from the fact that I fall prey to an extreme dualism of *good* and *ought;* he thinks that I isolate ought from good in the sense that all of our understanding of goods and values makes no contribution to our understanding of what we morally ought to do. When then I try to explain the moral ought as coming from God, I seem to be arguing for a blind obedience to God, and thus to introduce God into moral obligation in such a way as to compromise our moral autonomy. "On Crosby's account of obligation, one is obliged, as a human moral agent, only as a subject of a higher authority. Even one's own conscience is not truly one's own, for when it issues its magisterial dictates it speaks, not with one's own voice, but with God's.... [O]ne's understanding of the good, of what would make it flourish in oneself and in others, is not enough to give one the power to truly direct one's action; that requires a special kind of divine causality, the causality of divine commands and prohibitions. Since that is so, one's autonomy as a moral agent is severely limited...."

1. Suarez on moral obligation

For our purposes we can formulate as follows the thesis of Suarez which I find to be wrongly attacked by Grisez,[4] Finnis, and May. Suarez considers the opinion of those who say that the natural law is nothing but a "legem indicantem, quid agendum, vel cavendum sit, quid natura sua intrinsece bonum ac necessarium, vel intrinsece malum sit" ("law indicating what is to be done or avoided, what is intrinsically good and necessary of its own nature, or intrinsically bad").[5] One might at first glance think that with these words nothing less than the natural law is characterized: but according to Suarez, in expressing this *lex indicans* one captures only the content but not the law-character of the natural law. Only the natural law understood not only as "indicantem" but also as "praecipientem," as commanding or prohibiting, is for Suarez natural *law.*

This preceptive character of law in general (whether of natural or of some other kind of law) lies for Suarez in the commanding or prohibiting will of some superior directing an inferior. In the case of the natural moral law this superior is God. Thus the natural law is law only insofar as those actions and attitudes that are good or bad by their very nature, are commanded or prohibited by God. This is why Suarez speaks of natural law as "lex divina praeceptiva."

---

(474) I have reworked this paper in a number of places so as to secure my argument against even the appearance of espousing any such blind obedience and thus undermining the rightly understood moral autonomy of persons, a truth about persons that is as important to me as to Tollefsen. See my "Autonomy and Theonomy in Moral Obligation: Response to Tollefsen," in *The New Scholasticism* 63.3 (1989), 358–70, for my full response to these criticisms of Tollefsen. I deeply regret that this capable philosopher died prematurely and that we could not continue the dialogue that he initiated.

4. Grisez, *The Way of the Lord Jesus, vol. 1: Christian Moral Principles* (Chicago: Franciscan Herald Press, 1983), ch. 4, question F, and fns. 19 and 20; though not mentioning Suarez by name in ch. 1, question D, Grisez definitely means to ascribe to Suarez much of the legalism and rationalism of which he there speaks. Since all references to Grisez are to this work, I will give the references directly in the text.

5. Suarez, *De legibus ac de Deo legislatore* (Coimbra, 1612), 11, ch. 6, para. 3. Since all of my references to Suarez will be to this ch. 6, which is entitled, "an lex naturalis sit vere lex divina praeceptiva" ("whether the natural law is truly divine preceptive law"), I will give the paragraph number directly in the text. The English translations of Suarez are taken, with small modifications of my own, from Suarez, "Selections from Three Works" J. B. Scott (ed.), *The Classics of International Law* 20 (Oxford, 1944).

Encounter with God in Moral Obligation 67

It is quite clear from the text of Suarez that it is this preceptive character of natural law that makes natural law a source of moral obligation (cf. para. 10). It is God's commanding and prohibiting that establishes the *vinculum* of moral obligation. I stress this by way of justifying the attempt I am about to make to clarify the text of Suarez by investigating some aspects of moral obligation.

Suarez means, to use a modern example, that there is a goodness, an intrinsic goodness or worth, in human persons, so that the act of using persons as mere means is intrinsically wrong, or *cavendum*, to be avoided; but that this *cavendum*, which is directly proportioned to the value of human persons, is itself not yet a moral obligation to respect them, it is not yet a moral prohibition on doing violence to them. The obligation can almost be said to be "superadded" to the value towards which we have the obligation; thus Suarez puts forth as the first of his three theses in chapter 6: "potest lex naturalis, ut est vera lex divina, addere obligationem propriam moralem ortam ex praecepto, ultra naturalem (ut sic dicam) malitiam, vel honestatem, quam ex se habet materia, in quam cadit tale praeceptum" ("the law of nature, as it is true divine law, may also superimpose its own moral obligation, derived from a precept, over and above what may be called the natural evil or virtue inherent in the subject-matter in regard to which such a precept is imposed") (para. 12).

Not even his critics think that Suarez is a voluntarist in the sense of holding that God could command or prohibit just anything. Though His commands and prohibitions superadd something "ultra naturalem malitiam vel honestatem, quam ex se habet materia," He can superadd it only in accordance with the value-character of this "materia," on which His commands and prohibitions therefore in a certain sense depend. Thus the second of his three theses runs as follows: "Haec Dei voluntas, prohibitio, aut praeceptio non est tota ratio bonitatis, et malitiae, quae est in observatione, vel transgressions legis naturalis, sed supponit in ipsis actibus necessariam quandam honestatem, vel turpitudinem, et illis adiungit specialem legis divinae obligationem" ("this divine volition, in the form of a prohibition or in that of an [affirmative] command, is not the whole reason for the good or evil involved in the observance or transgression of the natural law; on the contrary, it necessarily presupposes the existence of a certain righteousness or turpitude in these actions, and attaches to them a special obligation derived from divine law") (para. 11). Suarez means that God could not only not give commands at odds with this "necessariam quandam honestatem, vel turpitudinem in ipsis actibus," He could also not fail to give commands in accordance with these value-characters of human acts (para. 8, 21).

A word, finally, on Suarez's teaching on our *knowledge* of moral obligation. There is some basis in the text of Suarez for reading him as teaching that we can first know moral obligation, and then come to know the divine will from which it derives. For example, at least twice he speaks of the natural law, which qua law binds as a matter of obligation, as a *signum* of the divine will (para. 10, 13); it could not function as a *signum* of the divine will if it could not be known prior to knowing the divine will. But perhaps more prominent in the thought of Suarez is the idea that we know obligation *on the basis of* knowing the divine will. Of course Suarez does not think that we need a special revelation from God in order to know what He commands and prohibits. We rather know this on the basis of knowing that He exists, and has dominion over us, and exercises a providence over us; we understand that in exercising this providence He cannot fail to command what is intrinsically good, and forbid what is intrinsically bad (cf. para. 24).

One of our main tasks in this paper will be to develop the first way of knowing, the one whereby we begin with the fact of obligation, and come to discern in it the divine will.

John Finnis rejects this whole teaching of Suarez; he holds that moral obligation exists without the support of divine commands and prohibitions. One has only to attend to what is objectively good for man, and to consider what means will lead to or will constitute this good, and one has already reached the phenomenon of obligation, which is nothing but the necessity of the means for achieving the good for man (pp. 40–41; 45–46). The principle of moral obligation is not the will of God, but the good for man. Finnis admits that from the point of view of revelation, actions that are already obligatory attract us in a new way as a result of being understood as willed by God (pp. 405–10). But this relation to God does not constitute moral obligation, but only adds a further dimension to it.

Finnis thinks that he understands why Suarez, in explaining moral obligation, so exaggerated the role of the will of God. Suarez supposedly lacks an adequate conception of the human good; instead of finding this good in its self-evidence, he speaks of what conforms to or is suitable to human nature and then rationalistically tries to deduce from this what is good for man. Finnis thinks that moral obligation cannot be understood in terms of the suitability of an act to human nature; he thinks that Suarez leaves himself open to the question, but why conform to human nature? He leaves himself open to the taunt of Hume that he is attempting the illegitimate deduction of what we morally ought to do from what is the case (that is, from relations of conformity with human nature). Since Suarez wants to make sense of moral obligation, and not to debunk it, but since he lacks a theory of the human goods—here I interpret Finnis slightly—he has to cast about for some other principle of it, and it is not surprising that he seizes on the will of God, and teaches that His will is the principle of all obligation. Finnis captures his objection to Suarez with the greatest possible succinctness when he calls the Suarezian position "rationalism eked out by voluntarism" (p. 47). Finnis thinks he can overcome the position of Suarez by rehabilitating the theory of human goods, thereby rendering superfluous Suarez's resort to the divine will in explaining moral obligation.[6]

Suarez also has a theory of the binding force of positive law that, according to Finnis, makes too much of the will of the lawgiver. Finnis thinks that just as the Suarezian theory of natural law makes too much of the divine will, so the Suarezian theory of positive law makes too much of

---

6. It seems that Finnis objects against Suarez in much the same way as Aristotelians and Thomists typically object against the value philosophy of Scheler, Hartmann, and von Hildebrand, and especially against the distinction which they make between being and value. It is said that such value phenomenologists uncritically take over what is nothing more than a positivistic idea of being—an idea of being as merely factual—and then, since they are after all not themselves positivists, they try to find a place for the riches of being which exceed this positivistic idea of being, and are thus led to assume a realm of value. In this way arises their untenable dualism of being and value. One has only to challenge the underlying positivism and to rehabilitate the metaphysics of *esse*, and the whole basis for the distinction between being and value, at least as it is made by these value phenomenologists, is eliminated. (One can find this line of thought presented by J.-B. Lotz in his "Sein und Wert. Das Grundproblem der Wertphilosophie," *Zeitschrift für katholische Theologie* 57 [1933], esp. 571–72.) In a similar way, Finnis thinks that the idea of the human good has been so rationalistically weakened by Suarez, that Suarez has to go beyond the human good in order to make sense of moral obligation, and to posit an untenable distinction between the moral law as *indicans* and *praecipiens*. Finnis wants to rehabilitate the theory of the human good, and thereby eliminate the basis for making this distinction and for going beyond human goods in explaining the binding force of moral obligation.

the human will of the legislator (ch. 11. 6, 7). But this legal issue will not concern us here; it is rather moral obligation in its relation to God that alone concerns us.

2. *The discrepancy between finite goods and moral imperatives*

Suarez's distinction between the moral law as *indicans* and as *praecipiens* is directly parallel to a well-known distinction that Cardinal Newman made with regard to conscience, a distinction that is absolutely central to Newman's thought.[7] What interests us is that Newman finds it possible to develop this distinction, and in particular to develop the sense of conscience corresponding to Suarez's *lex praecipiens*, on the basis of our moral experience and without constantly referring to God as Suarez does. There is a phenomenological orientation in Newman that (as far as I can tell) is foreign to Suarez.

Newman made a great point of distinguishing between conscience as a "judgment of reason" and conscience as a "magisterial dictate" (p. 105), or as he also put it, between conscience as a "rule of right conduct" and conscience as a "sanction of right conduct" (p. 106). Conscience in the first sense seems to apprehend the *lex indicans*, that is, the goodness or badness that actions have in relation to their objects. Conscience in the second sense, since it apprehends a dictate or imperative, would seem to apprehend Suarez's *lex praecipiens*. Here Newman brings out the second sense of conscience, which he always regarded as its most proper sense, by contrasting it with the first:

> Here I have to speak of conscience . . . not as supplying us, by means of its various acts, with the elements of morals, such as may be developed by the intellect into an ethical code, but simply as the dictate of an authoritative monitor bearing upon the details of conduct as they come before us . . . one by one. (p. 106)

Now the phrase, "the dictate of an authoritative monitor," hardly serves to express the attractive power of some human good, not even of the greatest human good; it is too strong for that, it obviously expresses something more, something fundamentally more. And the phrase is not

---

[7]. Newman, *An Essay in Aid of a Grammar of Assent* (London: Longmans, Green, and Co., 1898), ch. v, sec. 1. Since all of my references to Newman will be to this work, the page numbers will be given directly in the text.

dropped in passing; Newman cannot stress enough this authoritative aspect of conscience. Thus conscience is "a voice imperative and constraining, like no other dictate in the whole of our experience;" the "prerogative of dictating and commanding . . . is of its essence" (p. 107). For the purpose of my discussion with Finnis I am very interested in the fact that the basic goods for man—let us suppose that they are just as Finnis and Grisez say—do not have out of themselves such power to dictate and to command.

Let us try to understand concretely Newman's magisterial dictate and a certain disproportion between it and the morally relevant goods that underlie it. We can recognize this dictate in the moral situation that Socrates describes in the *Apology* (32 c, d, e). The Thirty Tyrants ordered Socrates to join four others in an action which Socrates regarded as completely unjust, arresting Leon of Salamis and bringing him to Athens for the purpose of executing him. Socrates ignored the order of the tyrants, and thereby risked his life. In fact Socrates survived only because the government fell before he could be punished for his disobedience. He found himself, or what is more to the point, we would in his situation find ourselves, bound by a moral obligation to do no wrong to a fellow human being who had done no wrong.[8] Let us reflect on the experience of being bound by such a moral obligation, considering first the obligation itself that confronts us, and then the way in which it appeals to us.

John Finnis is surely right that life is a basic human good; he is surely right that no one in the situation of Socrates may act against this good of another. But the question is, does this good completely explain the obligation, or rather the force of the obligation, with which we are bound in conscience when we come into the situation of Socrates? Notice that while Socrates is unconditionally committed to respecting Leon's life, he is perfectly willing to put his own life at risk. In performing his act of refusal he seems to be far more committed to the good of Leon's life than to the good of his own, or rather committed unconditionally to Leon's good and committed only conditionally to his own. But change the circumstances somewhat, and Socrates ceases to show this apparently one-

---

8. I think that the dialogue with Finnis is well served by working precisely with this Socratic example, for in his *Fundamentals of Ethics* (Washington, D.C.: Georgetown University Press, 1983), 112–20, Finnis, in developing his critique of proportionalism, makes a use of it with which I entirely agree. We make the same moral assessment of the refusal of Socrates.

sided preoccupation with the good of Leon's life. Let us suppose that Socrates has not been ordered to participate in the crime against Leon; let us suppose that others have been ordered, others who unlike Socrates will be quite compliant, and that Socrates knows about this. The only thing Socrates could do on Leon's behalf would be to try to reach him first and warn him of the plot against him. But we will further suppose that Socrates can attempt this only by putting his own life at risk. In this case, and assuming that Leon is not bound to Socrates by some special bond, Socrates will surely *not* think that he has to do absolutely everything in his power to protect Leon and to have little regard for his own life, willingly giving it up if that is what is needed to protect Leon's life. Socrates will surely not think this way; he will rather consider the good of his own life too, and will ask himself whether he really wants to endanger it for the sake of Leon. He might well come to the conclusion that his mission as a philosopher is so important, or that Leon, though not guilty as charged, is nevertheless simply so unknown to him that he ought not undertake anything on Leon's behalf. But even if he does decide to intervene on Leon's behalf, thereby risking his life, he will not decide this in the consciousness that it is unconditionally required of him, required by a dictate or command that completely overshadows his interest in his own life. His decision seems to be based on all the relevant human goods and not on the unconditional affirmation of one human good and a completely subordinate interest in all the other human goods at stake. And why does the basis of Socrates' decision undergo this change? Because in the new set of circumstances that we have imagined, he is no longer subject to a moral obligation. He is not morally obliged to risk his life to try to save Leon's. In the situation as described in the *Apology*, Socrates does have a moral obligation not to harm Leon; and it is this presence of the obligation that binds Socrates so unconditionally not to lay violent hands on Leon. Thus the moral obligation to do no harm to Leon is a factor that goes far beyond the good of his life. This good exercises the attractive power proper to itself[9] in the situation where Socrates has no obligation to take ini-

---

9. By the "attractive power proper to some good" I mean that power of the good thing to move me and to motivate me that is entirely intelligible in terms of the goodness of the good thing. This attractive power certainly includes the power of the good to say "ought" to me; in virtue of its attractive power the good thing not only draws me but can also bind me. Thus there is a moment of obligation that is entirely proper to a good and intelligible in terms of it. My purpose in this paper is not to deny this moment of obli-

Encounter with God in Moral Obligation

tiative on behalf of Leon. As soon as the obligation arises, Socrates is bound by something more than this good. The obligation to respect Leon superimposes itself on the good of Leon's life as something incomparably more powerful than the intrinsic appeal of this good; it is nothing other than Newman's magisterial dictate.[10]

There are of course ways in which an obligation can go beyond the intrinsic goodness of the being towards which one has the obligation, yet without amounting to a magisterial dictate. One might on consequentialist grounds consider that the best way to protect innocent lives is to act on the maxim *primum non nocere* (above all else do no harm). One would in this case refuse to harm Leon not merely out of respect for Leon but as a way of promoting a certain state of society in which innocent people are safe; one would be bound to the act of respecting Leon's life, but be bound more strongly than if one (deliberating in this consequentialist way) were motivated only by the good of Leon's life. But here the factor that heightens my interest in Leon's life is a consideration of good which belongs to the same order as the good of Leon's life; there is no question of a magisterial dictate to respect his life, no question of a fundamentally different way of being bound to respect it. What interests us in this study is that the moral obligation not to harm Leon goes beyond the good of Leon's life in the manner of an imperative or a dictate.

One might think that to speak of a magisterial dictate as we have been doing is simply a consequence of holding that there are norms that admit of no exception. One might think—and with this I quite agree—that Socrates acts on the principle *primum non nocere*, and that he understands this principle in a deontological and not in a consequentialist sense. One might say that my magisterial dictate is nothing other than the absolute prohibition that follows from deontological norms, and that the whole question which we are raising in this paper is nothing but the much-discussed question whether there really are such norms. But this would be a mistake, as we can see from the fact that one can find a magisterial dic-

---

gation but to bring out that further moment that is not completely intelligible in terms of the finite good. Tollefsen's paper helped me to think more clearly about these two moments of obligation.

10. On this discrepancy between obligation and the goods which ground it, see the very important discussion in Josef Seifert, *Was ist und was motiviert eine sittliche Handlung?* (Salzburg: Anton Pustet Verlag, 1976), 39–44; see also von Hildebrand, *Moralia* (Stuttgart: Kohlhammer Verlag, 1980), 407–9.

tate in obligations that are not based on exceptionless norms. Let us vary again the circumstances in which Socrates finds himself, and let us suppose that others have been sent to apprehend Leon, and that Socrates can, without any risk to his life and even without making any weighty sacrifice—this is the new circumstance—alert Leon to the danger which threatens him so that he can save himself. This action of alerting Leon is undoubtedly strictly obligatory for Socrates, but it is not an action based on a norm that admits of no exception. If, for example, the act of alerting Leon would have the foreseeable effect of exposing many other innocent persons to the violence of the Thirty Tyrants, then Socrates should consider omitting the act. Socrates' obligation seems to be sensitive to teleological considerations (without of course being completely explicable in teleological terms) in a way in which his obligation not to cooperate in the murder of Leon is not sensitive, and it does not seem to involve any one-sided preoccupation with one good at the expense of others, as this other obligation seems to involve. And yet, for as long as Socrates is obliged to intervene on Leon's behalf, he finds himself bound with imperative unconditional force; the fact that he does not act on some principle admitting no exceptions, in no way eliminates this imperative force.

John Finnis, in any case, will not reduce the issue of moral imperatives to the issue of exceptionless norms, for he recognizes (as I do) the existence of such norms, though he does not seem to recognize the existence of moral imperatives and dictates in the sense explained. On the other hand, there are some thinkers who reject the existence of such norms but who are nevertheless aware, at least to some extent, of what I have called the imperative force of moral obligation.[11]

Thus we are led to distinguish two kinds of absoluteness found in moral obligations: the one is the absoluteness of norms admitting of no exceptions, and this is found only in some obligations; the other is the absoluteness of an imperative dictate, and this is found in all obligations. I am here trying to bring to evidence the latter absoluteness; I am not trying to make a contribution to the debate over intrinsically wrong actions.

The reader will perhaps now understand why I claim to find a certain disproportion between moral obligation and the underlying morally rel-

---

11. Thus for instance Hans Küng in his *Existiert Gott?* (Zürich and Munich: 1978), 635–40, esp. 639–40.

evant goods. Having made this claim I hasten to add that I am in no way denying what is of such concern to Grisez and Finnis, namely that moral obligation does not flash up unpredictably and irrationally but is intelligibly rooted in the natures of things, and that we come to discern our obligation only on the basis of understanding what is intrinsically good and intrinsically bad. Thus if Leon's life were not a fundamental objective good for him, and if this good did not participate in the dignity of the human person, there would be no obligation not to destroy his life. Nor could Socrates apprehend this obligation without understanding this good and this dignity. Socrates could never find himself bound not to cooperate in killing a sub-personal animal as he finds himself bound not to cooperate in killing Leon, nor could he find himself bound not to interfere with the comfort of Leon as he finds himself bound not to interfere with the continued life of Leon. But this grounding of moral obligation in goods and values, to which I am as committed as Grisez and Finnis,[12] does not mean that moral obligation is nothing but the binding power proper to concrete goods and values. To make such a claim and to deny the phenomenon of obligation which Newman calls a magisterial dictate, would be no less at odds with our moral experience, than to deny that moral obligation intelligibly grows out of goods and values.

I admit that Kant, at least in one main strain of his moral philosophy, stressed the imperative force of obligation at the expense of recognizing

---

12. Differences between me and Finnis/Grisez, however, arise when it comes to determining more exactly that which grounds moral obligation. They seem to me to conceive of good as too exclusively *good for the moral agent*, and thus in my opinion to go too far in conceiving of the moral life as the search for self-fulfillment and the avoidance of self-mutilation. They lack the idea of value in the sense of von Hildebrand (*Ethics*, [Chicago: Franciscan Herald Press, 1972] chs. 1–3), R. Otto (*Aufsätze zur Ethik*, "Wert, Würde und Recht" [Munich: C. H. Beck Verlag, 1981]) and others: value as that which is not just objectively good for someone, but objectively good in itself. And thus they lack the idea of responding to a being not just for the sake of my fulfillment but for the sake of giving the being what is due to it in virtue of its value (on this dueness see von Hildebrand, *Ethics*, chs. 17, 18). Consider the value or dignity proper to the person. When I respect another person in virtue of his value and refuse to manipulate him for my purposes, my respect is permeated by the consciousness that the other is worthy of my respect; I am not primarily striving for my own fulfillment. I am not even primarily striving for his fulfillment; I respect him, not just because it is good for him to be respected, but because he as person is worthy of my respect. Now very many obligations are grounded in such value data, and it seems to me that Grisez and Finnis lack the axiological categories to do justice to these obligations. It would be worthwhile to inquire whether this deficiency in their teaching on good has something to do with their failure to do justice to the moral imperative.

an axiological foundation of obligation, but this is a weakness in Kant and not an inner necessity in the subject matter. If it is not easy to overcome this weakness in Kant, as I also admit, if it is not easy to hold fast both to the imperative force of obligation and to its axiological foundation, this should be taken as nothing more than a confirmation of our thesis that moral obligation, however much it grows out of certain goods, is essentially irreducible to them.

3. *This discrepancy as shown in the subjectivity of the person who is morally bound*

We turn now from the objective to the subjective side of moral obligation; having considered its imperative force, we will now consider the way in which it appeals to us. It appeals to us in our conscience, indeed in a sense it creates conscience in us, that is, it awakens for the first time that most intimate inviolable center in ourselves that we call conscience. (The term "conscience" is now being used in a sense closely related to but still distinct from either of Newman's ethical senses; it now refers not to an organ of ethical cognition but to the very center of the person.) When we find ourselves challenged by a moral obligation, we not only encounter the obligation and the good in which it is intelligibly grounded; as Karol Wojtyla has recently shown with great originality,[13] we also encounter ourselves. There is something paradoxical here; though the obligation breaks in upon us from without and binds us to some action with an awe-inspiring imperative force, it at the same time binds us without any least violence, for it sets us in a unique relation to ourselves, makes us come to ourselves as persons, makes us quicken as personal selves. We are aware that in being morally bound, we are handed over to ourselves in a unique way, and that our response to the obligation will determine who we ultimately are as persons, what kind of persons we ultimately are. We are aware that in submitting to the obligation, we affirm and secure our ultimate well-being as persons, just as we are aware that, in disregarding the obligation we compromise our ultimate well-being.[14]

---

13. Karol Wojtyla, *The Acting Person*, Anna-Teresa Tymieniecka (ed.). Translated by Andrzej Potocki. Vol. 10 of *Analecta Husserliana* (Dordrecht: D. Reidel, 1979), ch. 3.

14. I have developed this whole subject out of the philosophical writings of Karol Wojtyla in my paper, "Karol Wojtyla on the Objectivity and the Subjectivity of Moral Action," in Francis (ed.) *Christian Humanism* (New York: Peter Lang, 1995), 27–36.

Encounter with God in Moral Obligation

Now the question that I propose for our consideration is this: can moral obligation shake us like this to the roots of our being, if in being obliged we are only dealing with some finite good, even if it is a good as weighty as the life of a Leon? Must not moral obligation, with its power of opening the depths of personal subjectivity in us, be more than the inherent appeal of such a finite good? *Abyssus abyssum invocat* ("depth cries out to depth"); but one might well wonder whether the good of Leon's life, morally relevant though it is, is really such an *abyssus,* and whether it really has the power of invocation that moral obligation has.

It is all-important to see that this power of invocation presupposes the very thing which Grisez and Finnis are so concerned with securing: the intelligible foundation of moral obligation in goods and bads (to use their terms). For if moral obligations presented themselves to us as arbitrary dictates with an arbitrariness which made possible only a blind submission on our part, then our response would not have the inwardness of which I was just speaking. Everyone knows what a burden it is to submit to demands that we do not understand, everyone knows that such demands are experienced as a foreign force entirely external to ourselves. Moral obligation can bind us, as it undeniably does bind us, from within as well as from without, and set us in a unique relation to ourselves as persons even as it challenges us to do something, only because we understand how it arises from morally relevant goods. We touch here on a most amazing relation between our understanding of the moral law, and a certain internalizing of it, a certain admitting of it into our very selves.

We have been speaking of what it is to have a moral obligation. Suppose that we disregard the moral obligation that we have. Suppose that, having been brought into the situation of Socrates, we concur in the murder of Leon so as to save ourselves from the harm with which we were threatened. If we still have a conscience, then, when the shabby deed has been done, we are haunted with remorse and shame and dread; we are unsettled and perturbed in the deepest depths of our being; all the things which used to give us pleasure and make us happy, lose this beneficent power, and when experienced they just let us feel all the more keenly our inner distress. Again we ask: whence this convulsion in ourselves? Is it not all out of proportion with the act of depriving some human being of some human good? If I exclusively had to do with Leon, a fellow human being, would it be reasonable that my wrongdoing, once I recognize it, should make me shudder with dread, should poison the well-springs of all my happiness, and deprive me of all peace?

I am aware of the objections that present themselves at this point. Some will say that the good of Leon's continued life is so great that it is entirely reasonable to shudder with dread at the thought of having wrongly deprived him of his life. And there is a deeper objection that might be raised. One might say that the good of Leon's life is not the only good that grounds the obligation of Socrates. One might point out that precisely the reflection of the last paragraphs shows that there is also the good of Socrates' moral integrity, and that it also enters into the foundation of Socrates' obligation. One would then put the objection like this: the good of moral integrity is undeniably distinguished from all other goods by a certain mysterious ultimacy for the moral agent, by what Kant called "goodness without qualification," but Crosby has confused this ultimacy with a magisterial dictate. Whenever Socrates cannot omit a certain action without compromising himself morally, he is subject to an obligation, but instead of locating the factor of obligation in this relation to the moral integrity of the moral agent, Crosby locates it in an imperative that confronts the agent.

These objections can, as it seems to me, be overcome if, continuing our inquiry into the subjective experience of being morally bound, we reflect on the consciousness we would have in conforming (like Socrates) to the moral obligation to do no harm to Leon. Our conformity is not just a positive interest in the life of Leon, for notice the highly significant fact—a fact of the very last significance for our analysis—that our *response to the obligation is an act of obedience, and includes in itself a gesture of submission.* The obedience does not refer to Leon; we neither obey him nor submit to him in refusing to do him harm. It would be completely out of place, indeed there would be something idolatrous in submitting unconditionally to Leon as we submit unconditionally to the moral obligation to do him no harm. Nor does Leon think that he is being obeyed or submitted to when Socrates follows his conscience and refuses absolutely to do him any harm. If the circumstances of the situation change, and Socrates has the opportunity to help Leon but without being morally bound to help him, and if in these new circumstances Socrates does help him, there ceases to be this element of obedience or submission in his action.

This same factor of obedience in our response to moral obligation also shows that in responding to it we do not have exclusively to do even with the incomparable good of our moral integrity. Despite all the ultimacy of this good, our commitment to it, insofar as this commitment is motivated precisely by this good, does not have anything of obedience in it. As soon as we discover this element of obedience in our striving to become morally worthy, we can be sure that something else is breaking through the good of our moral worth and is binding us in a way in which this good itself could never bind us; in this something else I recognize Newman's magisterial dictate.

4. Back to Suarez and his critics

Much more might be said about moral obligation, both about its unconditional binding force, as well as about the way it addresses us. But perhaps we have said enough to show that there is after all something to Suarez's statement that the natural law adds obligation "ultra naturalem malitiam, vel honestatem, quam ex se habet materia" ("over and above the natural badness or worthiness which the material values have out of themselves"). He can be understood as expressing a fact about moral obligation that is susceptible of a thoroughly phenomenological foundation, that is, a fact to which our moral experience clearly testifies. We do not have to presuppose a rationalistically impoverished account of human goods in order to find moral obligation adding something above and beyond the goods towards which we have the obligation. (Indeed, we are about to try to show why we esteem the human goods more highly than Finnis does.) We do not have to try to derive the goodness of continued human life (to stay with the good which is at stake in the case of Socrates and Leon) from the fact that continued existence is suitable to human nature; we can fully recognize all the deep and important things which Finnis says (ch. 3) about the self-evidence of the basic human goods and yet still find this disproportion between moral obligation towards human life and the good of human life. For in my opinion, the unconditional force of moral obligation, which gives rise to this disproportion, is one of those elementary moral phenomena which imposes itself on us prior to any particular theories and interpretations about the status of the underlying goods.

The case of Newman is instructive. Newman had no developed theory of goodness/badness, and so one cannot possibly suspect him of trying to deduce goodness/badness from suitability/unsuitability to human nature in the way in which Finnis claims to find this deduction in Suarez. And yet Newman powerfully experienced moral obligation as a magisterial dictate. Apparently one can quite well hold the position of Suarez on obligation, yet without drawing support for this position from a rationalistically deformed theory of goodness/badness.

Let us suppose that the basic human goods which underlie obligation are just as Grisez and Finnis say they are, and that we get to know them just as they say we do: what they say simply helps to secure the axiological foundation of obligation in the sense of Suarez (and perhaps—let us grant it for the sake of argument—to improve on what Suarez said regarding this axiological foundation), but in no way does it tend to call into question the discrepancy that exists between moral obligation and the underlying goods.

One might have thought that the issue between Finnis/Grisez and Suarez is whether moral obligation is divine preceptive law, but we see that the issue is in fact more fundamental. They do not even agree on how to characterize moral obligation. Let us try to show this by looking somewhat more closely at the positions of Finnis and Grisez.

I do not find in Grisez's *Christian Moral Principles*, the most recent and also the most comprehensive work by him on the moral life, any recognition of what Newman calls the magisterial and imperative character of conscience. Grisez is extremely concerned with overcoming what he perceives as the legalism of post-Tridentine moral theology (p. 13). This legalism is for him characterized by the fact that it puts forth moral norms without sufficiently showing how they are intelligibly grounded in human goods. As the reader will by now realize, I am as committed to this intelligible grounding as Grisez is. I think that it really is a great task of moral philosophy to overcome what he calls legalism. But as far as I can see, Grisez seems to be led by this legitimate concern to go on to portray the response to moral obligation (or the acceptance of moral responsibility, as he prefers to say) as a response referring exclusively to human goods; that is, this response is never understood by him as containing an element of obedience that responds to a factor which, being something like a magisterial dictate, is as it were superadded to the human goods.

Encounter with God in Moral Obligation

Thus we have the unhappy situation where the legitimate concern of an important thinker tends to obscure for him the sight of a phenomenon with which one would expect him to have a natural affinity.

Furthermore, he goes so far (as does Finnis) in treating the moral life as centering around the pursuit of one's integral human fulfillment and the avoidance of self-mutilation (cf. for example ch. 13-C and ch. 24-E), that an imperative requiring a kind of obedience, even if it grows intelligibly out of human goods, seems to him to be at odds with the goal of integral fulfillment. Of course I would heartily agree with Grisez that in the response to moral obligation we fulfill ourselves as human persons, but as I tried to show above, our moral experience teaches us that an important part of this fulfillment occurs, and preeminently occurs, in an act of obedience to the magisterial dictate of conscience.

As for Finnis, who is after all our main interlocutor, I cannot find in his *Natural Law and Natural Rights* any recognition of the disproportion between moral obligation and the underlying morally relevant goods that intelligibly give rise to it. I am well aware that for him moral obligation does not follow directly from basic human goods but rather follows from them through the mediation of what he calls the principles of practical reasonableness; but this does not lead him to a recognition of anything like a magisterial dictate in obligation. He in fact makes it quite clear that he knows nothing of such a dictate. In a deep and thoughtful passage of his work he observes that all the human goods are ended by death:

> Our health fails, our stock of knowledge fades from recall, our making and appreciation of play and art falters and finishes, our friendships are ended by distance, time, death; and death appears to end our opportunities for authenticity, integrity, practical reasonableness, if despair or decay have not already done so. (p. 372)

Finnis observes that, given this mortality of all human goods, and certain other limitations of them which he discusses, they

> will seem, to any thoughtful person, to be weakened, in their attractiveness to reasonableness, by a certain relativity or subjectivity—not so much the "subjectivity" of arbitrary opining, but rather the "subjectivity" of the "merely relative to us." (p. 373)

As we learn subsequently (ch. 13.5) Finnis thinks that it is only through accepting revelation that we can overcome this relativity of morally relevant goods. This means that, as far as our moral *experience* goes, morally relevant goods, and the obligations that they ground, are fundamentally problematical, questionable; they leave us asking, "But what is the point of it all?" Now to experience morally relevant goods in this way is the very opposite of experiencing them as mediating obligations which are imperative, magisterial, and constraining.

We can appropriate for our own purposes something of this train of thought from Finnis. The more deeply one understands the ultimate metaphysical frailty of morally relevant goods, a frailty deeply experienced precisely in their mortality, then the more clearly one apprehends the disproportion between these goods and the imperative force of moral obligation.

I cannot, however, go as far as Finnis does in stressing this frailty. Take for instance the moral goodness of a person: it seems to me that, as I was saying above, this goodness has an ultimacy, a "goodness without qualification," which sets it in a certain contrast with the oppressive contingency of many aspects of human existence, and which forbids us from calling it subjective or problematical. Or take the worth that is proper to the human person as person, a value datum that tends to escape Finnis's attention since it is not a *good for* the person like the human goods that stand at the center of his value theory. This worth also has an ultimacy and an unconditionedness (even if different from that of moral goodness) which forbid us from assimilating it to that which is contingent-all-too-contingent. In saying all this I have now explained why, as I intimated above, I esteem (in one respect) more highly the goods and values underlying moral obligations than Finnis does. I think Finnis is right to feel deeply the metaphysical frailty that they have because of their mortality, but it seems to me that he tends to overlook certain extremely significant value phenomena in declaring all mortal goods to be, prior to being seen in the light of revelation, fundamentally problematical and subjective. Of course, I still find the mentioned disproportion between these goods and values on the one hand, and the moral obligations arising from them on the other.

By now we know well enough Finnis's main motive for wanting to have nothing to do with an imperative dictate; it is well expressed in his eloquent protest against "that vast movement of thought which has sought, with overwhelming historical success, to expel from the analysis

Encounter with God in Moral Obligation 83

of individual and political action all systematic attention to the intelligibility of the goods which are realizable in action" (p. 342). Finnis wants above all things to recover for moral philosophy this intelligibility of goods, and he would undoubtedly hold that the imperative dictate, of which I have been speaking, cannot possibly be intelligibly grounded in goods. In a later work he once refers to "sheer categorical imperatives" and then immediately qualifies them as "unrelated to any particular intelligible good(s),"[15] as if he cannot conceive of imperatives except in a state of detachment from intelligible goods.

It is instructive to note that this is just the way Max Scheler objects against Kant; he too thinks that imperatives and duties can exist only as separated from any value-foundation, and so, since he is as concerned with vindicating "values" in ethics as Finnis is concerned with vindicating "the basic human goods," he excludes imperatives and duties from his ethics.[16] It seems to me that both Finnis and Scheler are more dependent on Kantian presuppositions than they know. They both agree with the Kantian formalism in holding that imperatives can exist only in the absence of an axiological foundation. They differ from Kant only in this: since they hold—each in his own way—for an axiological foundation of moral obligation, they reject moral imperatives, whereas since Kant holds for the existence of moral imperatives, he gives up (at least in the formalistic strain of his thought) any axiological foundation of obligation. I would propose breaking out of the Kantian dialectic more radically and considering the possibility that moral imperatives grow intelligibly out of goods and values.[17]

---

15. Finnis, *Fundamentals of Ethics*, 149.

16. Scheler, *Der Formalismus in der Ethik und die materiale Wertethik* (Bern: Francke Verlag, 1966), 199–203. *Formalism in Ethics and Non-Formal Ethics of Values*, trans. by Manfred Frings and Roger Funk (Evanston: Northwestern University Press, 1973), 190–94.

17. This is exactly the direction in which Karol Wojtyla goes in his study of Scheler, "Über die Möglichkeit, eine christliche Ethik in Anlehnung an Max Scheler zu schaffen," *Primat des Geistes* (Stuttgart: Seewald Verlag, 1980). At 134–49 he reproaches Scheler with having developed "an ethics without duties," and for failing to see that the ought of a duty is something quite different from the inherent appeal of the values from which the duty originates. He adds the important thought that the ought of duty challenges our freedom in a way in which the attractive power of values cannot. At the same time Wojtyla so stresses that obligation arises from the "truth about good" (cf. *The Acting Person*, 135–39) that this is a distinguishing mark of his thought.

The reader will notice that I have hitherto carefully refrained from speaking of God or of God's will. I have had two reasons for this. First, I have wanted to find the origin of the disagreement between Finnis/Grisez and Newman, Suarez, and many others (including myself). It does not begin with the question whether moral obligation derives from the divine will, but rather with the more basic question whether moral obligation has imperative force; and with the question how obligation is related to the morally relevant goods out of which it arises; and even with the still more fundamental question as to the weight and seriousness of morally relevant goods. We could not have clarified the issue in this way if we had constantly expressed the Suarezian position in terms of the divine will.

Secondly, since I want to show in the next section of my paper how we can come to discern the divine will in the moral life, I would argue in a circle if I were to presuppose the divine will from the very beginning of my analysis. Moral obligation must be first investigated without reference to the divine will. It is very important that I make it as clear as possible that I am avoiding this circular argument, because one can easily suspect me of committing it. This is because the imperative force of moral obligation is so full of religious significance—we are about to discuss this—that it is very hard to recognize this imperative force without experiencing its religious significance; but this very fact, which makes moral obligation such a promising source for encountering the divine will, gives rise to the suspicion that God has been presupposed by one who finds imperative force in moral obligation, so that one argues in a circle in trying to attain to God on the basis of this imperative force.[18] I lay great stress, then, on the fact that I have been investigating moral obligation as it presents itself in our moral experience, and that I have found its imperative force in this experience.

5. The encounter with God in moral obligation

As I proceed now to draw out the religious significance of moral obligation I need to make clear in exactly what sense I try to pass from the moral to the religious sphere. I do not say that if someone is religiously

---

18. This is just what Schopenhauer objects against Kant; he thinks that Kant is unaware of all the theological assumptions which he makes in speaking of the imperative force of obligation (*Preisschrift über die Grundlage der Moral*, in *Sämtliche Werke* IV

Encounter with God in Moral Obligation   85

unawakened and lacks any sense of God he can acquire this sense by analyzing the moral imperative. As Rudolf Otto showed in an unforgettable way in *The Idea of the Holy*, the religious sphere is a realm of its own and not a mere derivate of the moral sphere; it can therefore not be disclosed in terms of the moral sphere but only be understood in terms of itself (though it may in the case of certain persons be disclosed *on the occasion of* a deep experience of being morally bound). And so all that I claim to show is that, if we are already religiously awakened but do not yet know where we encounter God, we can discern Him as the one from whom our moral obligations derive and with whom we have to do in being bound by them.[19] We require no special revelation from God about His presence in the moral law; we have only to be alive to moral obligation and to possess a *sensus numinis* ("sense of the divine") and on this basis we can encounter God in moral obligation. This is in any case what I will now try to show.

Above we divided our discussion of moral obligation into the objective and the subjective aspects of obligation, that is, into the imperative force of obligation, and the impact of obligation in our conscience. The same division can serve us now that we are looking for the religious significance of moral obligation. And first, the imperative force of obligation.

1. Let us ask what this force is grounded in. As Finnis and Grisez rightly see, there is a fundamental relation between obligation and good, such that obligation cannot exist without some foundation in good. But as we saw, the finite morally relevant goods towards which I typically act in fulfilling my obligation cannot entirely explain my obligation; or rather, while they explain *what* I ought to do (or the content of my obligation), they cannot explain the imperative force with which I am bound to do it. Where, then, is the good that can explain this binding force?

I answer with another question: if our obligation really were grounded in God, if He really were ultimately the one requiring of us the content of our obligation, would our obligation not be just as we have found it to be, "imperative and constraining," a "magisterial dictate?" I find that, of the many philosophers who would agree with me in answering this ques-

---

[Wiesbaden: 1950], 117–84; English: *On the Basis of Morality* [Indianapolis: Bobbs-Merrill, 1965], 49–119).

19. Cf. Louis Dupré's comments on Newman's approach to God through conscience, in his *A Dubious Heritage* (New York: Paulist Press, 1977), 166–69.

tion affirmatively, there is, surprisingly enough, William James, who explains well the affirmative answer.

> ... in a merely human world without a God, the appeal to our moral energy falls short of its maximal stimulating power. Life, to be sure, is even in such a world a genuinely ethical symphony; but it is played in the compass of a couple of poor octaves, and the infinite scale of values fails to open up.
> When, however, we believe that a God is there, and that he is one of the claimants, the infinite perspective opens out. The scale of the symphony is incalculably prolonged. The more imperative ideals now begin to speak with an altogether new objectivity and significance, and to utter the penetrating, shattering, tragically challenging note of appeal. All through history, in the periodical conflicts of puritanism with the don't care temper, we see the antagonism of the strenuous and genial moods, and the contrast between the ethics of infinite and mysterious obligation from on high, and those of prudence and the satisfaction of merely finite need.
> Our attitude towards concrete evils is entirely different in a world where we believe there are none but finite demanders, from what it is in one where we joyously face tragedy for an infinite demander's sake. Every sort of energy and endurance, of courage and capacity for handling life's evils, is set free in those who have religious faith.[20]

James here well understands the close relationship between the ultimate seriousness of moral obligation, and the consciousness of directly encountering God in responding to obligation. If we think that God is requiring something of us when we are morally bound, then surely our obligation becomes "infinite and mysterious obligation from on high."

But what if I begin only with a keen sense of moral obligation but with no sense of God and the divine will? May I not experience moral obligation as a "magisterial dictate," as having a mysterious ultimacy about it? May I not sense in all moral obligation a transcendence towards something higher than man? May I not sense the discrepancy between finite morally relevant goods and the urgency of being morally bound? Suppose now that I, having lived until the present only in the moral sphere of existence, break through to the religious sphere. I am touched by God and I awaken religiously. I want to say that in experiencing moral obligation in all its ultimacy and transcendence I have a uniquely favorable occasion for achieving this breakthrough. But suppose that this breakthrough occurs apart from the experience of moral obligation. Then

---

20. William James, "The Moral Philosopher and the Moral Life," in *Pragmatism and Other Essays* (New York: Washington Square Press, 1963), 233–34.

Encounter with God in Moral Obligation

I want to say that, once I am in this new religious position, I can effortlessly discern God somehow addressing me in moral obligation. My encounter with God gives me the key to what must have puzzled me about moral obligation, namely the key to its ultimacy and its transcendence. It is only natural for me to think, "How else should obligation become infinite and mysterious, imperative and constraining, except in relation to God?" Of course now that I am a religious person moral obligation becomes transformed for me, or perhaps we could say "potentiated," which means raised to a higher power of ultimacy and seriousness; only now will I speak with James of "infinite and mysterious obligation from on high." But this new enhanced sense of moral obligation is continuous with, indeed the fulfillment of, the sense of obligation that I began with. James does not consider this path; he considers only moving from the idea of God as an infinite demander to obligation experienced as imperative. But my analysis of obligation opens up the possibility of the reverse path, that is, of starting with moral obligation as deeply experienced and then coming to discern God in it.

2. Then there is the subjective side of moral obligation that we investigated above. Consider the moment of obedience in our response to an obligation, as well as the ultimacy of our commitment in obeying an obligation: could any finite good deserve this kind of commitment? Would there not be, as we were just suggesting, an element of idolatry in our relation to a finite good, especially a finite good destined, as Finnis reminds us, to be destroyed in a short time, if we willed that good with the ultimacy of commitment with which we will to fulfill our obligation? Is there any other way to avoid this idolatry than by submitting to God in the act of willing to fulfill our obligation?

Consider also that convulsion in ourselves which occurs when we are aware of having violated our obligation. Would the shuddering which goes with having a guilty conscience not be absurdly out of proportion with the wrong we have done if that wrong were only directed against some good having the mortality and contingency felt so keenly by Finnis? Would the guilty conscience not have to be judged pathological, a kind of neurotic obsession or phobia? On the other hand, does not the shuddering of a guilty conscience make eminent moral sense if we have in fact turned against God and estranged ourselves from God through the act of violating our obligation?

There is something else which was discussed above and which needs to be recalled here. A moral obligation takes us seriously, ultimately seriously as persons, for it appeals to our freedom, and actualizes in us the inwardness of conscience. In being morally bound we come alive as persons, we "quicken" as persons, we become present to ourselves in a unique way, and we experience, as no where else, the reality, the incommunicability, the worth of our personal selves, we experience the "infinite abyss of existence" (Newman) in ourselves. Now considering our creaturehood, our existing not through ourselves but through God (which as I say we can assume here and which Finnis too thinks can be philosophically established, ch. 13.2), one might expect that in thus coming to ourselves as persons, and in thus living through the truth of ourselves as persons, we would encounter Him in whom and through whom we exist. And it is not only our creaturehood that leads us to expect this; there is something else that awakens this same expectation, I mean the interpersonal structure of personal existence. This needs further explanation.

We know that all kinds of possibilities and powers in ourselves can awaken only in the encounter with another person, and in knowing this we understand how fundamental it is to personal existence to live in communion with other persons. How then could we be alone with ourselves, in solitude, when we undergo that profound actualization of our personal being that occurs in being bound in conscience? Either we undergo this actualization under the gaze of and in the encounter with some person, or else the interpersonal is after all only accidental to personal existence and does not radically determine it. But if the fullness of personal existence which is achieved in conscience does presuppose another person, then which other person? It is a matter of empirical fact that we are often not in the presence of, are often not in touch with the person towards whom we act in fulfilling our obligation—Socrates is not in the presence of, does not encounter Leon in the act of refusing to do him any wrong. And even when we do encounter the human person towards whom we act, and encounter him ever so closely, the question remains whether this person is really the one, and could ever be the one, who is present to us and enters into us and engages us in such a way as to effect that quickening of our personal being which occurs under the impact of a moral obligation. And so we are led to expect, on the basis of our ordination to other persons no less than on the basis of our creaturehood, that there

Encounter with God in Moral Obligation

must be some encounter with God precisely under the aspect of *Deus vivens et videns*.

Is this expectation not entirely fulfilled? When under the impact of a moral obligation "the infinite abyss of existence" is actualized in ourselves, can we not glimpse a personal God as Him to whom this abyss of personal existence responds, as Him in whose presence it resonates? Does it not come very naturally to speak of being "alone with God in conscience?"[21] Does not the solitude with respect to other human beings that we experience as we enter into ourselves at a time of moral crisis, does not this solitude open up to an Absolute Person with whom we have to do?[22]

The reader will see that my attempt to find God (whose existence is assumed to be already known) in moral obligation is not an inference from an effect to a cause, as when we infer (quite rightly, as I am convinced) from the contingency of the world to the absoluteness of the being through which the world exists. It is not a moving from one thing to another thing; it is rather an attempt to recognize explicitly in moral obligation the God who was from the beginning implicitly present in it. And so we can say that what my approach to God loses in the way of logical stringency, which is possessed to a very high degree by the contingency proof, it gains in the way of immediacy, since it enables us almost to glimpse God rather than just to reason that He must exist. Thus it has a far greater religious potency than the contingency proof has, which is why Newman called our sense of moral obligation "the creative principle of religion" (p. 110).

This is the place to mention one way in which Tollefsen misunderstood my argument. He does not notice that when I speak of a disproportion or discrepancy between good and ought, which is indeed the basis of my analysis, I am speaking only of finite goods. He thinks that I hold that obligation necessarily exceeds good in principle, whether the good be finite or infinite, and that therefore not even obligation directed

---

21. Cf. the words of Vatican II: "His conscience is man's most secret core, and his sanctuary. There he is alone with God whose voice echoes in his depths." (*Gaudium et spes*, para. 16)

22. The American philosopher, W. E. Hocking, expresses the same intuition when he writes: "... there is no obligation which is not an obligation *to* some living self, other than myself. The I-ought implies a Thou-art, co-extensive with the world I am bound to think. That Thou is the self within the world, the one elemental Other. Its common name is God." Letter of Oct. 14, 1954, quoted by Dupré, *op. cit.*, 175.

to God can be grounded in the goodness or holiness of God, as if even here there remained a fatal discrepancy between good and ought. This is a serious misunderstanding of my argument. I claim nothing more than to find the mentioned discrepancy with finite morally relevant goods. In fact Tollefsen, when he extends even to God the discrepancy of good and ought, overlooks the whole dialectic of my argument. *The very reason why I introduce God to explain the full extent of moral obligation is that for me there can be no ultimate discrepancy between good and ought.* Whenever then I find an ought which goes beyond the goodness of a finite good, I recognize the ought as coming from the infinite good; for some good or other there must be at the basis of every ought. The discrepancy, or disproportion, between a finite good and a moral ought calls for an explanation, and this explanation, according to my argument, is nothing other than the non-discrepancy, or the intelligible proportion, between the infinite good and the ultimacy of the moral ought.

There remains just one last step to take before returning to Suarez. Since we encounter God in moral obligation, and since in conforming to our obligation we perform a kind of obedience, it is natural to say that in conscience we find God demanding something of us, and thus to say that it is the divine will which seems to be the basis of our obligation. In the following Scheler explains the basis of this acknowledgement of the divine will:

> In order for the ideal ought [this ideal ought is an ought which does not address anyone, as for example, "justice ought to prevail"] to become a demand for a will, an *act of commanding* is always *presupposed*. Herbart has correctly stressed that every idea of duty is based on the obligation of an order. It makes no sense to speak, as Kant does, of a duty that is floating in the air, as it were, a duty vis-à-vis no one, and which is not imposed by the order of an authority.[23]

On this basis we can understand why it is so natural to speak of the divine will as the aspect that God presents to us when He is discovered as grounding the moral imperative.

But this talk of the divine will can be misunderstood. I do not mean that it is the divine will alone that explains the mysterious ultimacy of

---

23. Scheler, *Der Formalismus*, 219. English: *Formalism*, 211. Hans Kelsen is well known for repeatedly making the same point throughout his many writings; one can agree with him here without making any concessions to his positivism.

moral obligation. If I were to mean this, then I would, as Tollefsen rightly reminded me, be open to the objection, "But why obey the divine will?" Return for a moment to what was just said about the person who starts with only ethical existence and then breaks through to religious existence. We can now add that the God whom he encounters is encountered as holy, as supremely worthy; it is this divine holiness that, once brought into contact with moral obligation, grounds the ultimacy and transcendence of obligation. A naked divine will explains nothing, but only the will of one who is worthy.

With this I complete my attempt to show how in my view one could support Suarez's thesis that moral obligation is divine preceptive law. I am of course aware of stressing more than he did the possibility of experiencing moral obligation prior to experiencing anything of divine law in it; but as it turns out, this just lets me come closer to the mainstream of natural law theory as regards our knowledge of obligation, even while the phenomenon of obligation leads me to hold with Suarez that obligation is indeed a thing of divine preceptive law.[24]

I have been speaking of the religious significance of moral obligation. I conclude now with some remarks on Finnis's understanding of this subject. He of course does not deny that there is a religious significance in moral obligation. In *Natural Law and Natural Rights* he indicates what this significance would be if Christian revelation were true; he explains how we would pursue integral human fulfillment not only for its own sake but also for God's sake, since He would have revealed Himself as favoring our fulfillment (ch. 13.5, especially p. 403); thus in fulfilling our moral obligations we would also be trying to please God. And in other of his writ-

---

24. It is perhaps worth noting here that if Suarez had approached his subject more phenomenologically, certain difficulties that he poses to himself would have been much easier to dispose of. Towards the end of his discussion in ch. vi (para. 20-24), he considers the double objection that God has perhaps not commanded us to do that which is intrinsically right and has not forbidden us to do what is intrinsically wrong, and that even if He has so commanded, He has perhaps not promulgated His will to us men. Suarez answers the objection in terms of *a priori* considerations of what is implied in God creating rational natures (para. 23) and exercising providence over them (para. 24). He quite overlooks the most obvious response to the objection; we find ourselves subject to moral obligation, it is an undeniable fact of our moral experience; and since this obligation is a *signum* of the divine will, we know from the existence of obligation in the moral life that God has commanded what is intrinsically good, and has promulgated His command.

ings, where he speaks more freely as a Christian to other Christians, he does not hesitate to speak of the natural law as a divine law.[25]

And yet his position clearly diverges from the one I have put forward, and it diverges most obviously on the question how we know the religious significance of moral obligation. Finnis seems to me to overlook the mysterious ultimacy and unconditionedness that can be experienced in moral obligation "prior" to hearing and accepting any revelation from God about how He stands towards human flourishing. Finnis says that we know of the ultimate significance of obligation only through revelation, whereas I have claimed to find it immanent in, intrinsic to the experience of being morally bound, and thus to have found it "prior" to revelation. Finnis says that revelation originates our sense of the religious significance of moral obligation, whereas I say that revelation only explains and potentiates our already existing sense of this. He thinks that the moral law is, in the sense explained, questionable and subjective when considered apart from revelation; he does not find God in the ultimate seriousness of the moral law, because he needs God in order to find ultimate seriousness in the moral law. I hold that we can grasp its ultimate seriousness before, and as the basis for, explicitly acknowledging its divine ground. Thus everything in this discussion turns on the phenomenology of moral obligation; if we can agree on what is contained in our experience of being morally bound, we shall be able to reach agreement on how it is that we encounter God in moral obligation.[26]

There is, however, an entirely different way of challenging our claims about moral obligation and its religious significance. One could accept our phenomenology of obligation and grant that we really do experience the "magisterial dictate" of Newman, but one could try to debunk it in a Freudian way, claiming that moral obligation derives from the superego, which results from a certain kind of internalization of human authority and can be exhaustively explained in psychodynamic terms and without any recourse to God. It is the aim of the following paper to encounter this challenge.

---

25. As in his "The Natural Law, Objective Morality, and Vatican II," in May (editor), *Principles of Catholic Moral Life* (Chicago: 1980), especially 1142–25.

26. My thanks to Josef Seifert, John Finnis, and above all Olaf Tollefsen for their critical comments on earlier versions of this study.

CHAPTER 4

Conscience and Superego

A personalist philosophy is bound to be particularly concerned with doing justice to conscience. It is widely understood that when some question affects us strongly in our conscience, we quicken as persons. We enter into the inner sanctuary of our personhood when we work through some question of conscience. We violate ourselves as persons when we compromise ourselves in some matter of conscience. We show respect for others as persons by abstaining from any coercion in all that concerns their own judgments of conscience. We need not waste many words on the special place that conscience has among the themes of a personalist philosophy.

But many psychologists and philosophers think that conscience is nothing more than what Sigmund Freud called the superego. Indeed, Freud himself thought this, or more exactly he thought that conscience is one of several functions of the superego. I want to argue that one can never hope to understand the deep personalist meaning of conscience if one reduces it to the superego, and that a truly personalist philosophy as well as a personalist psychology have to distinguish between superego and conscience as fundamentally different things. I call my paper a phenomenological study, because it belongs to the genius of phenomenology to resist all forms of reductionism, and to let each thing be itself. I want to show why we have to let the superego be the superego and let conscience be conscience and must never reduce the one to the other. My paper is phenomenological also in the sense that I do not offer a critical study of

* This paper originally appeared as "Conscience and Superego" in *Logos* 1.4 (1998), 125–39. It has been somewhat expanded for the present publication.

Freud, but I attempt instead to clarify "the things themselves" that are at issue in these well-known Freudian claims.

In discriminating between conscience and superego I will also complete the analysis of the previous paper. For I mentioned there but did not fully discuss the objection that moral obligation as I described it is nothing but the pressure of the superego.

But though I want to defend conscience against being absorbed into the superego, I think at the same time that there is such a thing as the superego, and so I begin the work of my paper with an attempt to characterize it. Only in the third and fourth parts of my paper will I come to conscience and its relation to the superego.

1. Scheler's thought appropriated for understanding the superego

Let us begin with the small child whose parents prohibit various things which the child would like to do. The parents uphold their prohibitions by threatening different punishments in the event that the child does not comply. At an early stage of moral development the child will of course do the prohibited things if it can escape undetected and go unpunished; but the prospect of being caught and punished usually suffices to deter the child from the prohibited behavior. One can find a very similar stance towards authority in the way many people relate to the law of the state; one complies in order to avoid state punishment, but otherwise one does what one wants, even if that means violating the law.

Such a child can proceed in its moral development to the point of understanding the reasons for the parental prohibitions and in this way it can make these prohibitions its own. Then the child, who may be an adolescent, avoids the prohibited behavior, but not because of the threatened punishment, but because the child, understanding what it now understands, does not for its part want such behavior. It now sees the behavior in question as the parents see it, and wants to avoid it no less than they do; and just as they do not need to be threatened in order to avoid it, so neither does the older child now need to be threatened. It is in his own name that the child wants to avoid such behavior, and no longer just in response to parental pressure. This is one way of developing beyond the stage of fearing parental threats.

Conscience and Superego

But if the child does develop in this way, it would not develop a Freudian superego; it is a very different moral development that leads in the direction of the superego. For this the child has to internalize the parental prohibitions in a way that is different from understanding them and learning to will them for himself. It has to perform what psychologists call an "introjection" of the parental authority. We know what it is to project our inner feelings on to another, as when we are irritated at someone and proceed to project something blameworthy onto him or her. Well, there is also the reverse movement—not projection but introjection—whereby we take some other into ourselves, identifying ourselves with that other.

For understanding introjection, I find it helpful to think about a certain way of living in the expectations of others that Max Scheler has described under the title of "heteropathic identification" with others.[1] A person can experience so strongly the expectations of others that he loses any expectations of his own for himself and comes to be dominated by, and to live only for and live only in, the expectations of these others. Their expectations replace the expectations that he would normally have for himself; he yields in a sense to the others the place in himself which should be occupied by his own self, and in this sense he identifies himself with them. He is as it were inhabited by the dominant others.

Such a process of identification is obviously different from the case where a person comes to understand for himself the justice of the others' expectations and on this basis expects of himself what they expect of him. This way of agreeing with others involves using one's own mind and thus experiencing oneself as distinct from the others; as a result, it involves no heteropathic identification with them, for this always involves a certain substitution of oneself by the dominant others. Heteropathic identification has also to be distinguished from the case of *being motivated by some authority*. To understand the authority and its claim on me, and to be motivated by something like respect for this authority, even if I cannot understand all the commands and prohibitions of the authority, is in any case a relation to the authority wherein I remain intact as distinct person. The element of understanding and motivation preserves this distinctness

---

1. Scheler, *The Nature of Sympathy* (Hamden, CT: The Shoe String Press, 1973), 18–23, and especially 42–45.

in me vis-a-vis the authority; it prevents anything that might be called "identification" with the authoritative person; it prevents that person from occupying the place in me that should be occupied by my own self, or from inhabiting me.

The pathology that we are describing is found in highly suggestible persons. In the presence of some strongly dynamic other person they may at first try to preserve their own view of things and their own judgment; but they cannot hold out for long, and soon they are seeing everything with the eyes of the dynamic other, their own view of the world having been suppressed by the force of the view of the other. It is not suppressed in the sense that suggestible persons fall prey to the illusion of thinking that they are the other; each suggestible person retains some consciousness of being himself and not the other, though this consciousness is somehow weakened by the way in which the experiencing of the other interferes with him having his own experiencing.

Scheler gives an intriguing instance of how heteropathic identification can occur even among animals.[2] He relates the case, which he read about, of a large snake opening its mouth and moving towards a squirrel to eat it. At first the squirrel wants to run away, but it hesitates, and then does the last thing we might expect it to do, it jumps into the mouth of the snake. Scheler interprets this as follows: the squirrel felt in an abnormally strong way what the snake wanted of it, and it began to want the same thing. But wanting to yield to the snake conflicted with the squirrel's instinct for self-preservation. It was this inner conflict that made the squirrel hesitate. As the empathizing of the squirrel with the desire of the snake continued, it began to suppress the squirrel's instinct for self-preservation; eventually it took over completely, and led the squirrel to act spontaneously in complete agreement with what the snake wanted. Scheler sees here in the animal world a case of something very like the human phenomenon that he calls heteropathic identification with others.

Scheler's concept of heteropathic identification seems to me to provide us with a helpful approach to the superego. As I understand it, the superego arises from a certain identification of the child with the parental authority, perhaps especially with the paternal authority. Freud describes the identification like this in *The Ego and the Id:* "When we were little children we knew these higher natures [that is, our parents], we admired

---

2. Ibid., 21–22.

them and feared them; and later *we took them into ourselves*"³ (my italics). Instead of remaining outside of the child and in need of being supported by threats, the paternal authority is now taken into the child in such a way that threats become superfluous. The child who introjects the paternal authority will comply with the paternal prohibitions all on his own, even at those moments when he knows that the father is not looking. The father now has his own representative in the mind of his son or daughter; this representative observes the child even in the absence of the father. It is not that the paternal authority *motivates* the respect of the child; such a relation would involve elements of intentionality and understanding that are foreign to the superego, which is spiritually too primitive to be explained in terms of intentionality and understanding. The paternal authority rather tends, insofar as it is a form of heteropathic identification, to take the place in the child that will one day be occupied by the self of the child.

There is, however, one danger in appropriating Scheler's concept of heteropathic identification for understanding the superego. Scheler has in mind a certain pathology of personal existence, whereas the superego is not as such pathological. In a small child the superego is a normal stage of early moral development and so should not be thought of as depersonalizing. It functions like a godparent, who stands in for a child at baptism and who professes the faith of the Church for the child. We could change the analogy and say that the internalized voice of the superego functions like a maternal womb; just as the mother takes over certain biological functions for the child she carries, so the parent through the superego takes over certain moral functions for the child whom the parent is forming. We should call the superego depersonalizing only if it continues in the child after the time at which the child might think for itself. In fact, it is depersonalizing in just the same way in which it would be depersonalizing for a godparent to continue to speak in matters of faith for a young person who is now able to speak for himself. In the present study we are primarily interested in the superego in this latter form, that is, as a certain pathology of personal existence.

It is understandable that someone might confuse conscience with the superego, for the latter is beginning to look like conscience in some

---

3. Freud, *The Ego and the Id*, trans. by Joan Riviere (New York: W. W. Norton and Co., 1962), 26.

respects. The superego as it emerges in our discussion seems to have the inwardness as well as the authoritativeness of conscience; it also has the element of someone watching me from above within myself. But let us not get ahead of ourselves; only later will we come to the question of discriminating conscience from the superego. We are not yet finished with our characterization of the superego.

2. Erich Fromm on the superego

In his elaboration of the superego, Erich Fromm,[4] a Freudian, explores the way in which the superego can interfere with a boy or girl acting as person. Recall that the introjecting of parental authority is something very different from understanding for ourselves the justice of the commands and prohibitions of our parents, or even from understanding the claims of parental authority. If a boy or girl is capable of some moral understanding of his or her own, and if the boy or girl acts according to norms and principles which they do not understand, and if the source of their acting is the introjected authority occupying the place in themselves that they themselves should occupy, then they suffer a certain depersonalization. One understands why Fromm in one place compares being oppressed by a superego with the situation of the man in Kafka's novel, *The Trial*.[5] This man, called K, is charged with a crime of which he knows nothing, and he is brought into a mysterious court whose laws and procedures are impenetrable to him. So it is, according to Fromm, in the inner life of someone who, while he is capable of some understanding of his own, has taken into himself norms that he does not really understand.

But there is more in Fromm on the depersonalizing tendency of the superego; he suggests that the superego can outlive its developmental usefulness only on the basis of a certain unwillingness of a person to be a distinct personal self.

He has found inner security by becoming, symbiotically, part of an authority felt to be greater and more powerful than himself. As long as he is part of that

---

4. Erich Fromm, *Man for Himself: An Inquiry into the Psychology of Ethics* (New York: Rinehart, 1947), 145–75.

5. Ibid., 171–75.

authority—at the expense of his own integrity—he feels that he is participating in the authority's strength. His feeling of certainty and identity depends on this symbiosis. . . .[6]

We can verify a certain truth of this if only we look in the right place in our own experience. Most of us have had the experience of a conflict between the pressure of the superego and what we ourselves understand to be good and choose on the basis of our understanding. We have felt parents' and other people's expectations pulling us in one direction, and we have felt something in ourselves resonating with their claims; but at the same time we felt our own insight drawing us in another direction, and we felt something else and something deeper in ourselves resonating with this insight. In this inner struggle, which may repeat itself in the course of a person's moral development, we are aware of being challenged to dare to be ourselves by following our own insight, and are aware at the same time of being exposed to the temptation to play it safe and to remain sheltered in the symbiotic relation to the introjected authority. Perhaps the conflict in us is heightened by the illusion that we commit a morally reprehensible rebellion against the superego by following our own insight against its demands. But at the same time we know that if we remain captive to the superego, we do so at the expense of fully living our distinct personal selfhood, or in other words at the expense of a certain personal integrity.

But this depersonalizing tendency of the superego derives not only from the person seeking shelter in the introjected authority; it can also derive from a certain possessiveness of the authoritative persons who are introjected. Fromm reminds us of the famous passage in the *Antigone* of Sophocles where King Creon speaks about the kind of children which every father wants:

So it is right, my son, to be disposed—in everything to back your father's quarrel. It is for this men pray to breed and rear in their home *dutiful offspring*—to requite the foe with evil and their father's friend with honour, as did their father. Whoso gets children *unserviceable*—what else could he be said to breed, but troubles for himself. . . .[7]

---

6. Ibid., 151.
7. Ibid., 157 (italics are from Fromm).

This expresses a parental attitude which does not regard children as distinct persons, but as extensions of the parents.[8] Perhaps we could invoke here, for understanding such parents, Scheler's concept of the *idiopathic identification of others with oneself*, which corresponds to the concept of heteropathic identification with others. Such parents are only too glad to keep their children tethered to themselves by means of a superego in their children; in this way the children are made to exist as moral extensions of the parents. These parents will be quick to interpret as ungrateful and immoral rebellion any attempt of their children to develop their own moral understanding and to act in their own name.

We can say, then, that a person can fear being a distinct personal self, and that others, too, can fear him being a distinct personal self, and that these two fears can support each other in the formation of the thing that we are here calling the superego of such a person.

It follows from our discussion that an authority can be depersonalizing not only in the obvious case where it remains outside of me and has to resort to threats against me to secure my compliance; it can be no less depersonalizing when it is inside of me and has been so internalized by me as to have no need of threats.

Let me mention just one further feature of the superego. Fromm observes that the superego can be a repressive force in the life of a person. The creative energies and the spontaneity of a person are crippled by the dependency on the introjected other. They might be released if the person were to learn to form and to act on his own judgment, but they remain painfully pent up in the person as long as his superego blocks such growth in moral independence. These frustrated energies of personal existence, denied their natural outlet, become inner demons; they give rise to a certain cruelty against oneself that is so often found in the working of the superego. Echoing ideas expressed already by Nietzsche, Fromm writes that the person who is dominated by a strong superego,

being more or less crippled in his productiveness, develops a certain amount of sadism and destructiveness. These destructive energies are discharged by taking over the role of the authority and by dominating oneself as the servant. In the analysis of the Super-Ego, Freud has given a description of its destructive com-

---

8. In his *Das Wesen der Liebe* (Stuttgart: Kohlhammer Verlag, 1971), Dietrich von Hildebrand returns again and again to the difference between really loving another and taking another as an extension of oneself. See, for instance, ch. 8, *passim*.

ponents which has been amply confirmed by clinical data collected by other observers.[9]

Here, too, we seem to touch upon a mark of conscience, especially of "bad" conscience, which, as we all know, can accuse a person in the most merciless and relentless way.

We can no longer defer the question whether conscience is nothing more than the superego, whether it is adequately and exhaustively explained in terms of the psycho-dynamics of introjection and heteropathic identification, as Freud and many others think. I am quite convinced that there is such a thing as the superego in many persons, I think in fact that most of us know it from past and perhaps even from present experience. I further think that for the cultivation of our conscience it is very important to know what a superego is. But I think that this is important for the very reason that conscience is not the same as superego. We turn now to conscience and the kind of contrast it forms with the superego.

3. Fromm and Newman on conscience

Fromm has the merit of marking a certain distinction between superego and conscience. On this point he is better than his master, Freud. Fromm calls the superego "authoritarian conscience," which he contrasts with "humanistic conscience," which is for him conscience in its healthy form. Let us see what he means by humanistic conscience.

Actions, thoughts, and feelings which are conducive to the proper functioning and unfolding of our total personality produce a feeling of inner approval, of "rightness," characteristic of the humanistic "good conscience." On the other hand, acts, thoughts, and feelings injurious to our total personality produce a feeling of uneasiness and discomfort, characteristic of the "guilty conscience." *Conscience is thus a reaction of ourselves to ourselves.* It is the voice of our true selves that summons us back to ourselves, to live productively, to develop fully and harmoniously—that is, *to become what we potentially are*. It is the guardian of our integrity; it is the "ability to guarantee one's self with all due pride, and also at the same time *to say yes* to one's self" (Nietzsche). If love can be defined as the affirmation of the potentialities and the care for, and the respect of, the uniqueness of the loved person, humanistic conscience can be justly called *the voice of our loving care for ourselves.*[10]

9. Ibid., 155.
10. Ibid., 163 (my italics).

It certainly seems to be true that in conscience we have to do with ourselves, with our integrity. We typically say in a crisis of conscience that we will not be able to live with ourselves if we act against our conscience. In Robert Bolt's play about the life and death of St. Thomas More, *A Man for All Seasons*, there is a scene in which Thomas More says to his friend, Norfolk: "I will not give in because I oppose it—I do—not my pride, not my spleen, nor any other of my appetites but *I* do—*I!*"[11] Just as Fromm suggests, Thomas More seems to be concerned with the integrity of his very self, his I. In authoritarian conscience, or superego, one loses oneself in a certain sense in the introjected authority, suffering thereby a serious de-personalization; here in conscience rightly understood, one preserves and protects one's self, and one thrives in one's personal selfhood.

But does this suffice on the distinction between superego and conscience? Has Fromm told us all we need to know about conscience in its contrast to the superego? I think not. On the basis of what Fromm has given us, one can hardly understand why conscience and superego have so often, and so plausibly, been identified; in his presentation they are obviously different and no one can miss the difference. Fromm has given us only one aspect of authentic conscience, and has left out another, all-important aspect of it, and has quite wrongly assigned this other aspect to authoritarian conscience, or superego. What am I referring to?

Do we not encounter in conscience something demanding, something unconditionally binding, something authoritative, something calling for a kind of obedience? In his famous phenomenology of conscience John Henry Newman speaks of conscience as a "magisterial dictate";[12] in another place he speaks of it as "a voice, or the echo of a voice, imperative and constraining, like no other dictate in the whole of our experience."[13] It is well known how Kant explained the imperativity of that which binds us in conscience. He distinguishes between categorical and hypothetical imperatives. The latter say to us in effect, "if you want to attain a certain result, then do this or that." Which means that if you do not care about the result, you need not bother about doing this or that. But categorical imperatives say simply, "do this" or "you shall not do that." No if-clauses,

---

11. Robert Bolt, *A Man for All Seasons* (New York: Vintage Books, 1990), 38–39.
12. Newman, *An Essay in Aid of a Grammar of Assent* (London: Longmans, Green, and Co., 1898), ch. 5, sect. 1, 105–6.
13. Ibid., 107.

no conditions, no way to get out of the imperative by declining the pursuit of some goal. The categorical imperatives do not even say, "since you want to be happy, fulfilled, integrated, then do this or that;" even such almost inescapable conditions play no role with categorical imperatives. Thomas More did not hear in his conscience, "if you want to be ultimately happy, then do not give in to the king, but if you don't care about your ultimate happiness, then be as compliant as you like with him." He heard instead the sterner imperative, the unconditioned imperative, what Newman calls the magisterial dictate: "thou shalt not give in, it is absolutely wrong to yield to the king." Or recall the great drama of conscience portrayed in the play of the Russian writer, Pushkin, entitled *Boris Godounov*, which was put to music in the great opera of the same name by Moussorgsky. Boris killed the child Dmitri, the true heir to the throne, and, as the opera opens, has been reigning as Tsar of Russia for some years, but always tormented by his conscience, and most of all when he is surrounded by his own children. He shudders at the vision of the dead child that keeps rising up to accuse him. We could never explain this shuddering of Boris on the assumption that he had only violated some hypothetical imperative; no, it all makes sense only on the assumption that he is aware of violating some higher law that bound him not conditionally but unconditionally.

We will not find in Fromm anything about this imperativity and this authoritativeness of the moral call addressed to us in conscience, or about the moral accusation heard in a guilty conscience. He has something much tamer in mind when he speaks of conscience as "the voice of our loving care for ourselves," which would be an absurdly harmless way of describing the conscience of Boris Godounov. Fromm expresses his own atheistic humanism by saying, "No power transcending man can make a moral claim upon him. Man is responsible to himself for gaining or losing his life."[14] Hence the title of his book, *Man for Himself*. Conscience should be a matter only of a person in relation to himself; it becomes deformed as soon as it involves obedience to an imperative, in fact it then falls back into authoritarian conscience, or superego.

It must be admitted that conscience as portrayed by Newman, or as experienced by Tsar Boris Godounov, has certain points of resemblance

---

14. Fromm, *op. cit.*, 174.

with a superego which Fromm's humanistic conscience lacks; looked at from the outside, Newman can be suspected more plausibly than Fromm of having described nothing more than a superego. How is it that the imperativity of a moral call differs from the pressure of introjected authoritative persons making their demands of me in the form of a superego?

Out of all that might be said by way of distinguishing these two things, I call attention to one supremely important point of distinction: we are capable of understanding moral imperatives, of understanding where they come from and why they can bind us; we are capable of approving them with our own insight. This means that in obeying them we need not be yielding to the pressure of another person, whether of another outside of us or of another introjected person speaking in our own mind, or rather speaking in place of our own mind; we are quite capable of obeying in such a way as to think with our own mind and act in our own name. One might have gathered this liberating power of our own insight, from Fromm's own characterization of authoritarian conscience. As we saw, he repeatedly points out that the person afflicted with this pathology of conscience lacks understanding for the inner justice of the commands and prohibitions that he accepts and so follows blindly. When this person introjects parental authority he is doing something utterly different from coming to understand the point of the parental directives and so to will them in his own name. The introjection leads to a certain blurring of the difference between his will and his parents' will; he wills what they will only because of the way in which their will tends to replace his own. But his act of understanding enables him to will what his parents will and to remain completely intact as a distinct person; his understanding lets him act with his own will. This remains true even when that which he understands is a moral imperative that calls for a kind of moral obedience, as we saw in the previous paper.

Notice that it is not exactly the moral truth that liberates our personhood in relation to moral imperatives; it is our understanding of moral truth alone that liberates. The norms that are internalized in the depersonalizing manner of a superego may well be perfectly true and valid moral norms, but they do not liberate; the truth liberates only through our understanding of it.

Of course, this understanding of moral truth is only the beginning of that internalization of the moral ought that distinguishes conscience from superego. I take a further step when I commit myself to the ought that I understand. With this commitment I take the moral ought far more deeply into myself, reducing still more the "distance" between myself and the moral ought, and becoming still freer in my moral existence. While this moment of commitment presupposes the moral understanding of which I have spoken, it is at the same time something entirely new. The moral ought still remains in a way outside of me as long as, though I understand it, I resist it and resent its claim on myself; the full freedom of conscience—the freedom that distinguishes it from superego—shows itself only in the person who has committed himself to the moral truth that he understands.

But one will ask, what exactly is it that we understand when we grasp a moral imperative in our conscience, or when, having violated an imperative, we are burdened with a guilty conscience? Kant gives a profound answer to this question when, after searching for the ground of a categorical imperative, he says that this ground will have to be something having absolute value; that which has value only in relation to our needs can bind us only hypothetically but never categorically. He asks where absolute value is to be found, and he answers that it is first and foremost found in persons; each human person has absolute value, which we commonly call "dignity" in contrast to "price."[15] We are, therefore, categorically bound to show respect for persons and never merely to use them for our own purposes. If we understand the worth and dignity of persons, then we understand the categorical imperative to respect them that makes itself felt in conscience. Boris Godounov understood the value that the child Dmitri had as person and so he understood perfectly—in contrast to the hero of Kakfa's novel, *The Trial*—why his conscience was accusing him so relentlessly. Thus it is that imperativity and obedience and accusation enter into our life of conscience without any least tendency to degrade our conscience to a mere superego.

But we have to go farther to show just how different Newman's sense

---

15. Immanuel Kant, *Foundations of the Metaphysics of Morals and What Is Enlightenment?* Translated by Lewis White Beck, (New York: Liberal Arts Press, 1989), 46–47. (In his profound commentary on this work of Kant, Rudolf Otto called this passage the great *Einbruchstelle* of the work, that is, the passage in which Kant breaks through to a train of thought different from the dominant formalism of his moral philosophy.)

of conscience is from a superego, and how wrong Fromm is to identify them. Notice that Thomas More says "I" so emphatically just at the moment when he responds with unconditional obedience to a moral imperative. It is too little to say that the imperative does not harm his I; we have also to say that it gives Thomas More a supreme experience of his I. This experience of the quickening of one's deepest self in relation to a moral imperative has been well described by Dietrich von Hildebrand:

> A moral call is addressed to someone to intervene in a certain situation; perhaps another is in danger, or perhaps he has to refuse to do some evil which is asked of him. He grasps the morally relevant value, he understands its call, he is aware of the moral obligation, which appeals to his conscience. On the one hand, we have here a high-point of transcendence in the pure commitment to the morally relevant good. But on the other hand, this call, insofar as it is morally obligatory, pre-eminently contains the element of "tua res agitur" ("the thing concerns *you* personally"). In a certain sense this call is my most intimate and personal concern, in which I experience the uniqueness of my self. Supreme objectivity and supreme subjectivity interpenetrate here. One can even say that we have here the dramatic high-point of the "tua res agitur" in our earthly existence. On the one hand, I commit myself to something which in no way stands before me as merely "an objective good for me," but rather as something which appeals to me as valuable in itself; but on the other hand, since a moral obligation in its unique impact is here at stake . . . my decision to follow the call or not, eminently reaches into the innermost center of my own existence *(Eigenleben)*. When the moral call is addressed to me and appeals to my conscience, then at the same time the question of my own salvation comes up. It is not just the [objective] "issue" which is at stake; I and my salvation are just as much at stake.[16]

We see that Fromm's talk of conscience as the "voice of our loving care for ourselves" is in a way present here in von Hildebrand's account of conscience; it is present in his talk of the supreme subjectivity that is stirred

---

16. My translation from von Hildebrand, *Das Wesen der Liebe* (Regensburg, 1971), 274–75. Here is the German text: "Es ergeht an jemanden der Ruf, in einer bestimmten Situation einzugreifen, sei es, dass sich ein anderer in Gefahr befindet, sei es, dass . . . jemand etwas Böses, das von ihm verlangt wird, zu verweigern hat. Er erfasst den sittlich bedeutsamen Wert, er versteht seinen Ruf, er wird sich der sittlichen Verpflichtung bewusst, sie appelliert an sein Gewissen. Einerseits liegt hier, in der reinen Hingabe an den sittlich bedeutsamen Wert in sich, ein Höhepunkt der Transzendenz vor. Andererseits aber enthält dieser Ruf in eminenter Weise das Element des 'Tua res agitur,' insofern dieser Ruf sittlich verpflichtend ist. Dieser Ruf ist in gewissem Sinne sogar meine allerintimste und persönlichste Angelegenheit, in der ich die Einzigartigkeit

up in conscience, as well as in his talk of the "tua res agitur" of conscience. But at the same time this concern of me with myself in conscience is placed in a new context and is in a way transformed in von Hildebrand because of the presence in his account of that which Fromm excludes, namely the imperativity of moral obligation and the call for a kind of moral obedience. Von Hildebrand wants to show that it is just this imperativity that potentiates the subjectivity of conscience, transforming Fromm's harmless "loving care for myself" into a concern with something much more ultimate for myself, a concern with a kind of salvation for myself. Far from drawing me off of myself, or absorbing me heteropathically into another, or in some other way doing violence to my distinct selfhood, the moral imperative reveals depths of my interiority and of my deepest well-being of which Fromm knows nothing. The subjectivity that resonates with the moral imperative is immeasurably deeper than the subjectivity that, as in Fromm, has only to do with itself. Conscience as portrayed by von Hildebrand does not, because of the strong theme of obedience, tend to become a superego, as Fromm thinks it must: just the contrary, it becomes more and more opposed to a superego as the theme of obedience grows, it becomes an ever deeper experience of personhood through the imperativity of the moral call.[17] Fromm's "man for himself" is a flat and one-dimensional creature compared to man as he really exists, namely as called to the service of that which is good in itself. Thus Fromm's "humanistic conscience" is a pale and anemic thing compared with the throbbing, living conscience that resonates with the moral law and its categorical obligations.

---

meines Selbst erlebe. Höchste Objektivität und höchste Subjektivität greifen hier ineinander. Man kann sagen, dass hier der dramatische Höhepunkt des 'Tua res agitur' auf Erden vorliegt. Einerseits gebe ich mich an etwas hin, das in keiner Weise als 'objektives Gut für mich' vor mir steht, sondern als etwas, das nur als in sich wertvoll mich anspricht; aber weil dabei meine sittliche Verpflichtung in ihrer einzigartigen Tragweite im Spiel ist, also im letzten der Ruf Gottes an mich, ragt anderseits die Entscheidung, ob ich dem Ruf folge oder nicht, in eminenter Weise in mein Eigenleben hinein. Wenn der sittliche Ruf an mich ertönt, an mein Gewissen appelliert, dann wird damit auch gleichzeitig die Frage meines eigenen Heils aktualisiert. Nicht nur die 'Sache' steht auf dem Spiel, ich und mein eigenes Heil stehen gleichfalls auf dem Spiel."

17. I have tried to show how this paradoxical truth about moral obligation is elaborated in the philosophical work of Karol Wojtyla in my paper, "Karol Wojtyla on the Objectivity and the Subjectivity of Moral Obligation," in *Christian Humanism*, Francis (ed.) (New York: Peter Lang, 1995), 27–36.

We can only marvel at the fact that obligation can weigh so heavily on us without harming us as persons—can be so demanding and at the same time so liberating. Let us repeat the principle that explains this paradox: we understand the goods and values out of which obligation grows. At the beginning of the passage just quoted from von Hildebrand we read: "He grasps the morally relevant value, he understands its call." This understanding lets us internalize the moral call, not in the sense of introjection, but in the sense of being able to will, all in our own name, the right response to the call. Everything turns on the capacity of persons to understand goods and values and to understand what kind of commitment we owe to them. This is why relativism and subjectivism regarding value and the good are so devastating to our image of the human person; if these philosophies are true, then there is nothing to be understood about good and value, and we have no way to go beyond the superego.

This is not to say that those who understand values and moral requirements will not find these requirements burdensome in some way. Perhaps they understand the right that they ought to do and the wrong that they ought to avoid but lack a single-minded commitment to do good and avoid evil. This commitment is, as we have already observed, something entirely new in relation to the understanding of which we have spoken; and without this commitment a person will find himself constantly at odds with what he knows he ought to do. But the moral disquiet that he will feel has nothing to do with being cramped by a superego that interferes with his conscience; there is no other person acting in him so as to disable him as person; he undermines himself as person but is not depersonalized by any other. Even when people do commit themselves to the moral law that they understand they can still experience the law as burdensome. For there is a brokenness of our moral nature that keeps us from willing the good with an undivided heart; however much we may try to commit ourselves to the good there remains a lawless principle within us that cannot be completely extirpated. In *Romans* 7 St. Paul gives unforgettable expression to the distress of the morally conscientious person who is unable to serve the good in the single-minded way he wants to serve it. As a result of this moral brokenness, of this vulnerability for the fascination of evil, the demands of the moral law may sometimes oppress us, so that we have to struggle to overcome ourselves to fulfill them. If we imagine a morally unbroken, morally unfallen human being, one who encounters no inner impediment when he wills the good, who can will it with his whole heart, undivided, who has what Kant calls a holy will, then we imagine someone who is beyond the burdensomeness of moral effort that still afflicts us. The moral law does not oppress him as it still oppresses us; he enjoys a moral freedom that is not available to us. The decisive point for the present discussion is that this oppressive aspect of the moral law has nothing to do with the oppressive aspect of the superego. For there is an element of heteronomy in the superego that is missing in the moral suffering of St. Paul. It is significant that Kant, who was as sensitive as any moral philosopher ever was to the danger of heteronomy in the moral life, even to the point of suspecting it where it does not really exist, was able to recognize with great clarity our moral brokenness, which he expressed in terms of our being torn between duty and inclination and of lacking a "holy will." More exactly, it is significant that it never occurs to him to raise the specter of heteronomy in discussing this brokenness; it never occurs to him to see heteronomy in a moral law whose only offense is that we human beings cannot respect it as resolutely as we want to respect it. What I am saying comes to this: there are many other moral deficiencies besides having a superego that has outlived its temporary justification, and there are many ways of growing in moral freedom besides overcoming such a superego. The moral understanding of which I have spoken, important as it is, does not necessarily put everything in order in one's moral existence.

One last question; one may wonder whether, after so much stress on the understanding of moral requirements, I have left any room for some moral authority to which one might submit in leading one's moral life, for the insight which liberates us for conscience seems to render moral authority superfluous. But it is not difficult to allow for moral authority on our principles, and in fact the careful reader will recall that we have already allowed for it. One has only to understand the trustworthiness of the authority that one follows; then one has enough of one's own understanding to avoid acquiring anything like a superego as a result of accepting norms that one does not yet entirely understand. Of course, any persons possessing genuine moral authority will foster in the person his or her own moral understanding about the norms themselves and will to that extent render themselves less necessary for that person.

4. The religious dimension of conscience

Finally, a word about the religious dimension of conscience, which is so prominent in Newman's analysis of conscience. Newman in fact regards the sense of being morally obliged as "the creative principle of religion,"[18] as the most promising source of a "real" apprehension of God, in contrast to a merely "notional" apprehension of Him. And indeed this much seems to be true in the teaching of Newman, that it is almost impossible to experience conscience in all its imperativity and yet not to experience a religious depth in it; it is almost impossible not to be aware of encountering God in conscience in just the way described by Newman. I know of no major thinker who recognizes the imperativity of moral obligation and who at the same time holds fast to a merely humanistic account of conscience. Once one finds in conscience Newman's "magisterial dictate," one cannot help also finding something like his God.[19] In the previous paper in this volume, "The Personal Encounter with God in Moral Obligation," I have tried to unfold this way of passing from the moral into the religious realm.

What concerns us at present is that with this breakthrough into the religious sphere, which we here assume takes place just as Newman describes, there need be no least movement towards a superego. Of course it will seem to some as if the resemblance with a superego has only increased; the God appearing in conscience may look suspiciously like an introjected human father. In response we can only remind the reader that this God appears in a situation that is personalistically sound; as we saw, the moral subject is thriving in his selfhood as he encounters his moral obligation. The God of conscience does not just abruptly appear, merely superimposed on moral obligation, but rather "grows" out of obligation, so to say, as one can see in what we just mentioned, namely that the imperativity of obligation hardly makes sense apart from the divine

---

18. Newman, *An Essay in Aid of a Grammar of Assent*, 110.
19. This point has been made by Elisabeth Anscombe in her famous paper, "Modern Moral Philosophy," in *Collected Philosophical Papers*, III (Minneapolis: University of Minnesota Press, 1981), especially 30–33. But she speaks more on the level of moral language than of moral experience, and she moves in the opposite direction; whereas I propose moving from the moral ought to the divine ground of it, she proposes giving up talk of the moral ought since most people, she says, no longer share the theological framework apart from which the ought makes no sense.

Conscience and Superego

ground of it. God is already "contained" in the moral imperativity; so that if we thrive in our personal existence in relation to moral obligation, we cannot fail to thrive when we proceed to understand that relation in an explicitly religious way. This is verified in the experience of every religiously awakened person, who finds that *the God appearing in conscience does not take over the place in me occupied by my self, repressing me as person; just the contrary, my conscience as religiously potentiated gives me an incomparable experience of my selfhood and subjectivity.*[20] Thus this God appears in conscience *completely apart from and even in opposition to the psychodynamics of the superego;* whereas the superego interferes with and represses my distinct personhood, I am never so alive as person as in the presence of the divine person who makes himself felt in conscience.[21]

We can further secure the contrast between conscience and superego if we recall something from the previous chapter. We know that all kinds of possibilities and powers in ourselves can awaken only in the encounter with another person. Indeed, we know that our existing for and towards other persons is so fundamental to our personal existence that there is a certain metaphysical absurdity in the existence of only one solitary person. Is it possible, then, that we are really alone with ourselves, really in solitude, when we undergo that profound quickening of our personal being which occurs in being bound in conscience? Either we quicken under the gaze of, in the encounter with, some person, or else the interpersonal is after all only accidental to personal existence and does not radically determine it. But if the fullness of personal existence achieved in conscience does presuppose another person, then which other person? It is a matter of empirical fact that we are often not in the presence of, are often not in touch with the person towards whom we act in fulfilling our obligation—for example, Antigone did not encounter her brother, who was dead. And even when we do encounter the human person towards whom we act, and encounter him ever so closely, the question remains whether this person is really the one, and could ever be the one, who is present to us and enters into us and engages us in such a way as to effect

---

20. One is expressing this experience whenever one speaks of conscience as the "inner sanctuary" of the person.

21. It is very revealing to see how William James expresses the fullness of personal life in relation to religiously potentiated obligation. See the quote from his "The Moral Philosopher and the Moral Life," in the previous paper in this collection, p. 86.

that quickening of our personal being that occurs under the impact of a moral imperative. But if no human person can elicit it, could it be a divine personal being? When under the impact of an imperative, "the infinite abyss of existence" (Newman) is stirred up in ourselves, can we not catch a glimpse of a personal God as Him to whom this abyss of personal existence responds, as Him in whose presence it resonates? Does it not come very natural to speak of being "alone with God in conscience"? Does not the solitude with respect to other persons that we experience as we enter into ourselves at a time of moral crisis, does not this solitude open up to an absolute person with whom we have to do? Does it not have to open up to religious transcendence, given the general truth that persons can live and thrive as persons only in intersubjective relation, only in communion with other persons? If one could elaborate and defend the answers that we are suggesting to these questions, one would show the necessity of recognizing the divinity of the person appearing in conscience. This would mean that we cannot take it to be a merely human person, present in us by way of introjection, and that, therefore, the theory of the superego has no application here.

Let us conclude. We have developed a personalist criterion for distinguishing between superego and conscience. The superego commonly represents a pathology of individual personal existence and always represents at least an immaturity of personal existence. Conscience, by contrast, which is fundamentally more than Fromm's humanistic conscience, represents the most authentic, awakened personal existence; it is, as we have said, the inner sanctuary of each person. And there are good reasons for saying that the person making his presence felt in conscience is not an introjected human person, but can only be a divine person. Precisely a personalist philosophy should never reduce Newman's idea of conscience to the Freudian superego. Such a philosophy will know how to distinguish these things in theory and in practice, and the psychologists and counselors whose work is based on this distinction will know how to help sufferers beyond the moral immaturity of the superego towards the fullness of personal life in conscience.[22]

---

22. My thanks to Richard Cross, James DuBois, and Maria Crosby for their comments on earlier drafts of this paper.

CHAPTER 5

The Estrangement of Persons from Their Bodies

"God does not care what we do with each other's bodies; He only cares whether we treat each other as persons." With this utterance an American feminist succeeded in giving succinct expression to a certain personalist sensibility: the supreme moral norm is to respect persons, and bodily actions derive all their meaning from the presence or absence of such respect. At first glance this may seem to be akin to the personalism so often expressed by John Paul II, and expressed quite memorably in 1980 when he said in an address (October 8), to the consternation of many, that the "adultery in the heart" condemned by Christ can be committed *even within marriage.* It is not enough if the man and the woman are married; they may, he said, still not be respecting each other as persons, they may be only using each other for their gratification. In that case the moral substance of their marital intimacy is "adulterous." John Paul will hear nothing of the idea that the mutual using is legitimated by openness to offspring: such using is morally intolerable no matter how many children the man and the woman bring into the world and raise. Persons must simply never use each other.

And yet this feminist said that "God does not care what we do with each other's bodies" by way of expressing her rejection of almost all of the moral norms of Christian sexual morality. How is this? We might understand such a rejection coming from a hedonist, but this utterance does

---

* This paper originally appeared as "The Estrangement of Persons from Their Bodies" in *Logos* 1.2 (1997), 125–39. It has been considerably revised for the present collection.

not express hedonism, for there are some sexual things that, according to those subscribing to this dictum, you ought not do; you must never use persons in the exercise of your sexuality, however pleasurable it may be to use them. How does it happen that this worthy concern with respecting persons can get turned against Christian morality?[1] Is there something depersonalized about this morality? How does it happen that John Paul affirms the person in such a way as to enrich the very moral teachings on sexuality that this feminist rejects? How can those professing respect for persons arrive at antithetical ethical positions?

1.

In the last few centuries the personhood of human beings has been experienced and understood as never before. Karol Wojtyla has captured the truth found in this rising personalism in his seminal little essay, "Subjectivity and the Irreducible in Man."[2] He says that for centuries the image of man in Western thought was onesidedly "cosmological." Man was thought to fit snugly into nature. We can see what Wojtyla means if we refer to the Roman jurists who spoke of the "law of nature" as one law that comprises both the moral law governing human actions and those natural laws describing animal instincts. They ran together in one order of law what for us are two radically incommensurable orders of law; they ran together the law that provides a norm for our freedom and the law that records patterns in nature. When one approached cosmologically the sexual union of man and woman, what one primarily noticed was the procreative power of their union, a point in which human sexuality strongly resembles animal sexuality. This is why Wojtyla says that cosmologically man was seen too much "from without" and too little "from within," that is, too objectively and too little in terms of his self-experience, or his subjectivity.

Wojtyla goes on to say that the cosmological view of man began to

---

1. Charles Curran has tried to explain how this personalist critique of a large part of traditional morality is possible, and indeed why it is quite in order. For a presentation of his position along with a critique of it, see John Grabowski and Michael Naughton, "Catholic Social and Sexual Ethics: Inconsistent or Organic?" in *The Thomist* 57.4 (1993), 555–78.

2. In Karol Wojtyla, *Person and Community: Selected Essays* (New York: Peter Lang, 1993), 209–18.

yield to a more personalist view when people began to notice in a new way their subjectivity, or interiority. With this they experienced each person not as a snugly fitting part of nature but as a "world for himself," his own center, existing in a sense as if the only person. The so familiar personalist idea that each person is his own end and no mere instrumental means, is born of this awakening to the inwardness of personal subjectivity. People experienced in a new way what it is to act through oneself in freedom, to possess oneself, to determine oneself. They could no longer live in certain archaic forms of tribal solidarity; each began to think and act in his own name. In the sexual union of man and woman they began to see not only procreative power but also the more specifically personal thing of the enactment of a self-surrendering love. And they began to see this because they were looking at man and woman more "from within," paying a new kind of attention to the evidence of spousal subjectivity.

This shift from the cosmological to the personalist view was bound to have consequences for our understanding of the moral life. And at first glance one might think that the consequence is bound to be just that personalist critique of traditional morality that we mentioned. For if the moral center of gravity is shifted into the interiority of persons, then the bodily form of moral action would seem to lose importance in relation to the interior intentions and motives of the agent. But in the work of Wojtyla we find the personalist idea unfolding in a way that does not disrupt but rather enhances traditional sexual morality. For instance, if we look into that rich early work of Wojtyla's, *Love and Responsibility*, we find, among many other things, an original personalist rethinking of the meaning of chastity.[3] In one place he enters imaginatively into the shame a woman feels when she receives the look of aggressive male sexuality,[4] sensing that in it she becomes only an object of his selfish sexual consumption. Wojtyla says that she shrinks back in a kind of shame because she feels violated as person; she subdues everything in her bearing that could be sexually provocative, and she does this, not in a puritanical cramp, but in the attempt to remove the occasion for the look which reduces her to an object. Her practice of chastity, Wojtyla concludes, is

---

3. Karol Wojtyla, *Love and Responsibility*. Translated by H. T. Willetts. (New York: Farrar, Straus, Giroux, 1981), 143–208.
4. Ibid., 174–80.

not in the first place a matter of temperance, as was traditionally taught, nor is it in the first place a matter of placing procreation in its true context: it is above all else a matter of securing for herself the love and respect due to her as person. My point is that the old virtue of chastity retains its place in Wojtyla's moral thought; his personalism does not subvert it but brings out a new dimension of it.

Here is another example of how the image of man, once it has been modified in a personalist direction, can enhance traditional morality. Well known are the old "physicalist" arguments that were sometimes made in the past to explain the wrong of things like contraception. There was, for example, the argument that intercourse performed at a fertile time tends to conception as the "natural" end of intercourse, and that you act "unnaturally" and hence wrongly by interfering with this tendency. Wojtyla has nothing to do with such "physicalist" or "naturalist" arguments, and in fact he explicitly warns against them in his encyclical, *Veritatis splendor* (cf. para. 50). He thinks that they are cut from the cosmological cloth and are inadequate to the truth about the person. His own preferred argument on contraception is altogether personalist; he says that the self-donation of the spouses is inevitably perverted into a selfish using of each other when the marital act is sterilized. Whatever one makes of the argument, however one develops it, it is in any case not based on maintaining the intactness of physiological processes or on making natural use of bodily organs, but rather on what it takes for spouses authentically to live their love for each other. To understand the argument, we have to look at spousal love from within, that is, at the way spouses live their bodily self-surrender one to another.

By the way, we see that Wojtyla's recourse to subjectivity in his personalism has nothing to do with *subjectivism*. In personal subjectivity he hopes to read the structures of personal being, which are for him objective structures underlying objectively valid ethical norms. We need not dissolve moral truth in a subjectivist way simply because we are doing greater justice to the interiority of man and thus to his personhood. On the contrary, Wojtyla affirms the objectivity of moral truth in proclaiming in his personalism "the truth about man," as he calls it.

But with all of this we have still not addressed the question we put above. Here it is again: why do many moral philosophers who call themselves personalists reject Wojtyla's understanding of chastity, why do they contest his position on contraception and even on abortion? Why does Wojtyla's personalism renew Christian sexual morality, whereas theirs subverts it?

2.

"God does not care what we do with each other's bodies; He only cares whether we treat each other as persons." Is it really true that God does not care how we treat each other's bodies? Are we not embodied persons? When we show respect for another, do we not show it for him or her as embodied person? Are there not certain actions directed to the body of another that by their very form are inconsistent with showing him or her respect? Surely a man cannot plausibly tell his wife that, though he went to a prostitute, he only did this with his body and that his personal commitment to her, his spouse, remained untouched by his excursion. Here is the reason why many a personalism gets derailed and becomes antagonistic to Christian morality: it does not know how to do justice to the embodiment of human persons, nor does it understand the place of the body in moral action. This is in fact a perennial temptation of personalism—to interpret the shift from the cosmos to the interiority of persons as implying a dualism of person and body—to think that internal motives and intentions now count for everything and that their bodily expression now counts for little. Joseph Fletcher gave a memorable expression to this dualism when he wrote: "Physical nature—the body and its members, our organs and their functions—all of these are a part of 'what is over against us,' and if we live by the rules and conditions set in physiology or another *it*, we are not *Thou*. . . . Freedom, knowledge, choice, responsibility—all these things of personal or moral stature are in us, not *out there*. Physical nature is what is over against us, out there. It represents the world of *its*."[5] Here we see a thinker yielding to the temptation to set the personal in opposition to the cosmological.

The dualistic personalists for whom Fletcher speaks of course grant that the human body can take on a more than physiological meaning; it can be drawn up into the world of the person, taking on human and personal meaning. But all such meaning is conferred by persons, just as

---

5. Joseph Fletcher, *Morals and Medicine* (Boston: Beacon Press, 1960), 211.

word-meanings are conferred by the speakers of a language on word-sounds. The human and personal meaning of the body is thus not rooted in the very nature of man as embodied person. In itself the body is just a raw material for the meaning-conferring activities of human persons; only from them does it receive any more-than-physiological meaning. A personalism based on this understanding of embodiment—I call it "spiritualistic" or "gnostic" personalism—can only wreak havoc with traditional sexual morality.

For example, according to this personalism the sexual union of man and woman is in itself not so very different from what is found in some sub-human animals. But man and woman can give their sexual union personal meaning. Perhaps they decide to reserve this union for marriage and to let it express a spousal commitment; perhaps they even decide to leave open its procreative possibility so as to enhance this expressive power. So they may decide—but they may also decide very differently. The man and woman might just as well decide to give their sexual union the meaning of light entertainment, of casual fun with no responsibilities. In this case they will of course sterilize the procreative potential of their union; bringing a new human being into existence is utterly incongruous with the kind of lighthearted fun they have in mind. And there are undoubtedly other meanings besides these two that they might choose. Thus the man and the woman may decide to deprive their sexual union of any intrinsic meaning at all, conferring on it a mere instrumental meaning; this is what happens when they think of it as a mere means for procreation. With this meaning there can of course be no question of sterilizing their sexual union.

Now what characterizes the spiritualistic personalism is not that one interprets sexual intimacy as light entertainment. Within the framework of this position one may after all interpret it as spousal commitment. *One thinks as a spiritualist when one thinks that any of these meanings is eligible, that any can be conferred on sexual union, any can be revoked, and that such union does not inherently, by its very nature, have any definite personal meaning.*

And in thinking this one may still understand oneself as a personalist, insisting that persons must never be used as mere instruments. Of course, it may seem as if any pretense to personalism had been given up; are man and woman not degraded to the status of a means when, say, their sexual union is said to be an instrument for procreation? But the spiritualist will respond that in this case only the bodies of the man and woman serve as instruments to be used; the persons who use the bodies respect each other as persons by freely collaborating for a common goal. He might explain himself saying that, since we are free to take a distance to our bodies to the point of making them mere instruments, then it is no more disordered for us to use them instrumentally than to use a hammer. The using refers only to the bodies and does not extend to the persons. And if the spiritualist wants to bring God into it, then he or she might add, "God does not care what we do with each other's bodies; He only cares whether we treat each other as persons."

Indeed, the spiritualist goes one step farther and says that you fall away from personalism precisely when you take the personal meaning of sexual union to be a meaning intrinsic to it. For then you make personal meaning follow upon physical facts, and this is as bad as attempting any of those "physicalistic" or "naturalistic" arguments mentioned above. He might add that it is a too cosmological view of man to claim that personal meaning is intrinsic to certain bodily activities; the only truly personalist view is the one that recognizes the freedom of persons to confer and to revoke personal meaning in relation to the body.

3.

What is it to take personal embodiment seriously and to hold what we might call an "incarnational personalism"? Let us stay with the example of the sexual union of man and woman. This personalist would say that sexual union intrinsically has an incomparable personal intimacy. In it man and woman expose their most intimate personal selves. Their sexuality extends its roots into certain depths of their personal being; these depths are stirred up in any sexual encounter between them.[6] If they encounter each other in a trivial way, not meaning anything personally

---

6. Cf. the rich phenomenology of sex and sexuality that Dietrich von Hildebrand offers in his early work, *Reinheit und Jungfräulichkeit:* "In a certain sense sex is the secret of the individual, which he instinctively hides from others. Every person feels it to be altogether intimate, touching in a unique way his or her innermost self. Every disclosure of sex opens up something hidden, something intimate in the person, initiating the other into the secret of the one who discloses himself. This is why shame has its natural place in the sphere of sex. One is simply ashamed to unveil this secret before others.... This

deep or significant by their encounter, then there arises a conflict between the intimate depth in themselves which is engaged by genital sex, and the triviality of their subjective intention. They commonly feel, and the woman typically feels keenly, that they have somehow squandered themselves as persons. They lose self-respect, as one can see unmistakably in the face of every sexually promiscuous girl. They have said too much with their bodies, they have said far more than they mean; they have committed themselves objectively beyond anything that they intend subjectively—hence the dishonesty evident to anyone who thinks closely about casual sex.

The all-important point to be made against the spiritualistic personalism is that man and woman cannot get rid of this dishonesty by deciding to change the meaning of sexual union. They cannot redefine this meaning so that it coincides with their trivial intention. They are impotent to disengage depth and intimacy from sexual union. They cannot repress the intimacy and let sexuality be merely physiological, or be only a medium for light entertainment. This act goes deep by its very nature; it either expresses spousal love and commitment, or it effects a self-squandering, a self-desecration; but it will not be neutralized, will not be rendered harmless. There is a sexual embodiment of the intimate center of each person that we did not ask for and cannot undo; it is a personal meaning of the body that no human person or human society conferred on the body and that no one can remove from it. It is the basis of all kinds of objective norms of sexual behavior, including the norm prescribing that sexual intimacy be reserved for the setting of an enduring spousal commitment.

But we cannot understand these norms merely by knowing that persons should always be respected as their own ends and never be used. *We must also know about the embodied personhood of man and woman.* Then it becomes clear that "God does indeed care how we treat each other's bodies, *and He cares for the very reason that He requires us to respect each other as persons.*"[7]

---

intimacy shows us again the particular depth of the sensual sphere in contrast to all other aspects of vital life. But most of all it shows the central position occupied by this sphere. And since sex is the secret of each individual, to disclose it and to give it away constitutes a unique form of giving oneself away." Von Hildebrand, *Reinheit und Jungfräulichkeit* (St. Ottilien: 1981), 16–18.

7. It would be fascinating to pursue the difference between man and woman with

Estrangement from the Body

Wojtyla would add that we do not fall into an excessively cosmological view of man by affirming the natural sexual embodiment of our intimate selves. He would say that our embodiment was often well understood in the cosmological view and has to be preserved in any personalist development of the image of man. He would say that he never advocated *replacing* the cosmological with the personalist; it is only a question of *completing* the cosmological on the basis of all the newly discovered truth about man and woman as persons.

4.

Men and women who take for granted the spiritualistic personalism have no scruples at all about the procedure of *in vitro* fertilization followed by artificial implantation. They see no personalist problem in using their reproductive systems to supply biological materials to a lab technician who assembles the materials so as to bring about conception. On the contrary, they think that this makes eminent personalist sense because it corrects a deficiency in nature for the sake of bringing into being a new person. "God does not care about the physiological fineprint; He only cares that we bring new persons into existence."

But men and women imbued by incarnational personalism think and feel differently. They instinctively feel the great value of embodied love serving as the cause of conception. They are distressed at how this incomparable way of living their embodiment gives way to an instrumental using of their bodies when these are taken simply as a source of gametes, which are extracted and brought together *in vitro*. They cannot believe that these are just two different methods for achieving conception and that they are to be judged simply on the basis of their effectiveness in achieving it: they feel sure that there must be some moral differences between them. They instinctively feel that with the *in vitro* method they are trying to step out of their bodies, objectifying and using them in a way

---

respect to the experience of embodiment. Scheler thinks that woman experiences a much more intimate embodiment of herself than does man, who "deals with his body at a distance, as if he were leading a dog on a leash" (Scheler, "Zum Sinn der Frauenbewegung," *Vom Umsturz der Werte* (Bern: Francke Verlag, 1955), 206. Thus for Scheler the estrangement of persons from their bodies, which is our subject in this study, can be understood as the expression of a disproportionately masculine culture—of a culture suffering from the lack of the feminine principle.

that violates the truth of their embodiment. It is not that they profess more respect for persons than the other kind of personalists; it is rather that their sense of our embodied personhood leads them to draw different consequences from the imperative to respect persons. It is certainly not that they idolize the "natural" way of achieving conception and have some irrational aversion to the artificiality of the *in vitro* method of achieving it, as if they were hankering after the simplicity of the pre-technological world. No, if the artificial method did not interfere with some great value of their embodiment as persons, they would have no moral qualms about it.

But there is a far more radical way of abandoning the embodiment of human persons in the raising up of offspring. Those who propose to produce new human beings by cloning go much farther in the way in which they would have us step out of our bodies, lay hold of certain biological materials produced by our bodies, and manipulate these into a human embryo. For they are proposing to take the sexual form of reproduction that is proper to human beings (based on haploid gametes uniting at fertilization to form the diploid zygote) and to turn it into an asexual form of reproduction, in which the male gametes, or sperm cells, have no role to play.

At issue not only are the bodies of the parents but also of their offspring. These new human beings are in a sense manufactured rather than begotten. One can see the difference in this, that those who make human beings *in vitro* feel entitled to unmake what they have made; they take for granted their right to destroy the work of their hands if it is found to be defective, that is they take for granted their right to weed out their failures by means of selective abortion. They understandably feel themselves to be fundamentally above the product of their making, with the result that this product is entitled to continue to exist only if they will its continued existence. Thus it is that persons—the persons coming into existence in the petri dish of the lab technicians—are not respected as their own end, even if they are among the lucky few who are implanted and brought to term. And it is a grievous mistake about the embodied personhood of the parents that gives rise to this lack of respect; they put themselves in an intolerable position above their offspring just because they step outside of their bodies and treat them as a source of biological materials. Only if the parents would live their embodiment by begetting children through their sexual intimacy, would they be able to respect their children as being the full equals of themselves.

5.

Consider the distinction so commonly drawn today between a human being as "biologically human" and a human being as "personal." One says, for example, that the very young human embryo is undeniably human in the biological sense but is not yet a person. To kill it is indeed to kill a human being but not a human person; it is therefore not the kind of killing that violates the imperative to respect persons. One says the same thing about human beings who have suffered cortical brain death and who as a result will never be able to recover personal consciousness: they too have died as persons and remain alive only as subpersonal human animals; to kill them by taking their vital organs for transplant is not to kill a person and so not to commit any wrong. In fact, those who speak in this way go on to say that it is even de-personalizing to claim that every biological human being is a person; they say that this is to make the higher thing of personhood follow upon the lower thing of biological life of a certain kind, and that this is akin to that ethical naturalism, mentioned above, which consists in making moral norms follow on physiological tendencies. They say that it expresses the old cosmological view to see a human person in every human being, whatever its stage of development, and that it is a far more personalist view to be more discriminating about which human beings really count as persons. Perhaps they will venture to take God's point of view and to say, "God does not much care what we do with biological humans; He only cares how we treat human persons."

They are of course right to say that there can be non-human persons and that in this sense "human" and "person" do not coincide. They are even right to say that there is no metaphysical absurdity in assuming a human being which is not a person; the medieval thinkers who taught some form of "delayed animation" assumed as much. But there is a way of affirming the possibility of a non-personal human being that is entirely born of spiritualistic personalism.

If one thinks of the person mainly as an experiencing subject, and thinks of the body mainly as an object of this subject, existing over against this subject, then it is only natural to identify the person with his or her experiencing and to think that in the absence of conscious experiencing there can be no person, and that human bodily life, taken apart from conscious experiencing, is nothing personal. But if we develop a more adequate understanding of the embodiment of persons—an important project that we cannot undertake here—we will recognize that there are other, more intimate ways of experiencing our bodies than as objects over against us. Indeed, the fundamental experience of being embodied is absolutely inexplicable in terms of experiencing the body as an object over against us, as many authors have shown. In striving to do more justice to our embodiment we will also recognize that there is an embodiment of ourselves as persons that is prior to all conscious body experience and that provides the basis for it. In other words, we will recognize that, just as the sexual embodiment of our intimate personal self is a work of nature, being wrought in us without our consent or collaboration, as we saw, so also the more fundamental thing of being embodied at all, is a work of nature, a given of human personhood, preceding and grounding all the conscious relations existing between ourselves and our bodies.

If we do justice to these and other aspects of the embodiment that we know in ourselves as consciously awakened persons, then we readily understand that living human beings lacking all personal consciousness, like the human embryo, may well be persons. For we will think that, given the depth and intimacy of our embodiment, the only safe assumption is that a new human person begins to exist as soon as a new human body is formed, and continues in existence as long as the body is alive.[8] To affirm this has nothing to do with naturalism, nothing to do with an excessively cosmological self-understanding: but it has everything to do with respecting the truth of our embodiment.

---

8. In the present paper I do not mean to try to settle the issue of the personhood of the embryo but simply to show how the issue is skewed by spiritualistic personalism. I have more to say about this issue in my book, *Selfhood*, ch. 4.

6.

The spiritualistic personalism also takes a great toll at a more fundamental level, at the level not just of sex ethics and of the life issues, but of moral first principles. It may at first sound surprising if I say that it underlies the ethical consequentialism that is so widely held today: but it is not hard to show a certain spiritualism at the heart of consequentialism. Or to say it the other way around: it is not hard to understand why John Paul II, in the course of rejecting ethical consequentialism in his encyclical, *Veritatis splendor,* found it necessary to affirm repeatedly the unity of the person with his body (see, for example, para. 49).

By consequentialism I mean the ethical thesis that the right and wrong of any moral action derives exclusively from the consequences of the action. Thus an action is right if it will be more productive of good results, or more exactly, will give a better balance of good over bad results, than any other action open to me when I perform that action. What, you will ask, is conspicuously spiritualistic here? Notice that the body of the moral agent is treated as an instrumental means for getting results, and the instrumentalization of the body is commonly a sign of the spiritualism I have been deprecating. But the spiritualism shows itself even more clearly when we take a further step in developing the consequentialist thesis. The consequentialist speaks as consequentialist *only of the right and wrong of moral actions.* But he is commonly aware that there is more to morality than right and wrong actions, that morality also comprises *the good and bad of inner responses and attitudes.* He typically holds that this moral goodness and badness has nothing to do with results and consequences; it comes from intentions, motives, ultimate loves, fundamental options, and the like. He thus posits two almost incommensurable spheres of morality: an intimate sphere of willing and loving, and an external sphere where our bodily actions are hardly more than causes in nature and are measured exclusively by their consequences. The spiritualistic dualism is now in full evidence. *He thinks that by dwelling in the intimacy of his ultimate freedom he is at such a distance to his body that his moral actions become nothing but an instrumental means for achieving good results.* He thinks he can place the center of his moral existence in a kind of acosmic inwardness and can detach from this personal center his external actions, almost to the point that their norm is nothing more than their technical efficiency. If you try to object to him that at least certain actions, however fruitful they may be in their consequences, are inseparable from bad intentions and disordered fundamental options, and must therefore never be performed, he will retort that you must not bind the interior act and the exterior action in this way; that this is akin to the naturalistic attempt to bind physiological tendencies and moral norms; that you are thinking cosmologically where you should be thinking more personalistically. He might even say, "God is not so concerned about the wrong we may do in our bodily actions; He only cares whether in our heart of hearts we are loving persons."

If, however, we take seriously our personal embodiment, then we will not for a minute think that in our moral actions we merely use the body as an instrument. We readily recognize in the acosmic inwardness just mentioned a radical estrangement of the person from his body. We know that being present in the body, being incarnate in it, we are far more than natural causes; we are acting persons, subject not just to laws of technical efficiency, but to moral norms. This is why we can realize certain "meanings" in our actions that can be realized only because we are present as persons in our actions. Thus an action of ours can have the meaning of "violating someone's right;" but no cause in nature, however destructive of the good of persons, can violate anyone's right. We incarnational personalists know that certain bodily actions, such as those having the form of using persons, can never be brought into moral order by good motives, or by good consequences, or by some combination of both; they are inalienably, incurably disordered. Thus if a man buys sex from a prostitute, we know all we need to know in order to determine that they both act badly; we do not have first to find out the fundamental option of their lives. It is not that we think that a physical event implies a moral condemnation; it is rather that the moral action of an embodied person is not only a physical but also a personal and moral event. We will assert our incarnational personalism by saying, "God cares about the wrong we do in our bodily actions *for the very reason* that He cares whether we are loving persons."[9]

---

9. We should also mention that it is possible to go too far in affirming the embodiment of human persons. It seems to me that St. Thomas Aquinas does this with his teaching (as at *Summa Theologiae* I, q. 29, a. 1, ad 5) that the human person is dissolved at death, that only the soul but not the person survives death, and that the human per-

Many of our contemporaries think that Christianity hates the human body and cannot really accept the sexuality of men and women. It should now be clear that it is in fact these contemporaries who hate the body, who chafe under their embodiment, who impotently try to undo it, who would rather use the body instrumentally than live embodied in it, who would cultivate a disembodied moral existence that does not befit human beings. It is only the Christian tradition for which John Paul speaks that knows how intimately the body is incorporated into the human person and what dignity it has as a result. He defends the human body against its modern detractors. In raising his voice in witness to the "truth about man," he protests not only against materialism, but no less against this spiritualism.

I am committed, then, to an incarnational personalism. It is a personalism that knows the whole man, the embodiment of man no less than his personhood. But the spiritualistic, or gnostic personalism, recognizing only personhood and doing little justice to embodiment, works with a caricature of man. Little wonder that the two personalisms, divided as they are over the embodiment of persons, often arrive at antithetical ethical positions.[10]

---

son is "re-constituted" at the resurrection of the body. I cannot here do justice to his reasons for holding this and to my reasons for disagreeing with him. But though I have this point of disagreement, I acknowledge at the same time that St. Thomas contributed tremendously much to an adequate account of personal embodiment, above all in his critique of the Platonic theory of embodiment.

10. My thanks to Patrick Lee for his comments on the first draft of this article.

CHAPTER 6

Person and Consciousness

My antagonist in this paper is Locke, who reduced "person" to "personal consciousness," holding that there can be no person in the absence of any conscious personal life, that is, of any willing, understanding, feeling, grieving, rejoicing, despairing, hoping. I will begin by speaking as a Catholic believer in objecting to Locke's reductionist thesis. Then I will proceed to offer an argument for the irreducibility of person to consciousness that believer and non-believer alike can understand. A subplot in this paper is showing what follows from this irreducibility for the question whether the human embryo is a person. I begin by clarifying the position that is antithetical to the one that I defend.

1. *Locke's reduction of person to consciousness*

As far as I can determine Locke was the first to make a full argument for the reduction of persons to consciousness.[1] In a famous discussion of personal identity, that is, of what it is that makes for the "same" person and for "different" persons over some time, he repeatedly affirms that "it is impossible to make personal identity to consist in anything but consciousness."[2] He explains that only those deeds that I can remember as my own really belong to me as person and can be imputed to me morally;

---

* This paper originally appeared as "Person and Consciousness" in *Christian Bioethics* 6.1 (2000), 37–48. It has been only lightly revised for the present volume.
1. John Locke, *An Essay Concerning Human Understanding*, II (New York: Dover Publications, 1959), ch. 27.
2. Ibid., 461.

whatever deeds there are that I could never recall as my own must belong to some other person and be the responsibility of some other. In the course of his discussion he is led to the more fundamental thesis that "without consciousness there is no person."³ This is more fundamental in the sense that it concerns not the identity of persons over time, but rather concerns what it takes for a person to exist in any moment of time. Here is the thesis again: "it is by the consciousness it [the person] has of its present thoughts and actions, that it is *self to itself* now."⁴ Locke grants that there is a body-soul substance in each human being, and he grants that its being is not reducible to consciousness; but he distinguishes the person in each human being from any such body-soul substance and does so on the grounds that only the person, but not the soul, exhausts its being in consciousness, existing only in conscious self-presence. He carries this distinction very far, even to the point of saying that it is not absurd for the same human body-soul substance to be inhabited (whether successively or simultaneously) by different persons, nor absurd for the same person to inhabit different human body-soul substances. Locke tells of an acquaintance who thought he had the soul of Socrates; Locke observes that nothing prevents his friend from really having the soul of Socrates, but he adds that his friend was certainly not the person Socrates was unless he can remember events belonging to the life of Socrates.⁵ One sees that the distinction between man as human being and man as person, which has had such a career in contemporary bioethics, is already in Locke.

If he had had occasion to address the question of the human embryo, he would have probably agreed that it is a human being and would have perhaps even granted that it has a rational human soul, but he would have surely declared that it is no human person since it has as yet no personal consciousness.⁶

Though I reject Locke's identification of person and personal con-

---

3. Ibid., 464.
4. Ibid., 451.
5. Ibid., 455.
6. It is important to distinguish Locke's dualism of person and human being from the Platonic dualism of soul and body; it is a question of two completely different dualisms. We have just seen how Locke contrasts person and the body-soul compound, and sometimes he draws the contrast directly between person and soul. As for the body, he reckons it to person to the extent that it is experienced.

sciousness, I do acknowledge some important truths about "persons" that are connected with his position. 1) I acknowledge the central position that consciousness has in the makeup of human persons, which can be seen in this, that there is in a sense hardly any difference between annihilating a person altogether and depriving a person of all consciousness forever. If someone tries to console you with the thought that, though you will never regain consciousness, you will nevertheless continue to exist as person, you will say that this is no consolation at all, that the perpetual deprivation of all consciousness is somehow equivalent to annihilation. It is not as if you are losing a little while retaining a great deal; you are aware of losing everything and retaining virtually nothing by retaining a nonconscious personal being. Only through conscious acting can a person really live, show himself as person, and achieve the greatest excellences of personal being. Personal consciousness is not the mere accident of a personal substance; it makes the difference between being alive and being dead as person.

2) And there is another fact about persons that connects person and consciousness. Locke does not make a point of it, but I would reckon it to the truth connected with his position. Since persons exist in freedom they determine themselves, they constitute themselves; a person is not a given of nature but a self-creation. In his encyclical *Veritatis splendor*, John Paul II quotes Gregory of Nyssa saying that,

> human life is always subject to change; it needs to be born ever anew ... but here birth does not come about by a foreign intervention, as is the case with bodily beings ... it is the result of a free choice. Thus we are in a certain way our own parents, creating ourselves as we will, by our decisions. (para. 71)

Since any such self-creation exists only in the conscious acting of a person, we see again why it is that depriving a person of all consciousness is almost the same as annihilating that person. Of course, as I have tried to show elsewhere in some detail,[7] a human person cannot be altogether a self-creation. For any act of creating presupposes someone who creates, someone who in that act of creating is precisely not created. A self-creation that presupposes nothing that is not self-created, is a metaphysical

---

7. John Crosby, "Evolutionism and the Ontology of the Human Person: Critique of the Marxist Theory of the Emergence of Man," *Review of Politics* 38.2 (1976), 208–43.

Person and Consciousness

absurdity. (Needless to say, the absolute self-existence of God is not rightly conceived of in terms of self-creation.) And yet the central place of a certain rightly-understood self-creation in the life of human persons brings with it the central place of consciousness in the makeup of human persons.

But have we now conceded so much to Locke on person and consciousness that we can no longer reasonably claim to find personhood in the early human fetus, which undeniably lacks any subjective self-experience and has as yet done no work of self-creation?

2. What the sacramental life of Christians implies about person and consciousness

Let us look into the sacramental life of an adult Christian. Suppose that one is baptized as an adult. Changes are wrought in him that fall entirely outside of his subjective self-experience. He does not experience in himself the remission of original sin; indeed, he does not even experience that solidarity with Adam in virtue of which he is infected with the sin of Adam. *The Catechism of the Catholic Church* (para. 404) says that "the whole human race is in Adam 'as one body of one man.'" He experiences himself much more individualistically. He can only believe, but certainly not verify in his self-experience, that he exists in this mysterious solidarity with Adam. He also does not fully experience in himself the baptismal remission of his personal sins. He does not experience the incorporation of himself into Christ and the Church. He has become a new creature in Christ—he is clothed in an innocence of which the white baptismal stole is a sign; but he does not experience this newness and this innocence. Nor does he experience the priestly dignity that he acquires through baptism. He may glimpse these things in moments of deep contemplative prayer, but even then they remain much greater realities than he can experience in himself. The dramatic transition from the defilement of the person before baptism to the purity and radiance of the person after baptism, does not register in the self-experience of the one who devoutly receives baptism. Mystics have said that we could not bear the sight of the beauty of the freshly regenerated person, but this sight is withheld from the person himself, as it is from others around him. He believes in faith that he has been transformed; but the demand on his faith is often so great that he can only marvel at the contrast between the baptismal regeneration of himself that he believes and the plainness and everydayness of his self-experience as he undergoes baptism.

The same holds for the Eucharist. Our Lord says, "He who eats my flesh and drinks my blood lives in me and I in him" (*John* 6:56). But one does not experience this indwelling of Christ in receiving communion. He continues saying, "As the living father has sent me, and I live by the father, so he who eats me shall live by me" (*John* 6:57). But we do not experience ourselves living out of Christ; we believe it, and constantly struggle against unbelief. If by some fraud an unconsecrated host were distributed at communion the devout believer would not detect this in his prayer of thanksgiving. And so with marriage. Christian spouses do not experience their incorporation into the mystery of Christ and the Church; they do not experience it as they experience their love for each other; they believe it with a faith that overcomes the world. And so with Holy Orders; "the indelible spiritual character" (*Catechism of the Catholic Church*, para. 1582) imparted by this sacrament is not fully experienced by the priest, nor is its indelibility. The Church acknowledges a difference between the valid and the invalid conferral of this sacrament, but the recipient of the sacrament will never find this difference in his self-experience.

I take it as self-evident that all these sacramental effects wrought in believers are wrought in them *as persons*. What I mean is this: I do not live as person in all that I do and receive. For example, insofar as I am a subject of instinctual urges, I do not act as person. And again: insofar as others take me as a mere specimen or instance of human nature, they are not taking me as person. Now I want to insist on the fact that the sacraments work their effects in me precisely as person; they do not affect me as anything less than as person. For it is surely self-evident that only a person can have sin remitted, can regain innocence, can live out of Christ as He lives out of the Father, or can be established as a priest. Non-persons, even the non-personal human beings assumed by so many bioethicists, could not undergo such sacramental effects; nor can human beings who are taken under some less-than-personal aspect. And so it is that the Catholic Christian, by living the sacramental life of the Church, knows that as person, precisely as person, he is vastly more than he experiences himself to be. If he relied only on his self-experience he would have no idea of the length and breadth and depth of the person he is in Christ.

Person and Consciousness

Let us try to understand this more deeply by having recourse to the fundamental difference between experiencing myself from within, as only I and not another can experience me, and experiencing myself from without, as not only I but also any other can experience me. It is the fundamental difference between experiencing myself as subject and experiencing myself as object.[8] If one brings this concept of subjective self-experience to the interpretation of Locke, one can understand him perhaps even better than he understood himself. For it is only by reliving some past deed from within, as my own, that I incorporate it into myself, and establish the identity of my present self with my earlier self. If I just look at some past deed from without, as anyone else can also look at it, I cannot yet tell whether I am identical with the person who did that deed. If we now express the Lockean reduction of person to consciousness using this concept of subjective self-experience, we can say that if Locke is right, then I as person cannot fail to experience from within all intrinsic elements and aspects of myself as person. If there were something in myself as person that escaped my subjective self-experience, then the Lockean reduction of person to consciousness would not hold.

We make a point of saying "intrinsic," because the extrinsic relations in which I stand would not all have to be experienced. The fact, for example, that I have a guardian angel would not have to be experienced, not even on the assumption that as person I am nothing but consciousness in the sense of subjective self-experience. I would not have to know who my parents or grandparents were; this knowledge would not be necessarily included in my self-experience. But all that belongs immanently, intrinsically to myself as person would have to be experienced. Let us assume that as person I exist in freedom; this fact could not remain unknown to me

---

8. I have explored this difference in some detail in my book, *The Selfhood of the Human Person* (Washington, D.C.: The Catholic University of America Press, 1996), especially 82–97, where I give particular attention to the fact that my relation to myself as subject is irreducible to my relation to myself as object. While it is possible to make myself an object for myself, this self-relation is something fundamentally different from my relation to myself in what I am about to call my subjective self-experience. For one thing, the objectifying self-relation has something cognitive about it that is foreign to subjective self-experience. As this self-experience becomes stronger, I become more alive as person, more recollected, more empowered to act through myself as person, and all of this lacks the cognitive theme of standing over against myself as object. As far as I know this distinction is made for the first time in Western philosophy by St. Augustine; see, for example, *De Trinitate*, X, 16.

in my self-experience. If it did, then my being as person would exceed my self-experience, and the Lockean reduction of person to consciousness would be defeated. Of course, not all relations are extrinsic relations; some are entirely constitutive for who I am, such as the relation of being an adopted child of God, or of being called to union with God. These relations I would also reckon to the intrinsic or immanent makeup of human persons; thus they too would have to be experienced in my subjective self-experience if Locke were right.

The reader will notice that in speaking of the sacramental life of the Catholic Christian, I made a point of referring to the impact of the sacraments on his immanent being. The innocence restored in baptism characterizes his immanent being as person; it is not just a new relation to Christ (a relation of extrinsic imputation, say), but also a new intrinsic character of himself as person. So is the indelible spiritual character wrought by Holy Orders in the priest. The baptismal incorporation into Christ and the Church is also not just an extrinsic relation; it involves some immanent change in the one who is incorporated. Now my argument is this. All of these sacramental effects wrought in me as person would have to be experienced by me in myself, if indeed I as person were nothing but my self-experience. But since most of them fall entirely outside of my self-experience, far exceeding my self-experience, I as person am far more than my conscious self-experience.

It goes without saying that I do not mean that, given the Lockean reduction of person to consciousness, each person must be able to answer all possible questions about himself, thus possessing all possible knowledge about himself and being invulnerable to error about himself. A Lockean person could well ask, "What is consciousness?" or "How is it possible for the same being to be subject to natural causes and to exist in freedom?" and be at a loss to give any satisfactory answer. But notice that with these questions one steps out of the mode of subjective self-experience, asking rather about the universal essence of certain aspects of persons, and looking for knowledge that is as much about other persons as it is about oneself. I only say that immanent elements of yourself as person such as your consciousness or freedom must be experienced subjectively by you if Locke were right. If they were completely hidden from your subjective self-presence, then the Lockean reduction of person to consciousness would be refuted. And so I do not make an argument against the

Lockean reduction out of the fact that the Christian believer cannot explain theologically the indwelling of Christ in the devout communicant or explain theologically the original sin that is remitted by baptism. But I do make an argument against this reduction out of the fact that any given believer does not fully experience this indwelling in himself and does not fully experience in himself the transition from having original sin to being freed from it.

I can perhaps explain more precisely the way in which the great realities of the inner life of the believer exceed the self-experience of the believer. We can distinguish between that in a person which falls essentially and necessarily outside of the subjective self-experience of the person (like the working of the brain or the processes that occur in blood clotting) and is always perceptible only as an object, and so is always as perceptible by others as it is by me, from that which falls indeed for the time being outside of the person's subjective self-experience but could yet be retrieved in his self-experience. Now I do not see why the supernatural glory of the sacramentally nourished believer should not in principle be of this latter kind and thus fall within the self-experience of the believer. With God in the next world we hope to know ourselves even as we are known. When the divine life that has been sown in us is manifested, when it shows itself for what it is, we will surely have an entirely new self-experience. We will experience in ourselves our living out of Christ and our incorporation in Him. The new life that we have as a new creature in Christ belongs to us so intimately as persons that it is only fitting that, once we have passed beyond the twilight conditions of earthly existence, we should be able to experience it in ourselves.[9] Perhaps the mystics anticipate even now this fuller self-experience in their mystical prayer.[10]

9. It would be a mistake to think that Locke's position comes closer to being the true one if it is referred to our fulfillment in eternity, where, as I suggest here, our personal being and our conscious self-presence coincide more than they do in our earthly existence. A *coinciding* of person and consciousness is something different from a *reduction* of person to consciousness. See my discussion of this difference in *Selfhood*, 128–31, esp. 131.

10. Cf. the chapter, "The Mystical Experience of the Self," in Louis Dupré, *Transcendent Selfhood* (New York: The Seabury Press, 1976). "If we may attach any credence to the revelations of the mystics . . . an altogether different layer of selfhood hides underneath the familiar succession of outward-oriented phenomena. . . . [W]e enter [through mystical experience] the sanctuary where God and the soul touch. It is also the very core of the self . . ." (93).

When, then, I acknowledge in the self an abundance of personal being that exceeds subjective self-experience, I am not locating it in some objective part of a person, as for example in the objective body that we distinguish from the lived body. I am locating it in a sense in the subjectivity of the person.[11]

And so the Catholic Christian experiences his personal consciousness as a kind of light at the center of his being. The light shades off into a darkness that encompasses him. This is not the darkness of the world outside of him, but of his own being, of his own personal being. The talk of darkness is not meant to express anything evil, or even anything lower, but only to express depths of our personal being mysteriously inaccessible to our conscious self-experience, at least in our present state of existence. Newman captures this mystery when he says of each human being that "he has a depth within him unfathomable, an infinite abyss of existence; and the [social] scene in which he bears part for the moment is but like a gleam of sunshine upon its surface."[12]

It follows that the Christian has a profound experience of his finitude and creaturehood; he does not just experience self-possession and self-determination and self-creation in his conscious life, but he also experiences himself growing out of a mysteriously hidden ground of personal being. His life as person is hidden with Christ in God; he is not yet revealed as who he really is. He is far from consciously living through the infinite abyss of existence in himself, of experiencing it in the intimacy of his self-presence. This is why he often experiences in his inner life energies and impulses flowing through himself that, while they are in him as person, do not originate in his conscious self and that sometimes empower him to do what he would have thought beyond his conscious strength.

If now the Catholic Christian, having that sense of himself that is formed by living the sacramental life of the Church, has occasion to reason about the status of the early human embryo, he will say that the

---

11. I trust that none of my readers will be tempted to introduce here the modern psychological category of the *unconscious*. The priestly dignity that I have as baptized Christian, for example, does not reside in my unconscious, nor is there any such thing as a psychotherapy that could bring this priestly dignity into consciousness in the sense of letting me live it in my subjective self-presence.

12. John Henry Newman, *Parochial and Plain Sermons*, IV (London: Rivingtons, 1870), 83.

Person and Consciousness

absence of personal conscious life in it does not tell against its personhood: for if so much of his own personal being is hidden from his conscious self-experience, why should not the entire personal being of the embryo be hidden from itself, that is, why should it not exist as person even in the absence of any self-experience? He will also point out that the reasoning to this conclusion need not be so indirect. People are baptized not only as adults but also as newborn infants, who lack all real personal self-presence; but the effects wrought by baptism make sense only if the infant in whom they are wrought is a person. The infant must be a person of a kind that Locke never envisaged, namely a person not reducible to consciousness.

3. What the moral consciousness of all human beings implies about person and consciousness

But it is not only the Christian living by faith who can discern the infinite abyss of existence in himself; the searching pagan can discern something of it and he can also realize that it far exceeds the conscious self-experience of persons. The Lockean reduction of person to consciousness is by no means the natural position of the non-Christian, or of the Christian who is surveying the human experience that he shares with all other human beings. Precisely the Catholic Christian is alive to this continuity of Christian experience and universal human experience and takes pleasure in showing how the former illuminates the latter, and also how the latter predisposes the mind for receiving the former. Let me offer just one specimen of our natural human experience of the irreducibility of us persons to consciousness.

I start from a certain fact, first recognized by Socrates, about moral good and evil.[13] In teaching that it is better to suffer than to commit injustice (see above all the *Gorgias*), Socrates teaches that nothing is so ultimately harmful for a human being as doing wrong. Being the victim of the worst wrong is as nothing when compared to the harm inflicted on oneself as a result of committing some wrong. This defiles the soul so grievously that it is for Socrates a wonder that it does not destroy the soul, as a similarly grievous bodily disease kills the body. I also assume with

---

13. Beginning with this sentence and throughout the next few paragraphs I take over some sentences from my book *Selfhood*, 135–37.

Socrates that doing the just thing is supremely beneficial for human persons, entirely surpassing any non-moral benefit they could receive.

I submit that one can connect this great Socratic discovery with our understanding of man as person by saying that wrongdoing is an incomparable evil for the human *person* and that right-doing is incomparably beneficial for the *person*. Of course Socrates had no conception of person, any more than Plato or Aristotle had, and I do not mean that what he calls soul is equivalent to what we call person. I just mean that if we bring to the study of the Socratic ethics our understanding of man as person, then we will understand that it is *as persons* that we are supremely harmed and supremely benefited by our own moral action.

Now I argue that if persons really could be reduced to their subjective self-experience, it would be impossible to maintain this fundamental ethical insight of Socrates. My argument begins thus: If persons had no being beyond their conscious self-experiencing, they could not fail to experience that harm to themselves that comes from wrongdoing. How could this exist "objectively" and without being experienced? I can readily admit that, on the assumption that persons are nothing but subjective self-experience, all kinds of facts could characterize persons without them being aware of the facts. For example, some persons could resemble others without having any awareness of the resemblance. Or the relation of consciousness to the normal working of the brain could remain entirely unknown to them. But I speak here of what is good for persons and bad for persons, and in fact of what is supremely good and bad for them: how can this thoroughly intrinsic moral reality fail to be experienced subjectively from within? Of course if the harm lay in the fact that punishment is coming for the wrongdoing, then the harm could exist objectively. But the idea of Socrates, and the insight of each of us, is that moral harm to oneself is nothing imposed on us from without but is rather something springing up within us. How can it, being so thoroughly immanent to my moral being, fail to be experienced subjectively by me if indeed I were nothing but subjective self-experience? There is no point in objecting that the harm to the person is nothing but the violation of some standard or norm, as if nothing but an extrinsic relation to the norm were involved and so nothing that needs to be included in the self-experience of a Lockean person. Such a violation would at most explain the moral wrongness of an action—not really explain even this, in my opinion, but at least plausibly explain it—but not even plausibly explain the *harm for me* accruing from the wrongdoing. For this harm does not lie in a relation of my action to a norm, but in the relation of my action to my very self. Such an objection would try to explain in extrinsic terms that which is entirely intrinsic to the person.

To complete my argument I need only one further fact, an entirely non-controversial fact, namely that persons who do wrong do not commonly experience themselves as harmed or do not experience the harm to themselves in proportion to its seriousness. Here now is the finished argument: since wrongdoing is not always experienced in all the harmfulness that it really has for me, it follows that I as person am more than my conscious experiencing. There must be a personal being of myself that can be really harmed even when the harm does not subjectively or experientially register in me. This being is, of course, not the body of the person, for the body is not a possible subject of moral guilt or of other moral predicates; no, this more-than-conscious being is found *within* the person, it is found at the center of personal selfhood. Nor is this being a *thing* that can always only be an *object* of consciousness; belonging as it does to the very center of the person it is destined to become consciously self-present. The harm done to myself by my wrongdoing is fully capable of being experienced from within and ought to be so experienced. But it need not be, and so it is not reducible to conscious self-experience.

Even if wrongdoers come to recognize the harm to themselves and to experience it, they are quite aware of having to distinguish between this experience and the harm which they experience. They will for instance be aware that the depth of their experience of the harm to themselves will vary considerably from one time to another, though the harm itself that they experience is not subject to any such variations. This means that it would be no argument against my position if someone were right in saying that a criminal can never be entirely and at every level of his being unaware of the unsoundness in himself as person. The very fact that this moral unsoundness, and in and through it the part of the person that is unsound, can be very incompletely experienced, and very variously experienced, means that this part of the person has a depth of being that does not exhaust itself in being consciously lived through.

Socrates himself points to the excess of being over self-experience that we can gather from our moral experience. He points to it when he makes one of his main arguments for the immortality of the soul, the one found in *The Republic* X (608d–611a). He argues that the soul must be immortal to be able to endure moral evil in this life without being destroyed by it. Comparable harm for the body, he says, leads to the death of the body; only an indestructible spirit could undergo a kind of spiritual death without being corrupted; in any case, it will hardly be the death of the body that destroys the soul, when an evil that is far more threatening to the soul does not destroy it. If there is merit in this argument, as I think there is, then we see again how far the full being of the person lags behind personal consciousness. For we can hardly verify our immortality in our subjective self-experience; many feel that their inner consciousness is like a flickering flame that is in danger of being extinguished at death. An indestructible spirit out of which our conscious life arises is not inescapably given within ourselves, which is why Socrates can only attempt an inference to it on the basis of moral evil.

If then, someone, not necessarily a believer, lives the moral life seriously enough to experience "a depth unfathomable, an infinite abyss of existence" in himself, which he is far from completely living through and experiencing from within himself, then when he turns his thoughts to the status of the early human embryo he will not summarily deny its personhood on the grounds that it lacks all consciousness. He will be used to the idea of persons far exceeding their conscious self-experience and so will see nothing surprising in the idea of a person being embodied in the human embryo and still awaiting the moment when it will quicken into consciousness. And if he is a believer, he will be all the more sensitive to the way persons exceed their conscious self-experience in their moral existence; his experience of the sacraments of the Church will have enabled him to see more in his moral experience.

The fact that persons can exist without yet being consciously awake does not mean that we are entitled to suspect their presence just anywhere. There is, for example, no reason to suspect their presence in the sperm or egg prior to fertilization. Human persons are embodied persons, and until the body is formed that is developmentally continuous with the adult human body, there is no reason to suppose the existence of a slumbering human person. But once this body is formed at fertilization, the body which will later be inhabited by a consciously alive person, it is entirely reasonable to suppose that this person already dwells in the body, is really there as a real person, only not yet consciously awakened.

Of course, I do not claim to establish fully the assumption that the earliest human embryo is indeed already a person, for to do this I would have to deal with all kinds of plausible arguments (like the argument from twinning) that fall outside the scope of this paper. I aim only at doing the negative work of clearing away one of the main obstacles that prevents people from acknowledging the human embryo as person. If we can defeat the Lockean reduction of person to consciousness, we open up for many people the possibility of a person who is already in our midst with a moral claim on us even though he or she is still awaiting the dawning of consciousness.

Sources of Personalist Thought

CHAPTER 7

Max Scheler on Personal Individuality

In his deep and significant study of the thought of Max Scheler (1874–1928), Hans Urs von Balthasar writes that "the realm of the personal was Scheler's innermost concern, more important to him than anything else, the sanctuary of his thought."[1] This is why Scheler again and again aligned himself with personalism in philosophy, as we can see from the introduction to his major work, *Formalism in Ethics:*

> The most essential and important proposition that my present investigations would ground and communicate as perfectly as possible is the proposition that the final meaning and value of the *whole* universe is ultimately to be measured exclusively against the pure being (and not the effectiveness) . . . the richest fullness and the most perfect development, and the purest beauty and inner harmony of *persons*, in whom at times all forces of the world concentrate themselves and soar upward.[2]

---

* This paper appeared originally under the title, "The Individuality of Human Persons: A Study in the Ethical Personalism of Max Scheler," in the *Review of Metaphysics* 52.1 (Sept. 1998), 21–50. It has been considerably revised in preparation for its publication in this volume.

1. Hans Urs von Balthasar, *Apokalypse der deutschen Seele*, vol. 3 (Salzburg: Anton Pustet Verlag, 1939), 152; the translation here and the translations in the subsequent citations from this work are my own. The study that von Balthasar gives here of Scheler (84–193) seems to be little known among students and critics of Scheler, even among those writing in German: and yet it is in my opinion the deepest critical study of Scheler that we possess. It is a particularly important study of Scheler's relation to Christianity.

2. Max Scheler, *Formalism in Ethics and Non-Formal Ethics of Values*, trans. by Manfred Frings and Roger Funk (Evanston: Northwestern University Press, 1973), xxiv. German: *Der Formalismus in der Ethik und die materiale Wertethik* (Bern: Francke Verlag, 1966), 16, which is vol. 2 of Scheler's *Gesammelte Werke*. I will cite this and other works of Scheler according to the English translation but will always give in parentheses the

We want to enter into the sanctuary of Scheler's thought by picking out a central theme of his personalism. He himself refers to it in the following:

> At no point does the ethical personalism to which our investigation has led us reveal its distinctiveness from other present ethical currents to a greater degree than in the position that it allocates to the becoming and being of the spiritual individuality of the person as the bearer of moral value.[3]

This is what we propose to examine here: Scheler's understanding of the radical individuality of persons, and in particular of the ethical significance of personal individuality.[4]

1. *The antagonists of Scheler*

We must first know against whom Scheler is turning in his discussions on personal individuality. I quote again von Balthasar:

> The basic situation of Scheler results very simply from the twofold negation in which he was involved: the "no" which he spoke to the declining *Lebensphilosophie* [of Bergson and Nietzsche], the insufficiency of which showed the urgent need to recognize a positive "spirit" that is independent from "life"; and the "no" which he spoke to the old idealism, which was still influential.[5]

It is precisely this latter adversary, German Idealism, that puts the individuality of the person in question. Scheler sees already in Kant's characterization of the person as *Vernunftperson* a depersonalizing *Logonomie*. He means that Kant and above all his followers tend to conceive of the *Vernunftperson* as something superindividual; when they relate the

---

corresponding pages in the German text as found in Scheler's *Gesammelte Werke*. One can see already in this citation that Scheler makes abundant use of italics. Unless otherwise indicated the reader should take the italics in the Scheler quotes as Scheler's own.

3. Ibid., 508 (499).

4. To give the reader a general orientation in the texts of Scheler let me indicate the ones that I have found to be the most revealing sources of his thought on personal individuality. In his *Formalism* ch. 6 A see section 1, "Person and Reason" and in ch. 6 B see section 2, "Person and Individual," and in ch. 6 B section 4 see the subsection also entitled "Person and Individual." In his *The Nature of Sympathy* (Hamden, CT: Archon Books, 1973) Part I see ch. 4, "Metaphysical Theories" and ch. 7, "The Interaction of the Sympathetic Functions," especially the last ten pages. See also his essay, "Ordo Amoris," in *Gesammelte Werke*, vol. 10, (Bonn: Verlag Herbert Grundmann, 1986) (all translations from this essay are my own).

5. von Balthasar, *op. cit.*, 85.

Vernunftperson to individual human persons they think of it as one and the same thing existing in all persons. Thus the individuality of human persons becomes a problem in just the way it is a problem for Averroes, whom Scheler repeatedly invokes as an intellectual antecedent of Kant and the German Idealists. As a result these thinkers are driven to offering purely extrinsic explanations of the principle of personal individuation; they say that individuality results from some relation to space and time, or they say that it results from a relation to a body or to the experiences of the person or to the sequence of the person's acts. In each case the principle of individuation remains extrinsic to the person. We shall see how Scheler argues for a radically intrinsic principle. Speaking of Fichte and Hegel, Scheler says that "the person becomes in the end an indifferent thoroughfare *(gleichgültige Durchgangsstelle)* for an impersonal rational activity."[6]

He even finds a similar dissolution of personal individuality in Schopenhauer; despite the fact that Reason gives way to Will in Schopenhauer, individuals are still sacrificed to a superindividual principle. According to Schopenhauer, it is fellow-feeling *(Mitgefühl)* which reveals the *unity of being* underlying the multiplicity of selves. It is this that destroys the illusion to which we are otherwise enslaved, whereby each of us considers himself as having an independent reality.[7] In other words, before experiencing fellow-feeling, I experience myself as different from you; in fellow-feeling I come to recognize that we are ultimately not two but one; the illusion of my (and your) personal individuality is unmasked.

We need not concern ourselves with the correctness of Scheler's interpretation of Kant and of German Idealism; his self-understanding of his polemical situation suffices for our task of understanding him.

We can identify another antagonist with whom Scheler is dealing in his teaching on the individuality of persons. Consider his sharp polemic against most theories of the equality of all human beings. He suspects that these theories rest on the assumption of a superindividual humanity which, once it has been individuated in an extrinsic way, becomes the individual human beings who are equal to each other; they are equal

---

6. Scheler, *Formalism*, 372–73 (372).
7. Max Scheler, *The Nature of Sympathy*, 51. German: *Wesen und Formen der Sympathie*, (61–62).

because of the "indwelling" in each of the same superindividual humanity. When he objects to theses asserting the equality of human beings, it is usually this underlying metaphysics that is the real target of his objection.

2. Personal individuality

We begin by dealing with a potential misunderstanding. Scheler does not posit the antithesis of "person" and "individual" that is found in many personalist authors, such as Maritain, Mounier, and (even if he is not usually reckoned to the personalists) Hans Urs von Balthasar. Maritain lets "individual" express the material, extensive aspect of man, with the result that "person" expresses the spiritual aspect of man.[8] Mounier lets "individual" express a meaning more distinctly moral, namely the grasping, acquisitive, self-assertive side of man, with the result that "person" expresses the generous, self-giving side of man.[9] Von Balthasar lets "individual" express man as an instance of human nature, with the result that "person" expresses man as incommunicable, unrepeatable.[10] But in each case "individual" forms some kind of antithesis to "person" and it expresses something lower in human beings, something in contrast to what is highest and best in them, which receives the designation "person." Now, as usual as this antithesis is among personalist authors, Scheler knows nothing of it: individuality for him is nothing but an aspect of personhood. When he entitles a section of his *Formalismus* "Person und Individuum," he means to suggest no least antithesis; on the contrary, "Individuum" expresses for him the very heart of "Person." It makes good sense from the point of view of Schelerian personalism to speak of "personal individuality," an expression entirely foreign to the authors just mentioned. It is his understanding of personal individuality that we mean to study in this paper.

If we let ourselves be sensitized to the many meanings of individuality by Jorge Gracia's important work on individuality,[11] we can discern in

---

8. Jacques Maritain, *The Person and the Common Good* (New York: Charles Scribner's Sons, 1947), ch. 3.

9. Emmanuel Mounier, *Personalism* (Notre Dame, IN: University of Notre Dame Press, 2001), 17–19.

10. Hans Urs von Balthasar, "On the Concept of Person," *Communio* 13 (Spring 1986), 18.

11. I refer above all to Jorge Gracia, *Individuality* (Albany: State University of New York Press, 1988), especially ch. 1.

Scheler on Personal Individuality 149

Scheler above all these two meanings. 1) Sometimes he refers to a certain antithesis to "general" or "universal," as when he protests against the dissolution of the person into some general *nomos;* in this case individuality is simply equivalent to concreteness (and comes very close to Gracia's "non-instantiability"). 2) In other places, he refers to a certain antithesis to "other" beings, as when he protests against the various pantheistic attempts to dissolve individual persons into God: in this case, individuality means standing in oneself in such a way that a being is set off against everything else (Gracia's "distinction").

Whereas Gracia thinks that only concreteness or non-instantiability is a true note of individuality, Scheler would also recognize distinction from other beings as a note of individuality; most emphatically he would recognize it as a note of personal individuals. These two notes of individuality, though not explicitly discriminated by Scheler, would represent for him two interrelated aspects of the *Urphänomen* of individuality.

And now to Scheler on the individuality proper to persons, which is the subject that above all concerns us here. He finds a particular strength of individuality in human persons, which he explains by saying that each person has an essence all his own, that is, an essence that could not possibly be repeated in a second person.[12] It is true that "human nature" is not restricted to one human being but is found in a certain sense in every human being, but this is in sharp contrast to the personal essence of a given person, which cannot be repeated again in any other person. Scheler deliberately breaks with the Greek idea that essence is always only something general or universal; more than once in his major ethical work, *Formalism in Ethics,* he says provocatively "essence has nothing to do with generality."[13] Scheler seems to mean that there is not only essence in the sense of a universal, and not only the universal essence concretized or instantiated in many individuals, but that there is also the radically individual essence, unutterable in general terms, where the talk of instantiating a universal essence has no meaning.[14] There is an essence in each person of which one cannot say that the person has it or shares in it, but

12. Scheler, *Formalism,* 489 (481).
13. Ibid.
14. Of course it has some meaning in light of the fact that each human person once did not exist, which implies that the concrete essence of any person "preceded" the coming into being of that person. One might therefore say that on coming into existence a person "instantiates" his or her concrete essence. But one should really not say "instanti-

of which one must say that the person *is* it. Of course, this is not said in the same sense in which God is said *to be* His essence; it is said only by way of affirming the unique unity formed by concrete essence and individual precisely in the case of persons. This is at least part of the reason why Scheler repeatedly emphasizes the *positivity* of personal individuality. He means that this individuality is not simply a "contraction" of something general or of something superindividual; it is based on a positive content that is unrepeatable in any other individual.[15]

It goes without saying that the individual personal essence, which for Scheler stands at the center of the individuality of a person, has nothing to do with logical constructions such as "the last soldier killed in the Civil War" or "the eldest son of Smith." In such cases, recently introduced into this discussion, we have indeed a kind of essence that can be instantiated by only one person, but it is not any special strength of individual being which explains the unique instantiability. In fact, we can find this one-time instantiability among non-personal beings whose individuality is as poor as could be, as for example in "the first copy of the *Times* printed today." The first copy is a mere instance of today's *Times*, and in fact just as much a mere instance as any other copy; it is fully replaceable by any other copy. The one-time instantiability of "the first copy" or of "the three hundred and twenty-third copy" seems to derive from an intention of the mind that picks out one thing; it does not seem to derive from any inherent strength of individual being. But with persons it is just this inherent strength of individual being that prevents multiple instantiations; indeed, so great is the individuality of persons that it is unutterable *(individuum*

---

ate" here, because an "instance" of a kind is always one of many possible instances, whereas a given person is the only possible one who can realize his or her concrete essence.

15. If one does not accept this view of essence, if one persists in thinking with the Greeks that essence can only mean universal, or the being that instantiates a universal, then one is driven to an existential account of personal individuality. See Richard Stith, "On Death and Dworkin: a Critique of His Theory of Inviolability," *Maryland Law Review* 56. 2 (1997), 289–383. He first focuses with great understanding on the mystery of personal individuality: "Even if God were to promise me that he would immediately substitute an identical person . . . for my wife if I would let him take her away, I would refuse. I do not want someone *like* her; I want *her*" (345; cf. 344). Then he says, "In searching for a way of thinking that can respect the individuality of people [persons], we are thus looking for a mode of thought that can take existence seriously" (346). In the previous pages he seems to think that a mode of thought relying on essence would in the end undermine personal individuality by justifying replacements of persons.

est ineffabile). That is, it cannot be translated into general terms; but general terms entirely suffice to give expression to the one-time instantiables, which are therefore entirely utterable.

Notice how the two aspects of individuality distinguished above flow together in Scheler's discussion of personal individuality. The unrepeatable essence of a person forms a contrast to every general or universal essence, as well as to every mere instantiation of a universal essence; and it also serves to distinguish one person from all other persons, none of whom can repeat or replace the first person.[16]

Scheler develops his account of personal individuality by saying that a human person is more or less individual according to the level of his being with which we are dealing.[17] Scheler sees the person as much less individual in certain social roles, as in being a mother, a German, a professor, or in holding some office, as in being a judge. After all, many different persons can play these social roles; everyone who does so shares in something general. Scheler distinguishes in every human being between what he calls "social person" and "intimate person," and he says that I can experience myself as intimate person only by prescinding from all such roles, which constitute the social person in me. Only in experiencing myself as intimate person do I experience deeply my personal individuality.[18] In this connection Scheler also mentions other generalities under which a human being can "fall." Thus in one place he speaks of our "common bondage to similar instincts, passions, and necessities of life."[19] These are for him so many "layers" surrounding the individual personal center; we have to go beyond these relatively general aspects of a human being in order to attain to the fully individual person.

16. In ch. 2 of *The Selfhood of the Human Person* (Washington, D.C.: The Catholic University of America Press, 1996), I defend an account of personal individuality that is very close to Scheler's. There is a terminological difference between Scheler and me: where he says "individuality" I say "incommunicability."

17. For all the different questions about individuality that Gracia recognizes and distinguishes, he does not take notice of the fundamental metaphysical question as to degrees, kinds, and perfections of individuality. One can pose this question with regard to the different kinds of individuality found in different beings, or with regard to the different levels of individuality found in one and the same being. It is above all this latter question that Scheler addresses in the following.

18. Ibid., 561 (548). Cf. Scheler, *Sympathy,* 121 (130): "Das heisst ein Mensch ist umso mehr Individuum, *je mehr er intime Person ist,* je mehr er zugleich schweigendes Erleben ist. . . ."

19. Scheler, *Sympathy,* 121 (129).

Scheler goes farther. He says that even the traits or qualities of a person, which are much closer to the person than the just-mentioned social roles, qualities such as intelligence or courage, still have something of this relative generality. This is why one cannot think of a person as being simply a composition of all of his qualities or properties; one would miss that which is most individual in the person. Thus Scheler says that

> the love which has moral value is not that which pays loving regard to a person for having such and such qualities, pursuing such and such activities, or for possessing talents, beauty, or virtue; it is that love which incorporates these qualities, activities and gifts into its object, because they belong to that *individual person*.[20]

The qualities appear in their full individuality only on the basis of being rooted in the person. We can say that it is this person that in a certain sense communicates full individuality to the qualities.[21]

Of course one can pick out such qualities and properties in a being as serving to mark it off against all other individuals (so that one formulates one of those one-time instantiables that we discussed above); but in this case the qualities and properties are only serving as *criteria for our knowledge* of individuality, that is, aids for our discernment of individuality; they are not that in which personal individuality consists. Gracia is perfectly right to distinguish between the question what individuality is and the question how we come to recognize it.[22]

Scheler distinguishes the different levels of individuality in human beings in such a way as to reverse a certain natural way of thinking about individuality. He traces this way of thinking back to "eighteenth century individualism," but it is by no means limited to a particular century.

According to this doctrine, men and their values are to be regarded all the *more* equal, the *more* their being approaches the *absolute* level of being (as "rational entity") and the *more* their values are compared to values of the *highest* ranks (salvation and spiritual values); and they and their values should ... appear all

---

20. Ibid., 166 (167).
21. Scheler finds that these different "levels" of individuality in man are reflected in our knowledge of man; as this knowledge "progresses from the associative level of the soul to the vital, and thence to the existence of the spiritual person, the impression of individual quality grows, increasing by leaps as each new level is reached, until full individuality is attained." Ibid., 123 (131).
22. Gracia, *op. cit.*, 16–21.

Scheler on Personal Individuality

the more *unequal*, the more their being approaches sensible states of the lived body and the more their values are compared to values of the *lowest* ranks. This connection between transcendental *universalism* and empirical aristocratism and individualism is the exact *opposite* of our opinion.[23]

Scheler's opinion is that we are much more different from each other as persons than we are say as bearers of a racial identity or as having a gender or as having certain bodily traits; our individuality is much more pronounced at the level of personhood than at the level of race or gender. Thus he makes his own "the notion of a spiritual individual *qua* spiritual and the notion that the *individualization* of being and value increases with the purity of spirituality."[24] Notice that Scheler is here taking individuality as difference from other beings; the stronger individuality goes with greater difference from other beings, and the weaker individuality goes with less difference.

We proceed now to consider a further claim that Scheler makes about levels of individuality in human beings. Central to his philosophical anthropology is a sharp contrast between "life" and "spirit," or in other words between the vital center and the personal center in each human being. He conceived the vital center as occupying a middle position between purely bodily life and properly personal life.[25] He drew the contrast between vital and personal so sharply because he was struggling to overcome all forms of *Lebensphilosophie* and all traces of vitalism in philosophy. Now for Scheler the real "seat" of individuality in a human being—individuality is taken throughout this discussion in the sense of difference from other beings—is the personal level and not the vital level of the human being.

When we live out of our personal center, we never lose ourselves in the beings with which we have to do; we remain intact as persons, standing in ourselves in relation to all other beings. Thus in the properly personal act of *Mitgefühl* (sympathy) I enter into another without losing myself in the other, or identifying myself with the other, or the other with myself; I and the other remain irreducibly two persons throughout the most heart-

---

23. Scheler, *Formalism*, 510 (501).
24. Ibid.
25. On Scheler's teaching concerning these three centers in each human being see the able study of John White, "Scheler's Tripartite Anthropology," *Proceedings of the American Catholic Philosophical Association* 75 (2001), 255–66.

felt act of sympathizing with the other. Sympathy does not imply my being identical with the other, as Schopenhauer thought, but rather just the opposite, it implies the irreducible two-ness of myself and the other. The same holds for love; it too is a properly personal act and so there can be no question of any amalgamation of two persons loving each other. Their irreducibility to each other, their inalienable two-ness is presupposed and in fact powerfully lived from within in all authentic love.

But I can also live out of the vital center in myself, as for instance when I experience a certain oneness with my people at the outbreak of war. Here I lose myself in my people, according to Scheler, feeling myself to be as it were of one piece with my people; I do not stand over and against them but am submerged in them. I feel small as being only a drop in a vast collective ocean, but also large and powerful as being a part of this vast collectivity. Here my individuality is weakened, for the boundary between myself and the others is effaced (Scheler speaks of my *Einsfühlung* with them), and not just in my self-experience but in very reality, that is, as a vital being I really can get absorbed in my national collectivity and my individuality really can be to some extent effaced. In sympathizing with another, by contrast, this boundary is presupposed and experienced and reinforced, and this is because of the distinctly personal character of sympathy.[26]

It will be noticed that individuality has a somewhat different sense here than it had above in connection with the unique personal essence of each person. Here individuality does not belong to the order of essence as it did there; it belongs more to the order of real existence and causality. What abolishes the essential individuality is to be just like some other who can replace me; what abolishes the existential individuality is to be really absorbed into some other. In this latter sense of individuality it is clear that for Scheler we human beings have a relatively weak individuality insofar as we live out of our vital center and that we have a much stronger individuality insofar as we live and act as persons.

---

26. Scheler thinks that the preeminent example of living out of one's vital level is the sexual union of man and woman lovingly performed. In the text I give a different example of vital existence, for Scheler seems to me to fail to do justice to the personal dimension of sexual union, giving a onesidedly vitalistic account of it and so exaggerating the tendency of man and woman to lose themselves in each other in their sexual union.

3. The principle of personal individuation

Gracia distinguishes this question of what individuality is from other fundamental questions about individuality. For the purpose of understanding Scheler we pick out from among these other questions the question about the principle of individuation. What the individuality of a being is, has to be distinguished from the question as to the principle or source of the being's individuality. In answer to the first question Gracia says that the individuality of a being consists in the "non-instantiability" of the being; in answer to the second, he says that it is existence that is the principle of any individual's individuality. The different answers reflect different questions. Gracia is surely right that philosophers discussing individuality have commonly conflated these two questions. Now some of Scheler's richest insights into personal individuality are expressed in terms of the principle of personal individuation, even if he does not distinguish the two issues as sharply as Gracia does.

Scheler rejects all extrinsic principles of personal individuation. He usually considers three such principles: the body of a person, the spatio-temporal position of a person, and the history of the experiences of a person. He says that the individuality of a person is established "prior" to these three aspects of a person.[27] It is established in and through the unique personal essence of each human person. "The spiritual substances inherent in persons or their acts are thus the *only* substances having a truly individual essence, and whose existence as separate entities follows directly from their intrinsically individual character."[28] This is what Scheler means in calling persons, and only persons, "absolute individuals."[29] If the whole essence of a given person could be repeated in another person, then it could hardly serve as a principle of individuation for the first person; it is because the first person, as we saw, has in his essence something incommunicably, unrepeatably his own that his essence constitutes him as *this individual*.

Scheler is not just rejecting extrinsic accounts of personal individua-

---

27. Scheler, *Sympathy*, 65 (76).

28. Ibid., 123 (131). It comes as a surprise—a pleasant surprise for me—to find Scheler using the category of substance in explaining personal individuality; in *Formalism* and elsewhere he sharply criticizes all attempts to think of persons in terms of substance.

29. Ibid., 65 (76).

tion in favor of an intrinsic one. He is also rejecting a metaphysical hypothesis that commonly goes with the extrinsic theories. He is rejecting absolutely and uncompromisingly the idea that the point of departure for an individual human person is some *Allgeist*, some superindividual personal spirit, which gets contracted to individual human persons by means of one or other of the extrinsic principles of individuation. The radical and intrinsic individuality that each human person has as a result of his or her unique personal essence excludes any such (often pantheistically understood) *Allgeist* as well as any of the extrinsic individuating principles that go with it. In opposing this metaphysics of individuation Scheler is opposing what he takes to be one of "the gravest of metaphysical errors."[30]

There is something else that Scheler teaches about the principle of personal individuation. The unique personal essence of each person not only serves to individualize the whole human being, marking it off against other human beings; it also serves to individualize those levels in a human being that are in a sense common to other human beings. Thus the body, the voice, the hands, the handwriting of a person are imbued with the mystery of the person's individuality and so are lifted beyond the limited individuality that they have when considered in themselves.

It is very interesting to set Scheler's thought on personal individuation in relation to Jorge Gracia's account of the *principium individuationis* (which is meant by Gracia as a general account for all individuals and not just for persons).[31] For Gracia a being is individual only through its existence. Scheler would remark that this existential theory of individuation is in any case no extrinsic theory, since the existence of a being is entirely intrinsic to it; but he would have a reservation about it, at least if it were meant as an exhaustive account of the source of personal individuality. He would say that with persons it does not suffice to invoke only existence; essence, too, is a *principium individuationis*. For there is an essential core in each person that establishes nothing at all in common with other beings; it establishes only the incommunicable person. This essential core of the person is so radically individual that it can no longer be thought of as the instantiation of some universal form, as we saw. I would think that Scheler is quite right to recognize not only an existential prin-

---

30. Scheler, *Sympathy*, 75 (86).
31. Gracia, *op. cit.*, 170–78.

Scheler on Personal Individuality

ciple of individuation, but also, at least in the case of persons, this essential principle of individuation.[32]

It is also interesting to set Scheler's account of personal individuation in relation to the Aristotelian theory of matter as the principle of individuation. It is clear that he does not hold this theory and in one place he contradicts it, saying: "the ultimate and authentic *principium individuationis* in man (and not in angels only, as St. Thomas supposed), lies in his spiritual soul (that is, the real substratum of his personal center). . . ."[33] Thus for Scheler we do not need one theory of individuation for human beings and an entirely different one for angels; all persons, whether human or angelic, are individual through their unique personal essence, which is always a spiritual and never, not even with human beings, a material principle of individuation. Needless to say, if the Aristotelian position on individuation gets elaborated in an Averroistic vein so that identically the same intellectual soul is assumed to exist in all human beings, Scheler will have much more to say by way of fundamental objection.

Now this account of personal individuation is strictly limited to the personal in man; it is not meant to apply to the vital part of the soul. Given the way Scheler contrasts the vital and the personal in human beings, it is not so surprising that he gives a completely different account of the individuation of our vital being. Though he will have nothing to do with the hypothesis of an *Allgeist*, he himself introduces the hypothesis of an *Alleben*, which he defines as "a collective, *unitary* and universal life-force, embracing all kinds and conditions of terrestrial life, and purposefully guiding and governing the empirical development of one species from another."[34] It is a superindividual life-force that transcends all living beings even while it inhabits and informs them, being the source of their life. Beings with vital life grow out of the *Alleben*, they exist as individua-

---

32. Gracia would be quick to point out, and would be right in pointing out, that this divergence of Scheler from his position rests on the underlying divergence of Scheler from him concerning what individuality is at all. As we saw, Scheler includes in his understanding of individuality that in virtue of which a being is itself and no other; Gracia excludes all such "distinction from others" in his determination of the intension of individuality. Thus Scheler is working with a somewhat different *explanandum* when he takes up the question of the principle of personal individuation.

33. Scheler, *Sympathy*, 123 (131). I have amended the English translation in a few places to bring it closer to the German.

34. Ibid., 74 (85).

tions of it; they may well have extrinsic principles of individuation. Thus the very scheme of individuation that Scheler combats so vigorously with respect to personal being and personal life, this scheme he himself introduces and develops with respect to vital being and vital life in human beings. Here we have the explanation for something observed above; on the level of vital experiencing, persons can dissolve one into the other. This is because as vital beings they are in some sense already one, being just differentiations of the same *Alleben*; in *Einsfühlung* they come to experience the oneness with others that comes from their common "descent" from the *Alleben*. Thus the positivity of personal individuality gives way to a certain negativity of vital individuality, which really does arise from a certain "contracting" of the *Alleben*.

We are now in a position to understand why Scheler declared himself in favor of the "profoundly true idea of creationism,"[35] that is, of the thesis that God creates each person immediately, or more exactly, creates immediately the personal center of each human being. In order to understand Scheler we have only to put ourselves into the above-mentioned position of those who conceive of individual persons as differentiations of an already-existing *Allgeist*. From this point of view one could ascribe the emergence of individual persons to the secondary causes governing the process of differentiation, and one would not need to assume any immediate intervention of God. This is why Scheler, when he speaks of the emergence of living beings out of the *Alleben*, does not dream of assuming any such divine intervention for each living being. But since the personal center has an individuality which immeasurably surpasses that of a living being and which is entirely immanent in the person, Scheler can only reject any emergence that is supposed to occur by means of contracting something that is already given; only an emergence from nothing, and with this a direct dependency on a creator-God, seems to remain.

In his study of Scheler, von Balthasar objects to something in Scheler that has emerged in our last few pages, namely to his "distributing the individuation problem over two spheres, so that individuation in the sphere of the spirit is purely positive, but in the vital sphere purely negative (because here it is only the *Alleben* which is the ultimate subject)." Then he goes on:

35. Ibid., 127 (135).

The purely positive individuation of the person raises him [man], in the end, beyond creaturely potentiality and passivity and lifts him in a Promethean way into the realm of the very ideas of God himself. The purely negative individuation, however, gives as an ideal only an *Einsfühlung* with the anonymous instinctual life of the *Weltgrund* in which the individual arises like a wave which loses itself in the sea.

The true concept of individuation, which Scheler sought but never found, lies in a certain middle position. Man is neither pure spirit nor pure nature; his individuality is indissolubly positive and negative, actual and potential.[36]

It exceeds the scope of this paper to test this challenging criticism of von Balthasar. He raises here a serious question about Scheler's anthropology, namely about the unity of man according to Scheler. We will, however, stay focused on specifically personal individuality.

4. Individual persons and community

One could at this point ask whether Scheler with his teaching on the radical individuality of each person is perhaps enclosing himself in a negative individualism. Strange as it would be if a thinker so well known for his penetrating critique of bourgeois individualism were to share in this individualism, one may still wonder, coming fresh from the ideas of his that we have just presented, whether he can still do justice to I and Thou and to the different forms of community.

Let us return to the two aspects of individuality that we distinguished at the beginning of this study. Insofar as "individual" expresses simply the antithesis to "general" or "universal," it need involve no least opposition to community. We have to recall that for Scheler the individual person *(Individualperson)* is not identical with the single person *(Einzelperson)*. For him individual person comprises both single person and collective person *(Gesamtperson)*. By collective persons he means the person-like unities formed by certain communities, such as the French nation or the Catholic Church. You and I, by contrast, are single persons. Now Scheler wants to say of collective persons too that they are radically individual; they are not just extrinsically individuated, nor do they first of all exist as something general. The concrete essence of the French nation can just as

---

36. Von Balthasar, *op. cit.*, 191–92. He thinks that Scheler glimpses for a moment the unity of the vital and the personal in man in the course of discussing the spiritual achievement of St. Francis of Assisi (*Sympathy*, Part I, ch. 5).

little be common to several nations as the concrete essence of an individual person can be common to several single persons. The individuality affirmed by Scheler, then, extends to community and therefore cannot stand in opposition to community.

But what about personal individuality in the sense of standing in oneself and being marked off against all other persons? Here, one may want to object, individuality is unavoidably affirmed at the expense of interpersonal communion. And yet here too Scheler will say that community can encompass individuality rather than be excluded by it, for he will say that each nation is itself and no other. It is not just single persons who are themselves and no other.

But one will want to respond that it is also single persons who are themselves and no other, and that their individuality cannot fail to play into the hands of that individualism that undermines community. Out of the writings of Scheler we could get various responses, including this one: the highest forms of interpersonal communion, such as sympathizing with another, or loving another, presuppose the person as individual, as we saw, and are undermined precisely as communion if persons become obscured in their irreducible individuality. How should we otherwise explain certain obvious disorders of interpersonal life, such as the thing that Scheler calls heteropathic identification with another, whereby one person is completely taken over by another, as in hypnosis as well as in certain hypnotic dependencies of one person on another?[37] How explain this obvious disorder except in terms of an irreducible individuality that persons should maintain even in the closest forms of interpersonal life?

From the heteropathic identification of oneself with another Scheler distinguishes the idiopathic identification of another with oneself. This is the opposite pathology: remaining so fortified in oneself and one's own experiencing that one never really attains to the other as other. Scheler argues that such an existential solipsism is a fundamentally disordered way of living one's personal individuality, which can never be really lived in this isolation from others. One can even find in Scheler elements of Buber's idea that the isolated I of the I-It relation is much poorer than the participating I of the I-Thou relation. In a separate study of Scheler's great work on sympathy one could discuss these and other ways of devel-

---

37. Scheler, *Sympathy*, 18–23 (29–33), 42–45 (53–56).

oping an adequate philosophy of the interpersonal precisely on the basis of Scheler's insights into personal individuality.

Let me also just mention here his so significant "principle of solidarity." "Every false so-called individualism, with its erroneous and pernicious consequences, is excluded in my ethics by the theory of the original *coresponsibility* of every person for the moral salvation of the *whole of all realms of persons*...."[38] Scheler explains being "originally coresponsible" by saying that each person is just as coresponsible for others as he is directly responsible for himself. Furthermore, we stand in such a solidarity one with another that we always have some share in the guilt of others. I discuss this theme in Scheler in the next paper in this collection. It suffices here to stress that for Scheler human beings are responsible one for another not insofar as they are parts of some whole *but insofar as they are individual persons*.

5. The knowledge we have of individual persons

Scheler has not only studied personal individuality, but also the knowledge we have of it. Here too he breaks with a certain Greek idea, namely, the restriction of knowledge to that which is universal. According to Scheler persons can be known in all their individuality. How is this possible?

It is possible through love for a person. Scheler says:

Indeed, the essence of another's individuality, which cannot be described or expressed in conceptual terms *(individuum ineffabile)*, is *only* revealed in its full purity by love or by virtue of the insight it provides. When love is absent the "individual" is immediately replaced by the "social personality," the mere focus of a set of relationships (being an aunt or an uncle, for instance), or the exponent of a particular social function (profession), etc.[39]

In other words, without love we can attain only to those aspects of a human being which are common to the human being and to others; only through love can we attain to the mystery of individuality in a person, that is, get a glimpse of the unrepeatable personal essence of a person.

There is a well-known paradox of love and knowledge that makes itself felt here. It would seem that the personal love of which Scheler speaks

---

38. Scheler, *Formalism*, xxiv (15).
39. Scheler, *Sympathy*, 160 (163).

presupposes some *prior* apprehension of the personal individuality of the one who is loved; it would seem that such love is engendered by the sight of the other as unrepeatable person. While Scheler quite acknowledges this more obvious relation of love and knowledge, he is here affirming that love for another also grounds our knowledge of the other as person, empowering us to see beyond all that the person shares with others, so that we attain to what the person is in his or her own incommunicable right.[40] The dialectical difficulty which goes with letting love precede and ground knowledge would perhaps be mitigated if this preceding love were that *Menschenliebe,* or love of humanity, of which he says in another place that it "merely regards individuals as lovable qua 'specimens' of the human race."[41] For then the preceding love would be different in kind from the properly personal love, which regards individuals as individuals, and we would be at liberty to interpret this personal love as grounded in a prior experience of the beloved person as human being. But Scheler does not let us simplify things in this way; while he recognizes that the *Menschenliebe* can stand in the service of properly personal love,[42] he still teaches, at least as I understand him, that the love which opens our eyes to the other as unrepeatable individual is not the *Menschenliebe* but a different and more properly personal love. I do not see that he attempts to resolve the dialectical difficulty of this position.

By the way, it accords entirely with the central place of the heart and the affections in Scheler's anthropology, and with Scheler's attempt to rehabilitate these, to say that the heart has a place even in the knowing operations performed by persons, even to the point of making some of them possible at all.

40. Cf. the kindred teaching of Scheler's essay, "The Nature of Philosophy and the Moral Preconditions of Philosophical Knowledge," in his *On the Eternal in Man,* trans. by Bernard Noble (Hamden, CT: Archon Books, 1972). German: *Vom Ewigen im Menschen* (Bern: Francke Verlag, 1968). In this essay Scheler argues that philosophical knowledge is grounded in a certain love of absolute value and being.

41. Scheler, *Sympathy,* 101 (109).

42. Ibid. Scheler is here trying to establish the principle, "love of humanity [*Menschenliebe*] underlies a cosmic personal love and the love of God." He explains himself by saying that I lose the chance of recognizing certain persons in all their uniqueness when I erroneously think that they are not even human beings. When, for instance, Aristotle divides human beings into free men and slaves, so that only the free men are really human beings, I can no longer encounter the slaves as persons. But as I say, this love only disposes me favorably towards personal love for others, it is not that love whereby I apprehend them in all their personal individuality.

Scheler on Personal Individuality

He grasps still more deeply this epistemic power of love by distinguishing the knowing of a concrete person from a merely empirical observation of the person:

> What mediates the intuition of the person's ideal and *individual value-essence* is, first of all, the *understanding* of his most central source, which is itself mediated through *love* for the person. This understanding love is the great master workman and ... the great *sculptor* who, working from the masses of empirical particulars, can intuitively seize, sometimes from only *one* action or only *one* expressive gesture, the lines of the person's *value-essence*.[43]

He goes on to say that even the most complete empirical observation of a person can never yield the value-essence *(Wertwesen)* of that person. Indeed, he thinks that it is rather the case that such observation commonly grasps things in a person that only obscure his value-essence. The understanding of the value-essence is so far removed from empirical observation that it in fact precedes and gives direction to all such observation; it is this understanding that lets us distinguish between valid and invalid, expressive and non-expressive, empirical facts about the person.

6. Personal individuality as a moral task

The reason that empirical observation gives us so little is that the individual value-essence of a person is usually far from being fully realized. Each person stands before the task of becoming himself, of realizing his individual value-essence. Scheler is presupposing this when he speaks of the power of love to effect a certain "emergence [*zum Auftauchen zu bringen*]"[44] of the value-essence of the beloved person. Insofar as a person is in any way unfaithful to his value-essence, the empirical observation we make of that person must clearly lag far behind a deeper understanding of his value-essence, which remains intact in spite of this unfaithfulness to it. Love calls the person back to his value-essence, but without any of that pedagogical intention by which one deliberately tries to improve the beloved person, as Scheler shows in keen and subtle analyses.[45] Thus the individual value-essence has something ideal about it, although nothing ideal in the sense of general, for it is the essence only of this unrepeatable person.

43. Scheler, *Formalism*, 488 (480).
44. Scheler, *Sympathy*, 157 (160).
45. See especially ibid., 156–59 (159–62).

Talking like this about the possible divergence of the ideal value-essence of a person from his factual condition, we arrive at the ethical significance of personal individuality. Here I see particularly original contributions of Scheler to a personalist philosophy, contributions which Scheler himself thought were central to his ethical personalism.[46]

Personal individuality is permeated by value. This is why it can only be grasped by one who loves the individual person. Scheler expresses this value dimension of it by using the expression, "individual value-essence." Thus there is for Scheler a personal value that grows out of personal individuality. Now since it is a fundamental principle of his ethics that value grounds the ought and not vice versa, it is only natural for him to say that in the moral life there are radically individual moral requirements, that is, requirements grounded in the individual value-essence of a person and valid only for that person. There are, in fact, for Scheler moral requirements which are just as little concretizations of a general norm as the personal essence is a mere concretization of a general essence. With this Scheler in no way holds the position of situation ethics, because he does not think that the moral life consists exclusively in such highly personal tasks and requirements. It goes without saying that he recognizes universally valid norms—how could he not, he who is constantly speaking of "the material *a priori*" in ethics, that is, of the essential necessity and essential impossibility proper to ethics? In no place does he say that the individual requirements can contradict the general ones. But he is of the opinion that the general norms represent a certain indispensable moral minimum, so that the fullness of moral existence is impossible without attending to the personal requirements. So we find no situation ethics in Scheler, and yet, as one sees, he is able to salvage a core of truth in what has come to be called situation ethics and to place it in a non-situationist frame of reference. Here is the central point: for Scheler there are individual tasks and requirements corresponding to the individual essence of each person.[47]

46. Cf. Scheler, *Formalism*, xxiii–xxiv (15). For a helpful discussion of this theme in Scheler see Peter Spader, *Scheler's Ethical Personalism* (New York: Fordham University Press, 2002), 136–38.

47. It would be interesting to consider how Scheler's thought on personal individuality is limited and qualified by his thought on the important place of exemplary moral persons *(Vorbilder)* in the moral life (see Scheler, ibid., 572–95 [558–80]). If his affirmation of personal individuality were simply unqualified, then persons would be too different from one another for any one of them to be exemplary for the others.

Scheler on Personal Individuality 165

He also develops the idea that the individual tasks are given at very definite times, not just at any time.

Every moment of life in the development of an individual represents at the same time a possibility for the individual to know *unique* values and their interconnections, and, in accordance with these, the necessitation of moral tasks and actions that can never be repeated; such tasks and actions are predetermined, as it were, in the objective nexus of the factual-moral value-order for this moment (and for this individual, for example) and, if not utilized, are lost forever.[48]

One understands why Scheler says that Goethe's *Forderung der Stunde* (call of the moment) represents a fundamental category of any personalist ethics.

Let me offer here a concrete example. When we read in the newly-published memoirs of Dietrich von Hildebrand concerning his life in the twenties and thirties, we see clearly that he felt a personal call to carry on his struggle against National Socialism in Austria between 1933 and 1938.[49] After he had lost everything in Germany in 1933, he could have saved his life by taking refuge in the United States, where in fact some years later he came as a refugee. But we cannot derive from any general norms, valid for all people, that obligation that von Hildebrand felt in conscience to carry on in Vienna his struggle against Hitler, living in constant danger of assassination. He felt himself personally called to make this commitment. It was not the case that he gladly went beyond the call of duty, generously ready to do something that was not strictly required of him. That interpretation does not do justice to the urgency of the call that he felt in conscience. This call went in the direction of a moral necessity—but only for him. Von Hildebrand could not have blamed a similarly-situated colleague who would have right away taken refuge in the United States. One should also not misunderstand the peculiarity of this moral call by offering a premature religious interpretation of it; one should not be too quick to say that von Hildebrand felt, as once Abraham did, directly commanded by God. No, the moral requirement that he responded to cannot be interpreted as a positive command of God. That would miss the decisive point, namely that this call was mediated through the personal individu-

---

48. Ibid., 493 (485).
49. *Dietrich von Hildebrand: Memoiren und Aufsätze gegen den Nationalsozialismus, 1933–1938*, Ernst Wenisch (ed.) (Mainz: Matthias Grünewald Verlag, 1994).

ality of the one who was called. Naturally von Hildebrand said that God was calling him, but not on the basis of a private revelation, rather on the basis of a personal encounter with God in conscience, where his consciousness of his own unique value-essence must have flowed into his deliberations about his opportunities for offering resistance to Hitler.

With this example in mind let us read what Scheler says about the moral evaluation of a person.

> If we try to assess fully and to take the measure of a person in a moral respect, we have to have before our minds not only the universally valid norms but also the idea of the individual calling that is proper to *him* and not to ourselves or to someone else.[50]

To take the moral measure of someone like von Hildebrand, to praise or blame his actions justly, one would have to know not only whether he fulfilled those universal norms binding on all moral beings but also whether he fulfilled the personal moral calling that he discerned in his conscience.

The polemical edge of Scheler's teaching about these highly personal tasks is turned above all against Kant, who cannot fail to be a main adversary of Scheler, seeing as he taught that we act morally only on the basis of a certain universalizability of the maxim of our action. We must always act so that the maxim of our action can be willed as a general law for all men, indeed we should so act that it is not so much the content as the universal validity of the maxim which is willed; Kant says that it is only this kind of willing that lets us become morally good. Scheler by contrast speaks of actions whose maxims can only be willed by one person, actions in which the person acts in the consciousness of precisely not positing a universal law for all others. Scheler is also aware that this is not just a problem of Kant's. We all inherit a certain tendency to identify the objective with the universally valid and to suspect that there must be something accidental, something capricious in that which is unique and happens only once. Scheler is surely right to hold that the personally unique, valid only for me, can be just as real and valid as the universal that repeats itself in many individuals. "... let a sharp distinction be made between the 'universally' and the 'objectively' valid, as well as between the 'personal' and the 'subjective.'"[51]

It is not only in his ethics that Scheler develops this personalist idea of

50. Scheler, "Ordo Amoris," 351.
51. Scheler, *Eternal*, 25 (19).

Scheler on Personal Individuality

something valid only for me; it is also found, surprisingly enough, in his epistemology.

Just as there is a good which is *intrinsically* of . . . objective universal validity, as well as a good intrinsically of . . . objective *individual* validity, so there can certainly be also an "intrinsically universally valid truth" *and* an "intrinsically individually valid truth."[52]

In order to clarify what he means by an "individually valid truth" he proceeds to ask rhetorically:

For what reason is there to rule out the possibility that certain objective entities or values are cognitively accessible only to *one* particular individual person, or to *one* particular *individual civilization or culture* or to *one* particular phase of historical development?[53]

One is perhaps at first inclined to object to Scheler that the two cases (of an individually valid good and an individually valid truth) are not as parallel as he thinks, for the subject matter which is at first knowable only to one person must in principle ultimately be knowable to others, and in the end to all others, even if through the mediation of that person. In this case the restriction to one person seems to be relatively accidental and to form a contrast with the essential restriction of a moral task to the person who has it.[54] But if we consider the vision I have of a person whom I love, then it seems after all quite right to say with Scheler that I may understand the loveableness of that person more fully than anyone else will ever understand it. In this case the parallel between a knowledge that only I have and a moral call that only I have is quite striking.

As for the way in which I come to know my personal moral calls, Scheler says, as we would expect, that this is a knowledge based on love. If it takes love to see the value-essence of a person, then it will take love to find the individual moral call growing out of the value-essence. Scheler distinguishes between *Eigenliebe* (a selfish self-love) and *Selbstliebe* (a

---

52. Ibid., 23 (18).
53. Ibid.
54. The difficulties that we feel even with a suitably qualified concept of "individually valid truth" are placed in historical context by von Balthasar when he writes: "Still at work [today] in the background is the mathematical and natural science ideal of a truth whose criterion is general availability and obviousness. The positive value, indeed the very possibility of something that exists in itself also existing as such for me, seems to be a hidden contradiction. . . . The philosophy of personality that draws its ideal of objectivity from Greek thought is here at the end of its resources" (von Balthasar, *op. cit.*, 153).

noble self-love) and sees in the latter love that which gives me eyes and ears for my personal moral tasks. But more significant is what Scheler says about the indispensable role of other persons who enable me to discern my personal calls. He brings his principle of moral and religious solidarity into his account of this discernment:

> ... another can understand my individual calling better than I can ... another can do much to help me achieve it. To be there for each other in the form of living, acting, believing, hoping *one with another,* belongs to the general calling of every finite spirit. It thus belongs to the essential nature of one's individual calling that one is *co-responsible* for everyone coming to understand and to realize his or her own individual calling. The idea of the individual calling, therefore, far from excluding the mutual *solidarity of responsibility* in both guilt and merit on the part of moral beings, includes this solidarity.[55]

This important passage should also be used in dispelling the suspicion, addressed above, that Scheler's teaching on personal individuality undermines important truths about the interpersonal and communitarian nature of human persons.[56]

Let us mention just one other thought of Scheler's about this moral self-knowledge: we commonly gain it through a certain *via negativa.*

Only by feeling again and again when and where we *deviate* from it [our personal moral vocation], when and where we yield to what Goethe called "false tendencies" . . . does the image of our vocation emerge.[57]

Before concluding our discussion of the unique moral tasks that a person has as a result of his or her value-essence, it is worth noticing how this issue turns up in Charles Taylor's recent study, *The Ethics of Authenticity.* Taylor wants to find certain noble moral aspirations at work in the culture of authenticity despite all the subjectivism, relativism, and narcissism that disfigure it. He thinks that such often-criticized aspects of this

---

55. Max Scheler, "Ordo Amoris," 352.
56. For a thinker deeply akin to Scheler on the personal calls see Mounier, *op. cit.,* 41–42. Mounier makes here the keen observation that these calls are neither simply given to me, like a temperamental disposition, nor are they simply devised by me.
57. Scheler, "Ordo Amoris," 354. The first section of this essay, entitled "*Umwelt, Schicksal, 'individuelle Bestimmung' und der Ordo Amoris,*" is one of the main texts in Scheler on the individual vocation of each person. Among other things Scheler makes an important distinction between the *Schicksal* and the *Bestimmung* of each person, arguing that it is really only the latter that fully expresses the person as person.

Scheler on Personal Individuality

culture are not the whole story and that in the midst of them important moral insights are struggling to be born. Taylor would clearly reckon to these insights what we have been studying in Scheler, the unrepeatability of each person both in his value-essence and in his moral vocation. At the same time Taylor provides helpful historical context for understanding Scheler's insights into personal individuality.

Herder put forward the idea that each of us has an original way of being human. Each person has his or her own "measure" is his way of putting it. This idea has entered very deep into modern consciousness. It is also new. Before the late eighteenth century no one thought that the differences between human beings had this kind of moral significance. There is a certain way of being that is *my* way. I am called upon to live my life in this way, and not in imitation of anyone else's. But this gives a new importance to being true to myself. If I am not, I miss the point of my life, I miss what being human is for *me*.

This is the powerful moral ideal that has come down to us. It accords crucial moral importance to a kind of contact with myself, with my own inner nature, which it sees as in danger of being lost, partly through the pressures towards outward conformity. . . . And then it greatly increases the importance of this self-contact by introducing the principle of originality: each of our voices has something of its own to say.[58]

We agree with Taylor that this powerful moral ideal is susceptible of all kinds of subjectivistic and self-centered corruption—we also agree that it is not itself a corruption but precisely a powerful moral ideal, an important new moral acquisition. How is it to be protected from degenerating into narcissism and individualism? If we were to answer on the basis of Scheler then we would say: it can be protected by Scheler's teaching on sympathy, love, and above all by his great principle of moral and religious solidarity. But as we remarked already, it would take a separate study to do justice to the rich communitarian side of Scheler's mind.[59]

---

58. Charles Taylor, *The Ethics of Authenticity* (Cambridge, MA: Harvard University Press, 1991), 28–29.

59. It would be interesting to inquire whether Scheler, with his teaching about the individual value-essence and the individual vocation of each person, does not look towards post-modernist ideas about the "face" of the "other" (Levinas). Certainly the other would be weaker in his otherness if he just instantiated kinds and types, and is that much stronger in his otherness as a result of having something unrepeatably his or her own.

7. Convergences with Maritain and above all Rahner

It is extremely interesting to notice that Jacques Maritain is in full agreement with Scheler here, though without in any way being influenced by Scheler. After he has listed several examples taken from the lives of the saints of extraordinary actions, he goes on:

> We utter something deeper than we realize when we say of such acts that they are admirable, but not imitable. They are not generalizable, universalizable. They are good; indeed, they are the best of all moral acts. But they are good only for him who does them. We are here very far from the Kantian universal with its morality defined as the possibility of making the maxim of an act into a law for all men.[60]

It is quite according to the mind of Scheler when Maritain distances himself here from Kant, making room within ethics for the strictly personal moral tasks.

The agreement of Karl Rahner with Scheler goes even further. In his significant and influential study, "On the Question of a Formal Existential Ethics," Rahner deals not with Kant but rather with a teaching that used to be found among many Catholic moral theologians; and yet Rahner is concerned with the same problem as Scheler. The teaching in question says: "Whoever knows the universal laws exactly and comprehends the given situation down to its last detail, knows also clearly what he must or may do here."[61] In other words, concrete moral tasks always result unambiguously from the application of general moral norms to the concrete situation in which I have to act. Rahner responds that while this is often the case, it is by no means always the case. He is not thinking of a contradiction of the general norms, but of moral tasks that are found within that which is allowed on the basis of those norms.[62] That is, when in my

---

60. Jacques Maritain, *Existence and the Existent*, trans. by Lewis Galantiere and Gerald Phelan (New York: Doubleday and Co., 1956), 64.

61. Karl Rahner, "On the Question of a Formal Existential Ethics," in *Theological Investigations* vol. 2, trans. by Karl Kruger (Baltimore: Helicon, 1963), 222. German: "Über die Frage einer formalen Existentialethik," in *Schriften zur Theologie* II (Einsiedeln: Benzinger Verlag, 1955), 232.

62. While at the beginning of his essay Rahner rejects situation ethics, he is at pains to preserve its core of truth in his existential ethics. Rahner rejects, just like Scheler does, the nominalism of situation ethics.

moral deliberations I see that there are several ways of acting that do not contradict any general norms and are therefore allowed, I am by no means at the end of my deliberations. It may still be the case that one of these ways of acting is personally required of me and that, therefore, the other ways of acting are not allowable—not for me. Such a judgment of conscience[63] cannot be derived from general norms. "The concrete moral act is more than just the realization of a universal idea happening here and now in the form of a case. The act is a reality that has a positive and substantial property which is basically and absolutely unique."[64]

What is the source of this uniqueness that belongs to certain moral acts? Rahner answers entirely in the spirit of Scheler's personalism, though without explicitly speaking of person: it is grounded in the uniqueness of the one who performs the act.

In him, the individual, there must rather be a positive reality; expressed differently: his spiritual individuality cannot be (at least not in his acts) merely the circumscription of an in itself universal nature through the negativity of the *materia prima*, understood as the mere repetition of the same thing at different points in space-time.

. . . anyone who cannot rise to the metaphysical thought that . . . God cannot even *de potentia absoluta* create a second Gabriel—in other words, anyone who cannot rise *at all* to the notion of something individual which is not [merely] the instance of some universal idea, of something repeatable—cannot follow our thought here from the very start.[65]

Later on Rahner formulates the thought in such a way as to bring out the profound connection between the positive individuality that he finds in human beings and the individual immortality of each human being:

At least in his actions, man is really also (not only!) *individuum ineffabile*, whom God has called by his name, a name which is and can only be unique, so that it really is worthwhile for this unique being as such to exist in eternity.[66]

---

63. Scheler too sometimes speaks of "conscience" in this connection, as in *Formalism*, 494 (486) and 509 (499). Indeed, he seems to think that this deliberation about my most personal moral tasks is the most proper function of conscience.

64. Rahner, 225 (236).

65. Ibid., 226 (236–37).

66. Ibid., 226–27 (237). Cf. also this: "God is interested in history not only in so far as it is the carrying out of norms, but in so far as it is a history which consists in the harmony of unique events and which precisely in this way has a meaning for eternity." Ibid., 228 (239).

If human beings were just specimens of the human kind, so that all that is found in one human being can be found as well in some successor human being, then an unending succession of human beings would provide all the immortality that could be meaningfully required. Only because with human persons the individual surpasses the species or kind, being far more than just a specimen of the kind, being something incommunicably, unrepeatably its own, does immortality have to be a personal, individual immortality.

Rahner draws some very interesting consequences from his existential ethics.[67] Let us pick out only one of them:

> In the usual theory of sin we treat sin too exclusively as the mere offence against a universal divine norm. Could not an existential-ethics help us to see more clearly that sin, over and above its property of being an offence against the law of God, is also and just as much an offence against an utterly individual imperative of the individual will of God, which is the basis of uniqueness? Would we not perceive sin more clearly in this way as the failure of the personal-individual love for God?[68]

The difference to Scheler is only that Rahner develops in a more religious vein the concept of personal moral tasks.

Conclusion

The phenomenology represented by Scheler is well known for reviving *a priori* knowledge and for recognizing more domains of *a priori* knowledge than had been traditionally recognized. When Scheler speaks of the material *a priori* in ethics he means that we do not just subsume ethical subject matters under formal laws of being, but that we find properly ethical laws that are underivable from the formal laws but are no less necessary than these. Scheler labored to advance the science of the material *a priori* in ethics. Now all *a priori* knowledge is universal knowledge, especially for Scheler, who as a realist phenomenologist stressed against Husserl the validity of the *a priori* "in any possible world." This is why many have suspected phenomenology of being the revival of a Platonic

---

67. An ethics that works only with general norms is for him an *essential ethics*, thus it is only natural for him to call the ethics that also recognizes strictly personal tasks an *existential ethics*.

68. Ibid., 232 (243).

Scheler on Personal Individuality

philosophy that is incapable of doing justice to individual being. The side of Scheler's thought that we have studied here, however, shows that phenomenology, for all its concern with essential necessity and essential impossibility, also has within itself the resources for illuminating the mystery of the concrete individuality of persons.[69]

69. My thanks to Jorge Gracia and especially John White for their critical reactions to earlier drafts of this study.

CHAPTER 8

Max Scheler on the Moral and Religious Solidarity of Persons

Richard John Neuhaus once said, "The great question, it seems to me, in the abortion debate—I've argued this for years—is not 'When does life begin?' When life begins is not a moral question. It is self-evident to all sane people on grounds of undeniable empirical scientific evidence. But the great question is who belongs to the community for which we accept common responsibility. . . ."[1] This caught my attention, for it was very challenging to me; I had always opened in abortion discussions with the personhood of the embryo, and here was Neuhaus saying that the real center of gravity in the debate lies elsewhere, it lies in a certain question of co-responsibility. In one point I disagreed with Neuhaus and still do disagree; in addition to the question when life begins *in utero*, which really is an empirical question, there is also the question when each human being as person begins to exist, which is not simply an empirical but a philosophical question. Nor is the answer to the question so obvious to all sane people as to render all discussion of it superfluous. Nor is it unimportant for our stance on abortion to be able to explain the personhood that the human embryo has from conception. And yet I thought at the time, and I increasingly think, that Neuhaus was right to object to a too exclusive preoccupation with the question of the status of the human

---

* This paper originally appeared as "Max Scheler's Principle of Moral and Relgious Solidarity" in *Communio* 24.1 (Spring 1997), 110–27. It has been somewhat revised.

1. Richard John Neuhaus, "The Divided Soul of Liberalism," in Joseph Koterski, S.J., (ed.), *Life and Learning: Proceedings of the Third University Faculty for Life Conference* (Washington, D.C.: University Faculty for Life, 1993), 7.

embryo, and was right to warn against an excessive individualism that prevents many people from understanding the position of those who defend pre-born human beings. He was aiming at the mysterious solidarity in which we exist one with another.

In what follows I propose to examine this solidarity with the help of the great German philosopher Max Scheler. In the earliest days of the phenomenological movement (at the beginning of the twentieth century), Scheler brought the methods of phenomenology for the first time into contact with Christian thought.[2] Except for the tragic last years of his life, Scheler did all of his so seminal work in philosophy as a convinced Catholic Christian. Of particular interest to us is his extensive work in philosophical sociology, such as his great study, *On the Nature of Sympathy*, and the sections on community in his *Formalism in Ethics*. By the way, Scheler is also the phenomenologist who influenced so profoundly the young Karol Wojtyla, who says at the beginning of *The Acting Person* that he owes the ideas of his book not only to St. Thomas Aquinas, but also to phenomenology in the interpretation of Max Scheler.

1.

In 1917 Scheler gave a lecture entitled "The Cultural Reconstruction of Europe," in which we read to our great surprise:

A cultural reconstruction is only possible if an increasingly large proportion of the European peoples learns to look upon this cataclysm [World War I] as resulting from *a common guilt* [*Gemeinschuld*] of European peoples mutually influencing each other....

First, therefore, must come the recognition that in the final analysis there is only *one* answer to the question, Who or what nation is responsible for this war? The answer is You, the asker of the question—by what you have done or left undone.[3]

---

2. The most important study of the relation of Schelerian phenomenology to Christianity is undoubtedly Hans Urs von Balthasar's chapters on Scheler in *Apokalypse der deutschen Seele*, vol. 3 (Salzburg: Anton Pustet Verlag, 1939), 84–192.

3. Scheler, "Vom kulturellen Wiederaufbau Europas," in *Vom Ewigen im Menschen* (Bern: Francke Verlag, 1954), 405–47. Translated by Bernard Noble as "The Reconstruction of European Culture," in *On the Eternal in Man* (Hamden, CT: Archon Books, 1972), 416–17. I do not think that the translator was well advised to translate *Gemeinschuld* as "collective guilt;" here and elsewhere I have amended his translation to read "common guilt."

This way of extending the guilt and responsibility for a war strikes us at first as an exaggeration beyond all measure. But let us set aside for a moment the obvious objections that leap to mind, so as to let Scheler challenge a certain individualism that we all tend to hold. In the following we find him distinguishing between the guilt that concerns him in this essay and the guilt that will concern the politicians who draw up the peace treaty after the war.

> I do not say that . . . the politician or historian must refrain from asking where the *political,* historical guilt for the definite occurrence lies, guilt for the outbreak of August, 1914.[4]

In other words, as we might say by way of rendering Scheler's thought more concrete, Serbia had a responsibility for the outbreak of the war that, for example, Belgium did not have; on this level of guilt, Serbia was guilty and Belgium was innocent. Scheler himself was capable of speaking on this level of guilt, as we can see from those war writings of his in which he pleads the cause of Germany.[5] But on the deeper level of guilt of which he speaks in the lecture we are quoting, the guilt cannot be localized so easily; the guilt is more diffused, and almost everyone has some share in it. Scheler proceeds to explain this deeper guilt as a guilt, not for starting the war, but for helping to create the moral milieu in which the war was possible at all.

> What forms the object of common guilt is not that the War did take place, still less the how and when of its beginning, but that it *could* take place, that *such* an event was possible in this European quarter of the human globe, that it was an event of such a nature as we know it to be. The object of common guilt is its possibility, then, and its quality, not its actual occurrence and real beginning. As you must be aware, within the individual the object of any deeper guilt-feeling is likewise not "that I did it" but that I *could* so behave, was *such* a person as could do it. Only this common act of insight into the *reciprocity* of the shared responsibilities of every belligerent nation and all its subdivisions down to the family and individual can produce the psychological atmosphere from which European culture can arise renewed.[6]

Scheler means that everyone who in the years before the war did any moral wrong, contributed in some way to the formation of the interper-

---

4. Ibid.
5. See for example his "Der Genius des Krieges und der Deutsche Krieg," in *Gesammelte Werke* IV (Bonn: Bouvier Verlag, 1982), 7–250.
6. "The Reconstruction of European Culture," 417.

sonal situation in Europe in which a world war was possible. The wrong that each committed did not stay with the wrongdoer but was able to spread throughout the European community, enhancing the possibility of a world war. This idea of Scheler is, of course, an idea that stands at the center of Dostoevsky's great work, *The Brothers Karamazov*,[7] and which is expressed as the "responsibility of everyone for everyone."[8]

In one place Scheler makes an attempt to understand more exactly one of the modes of transmitting good and bad by which we become co-responsible for so many others.[9] He tries to think through what is involved in me failing to show love to another to whom I should have shown love, and sees typified in this at least one mode of acquiring co-responsibility for others. He says that the other, whom I should have loved, would have been "called" to love me in return if I had loved him, since all love, by its inner logic as love, calls for some requital. My failure to love the other leaves him with one less reason for loving, for it deprives him of the call to requite my love. But in having one less reason for loving, the other grows that much less in the power to love, for the power to love grows by performing acts of love (as Aristotle recognized in his theory of moral virtue). When the other turns to all those who are his others, he turns to them with less power to love than he would have had if I had loved as I should have loved; in this way my failure takes its toll on all of his relations to others, thus making itself felt far beyond anything that I can track, just as the stone falling in the water sends its ripples across the lake and out of the sight of the one who dropped the stone. On the other hand, if I had loved as I should have loved, then I would have been co-responsible for the growth in the power of another to love, and thus co-

---

7. On Scheler and Dostoevsky see Hans Urs von Balthasar, *op. cit.*, 187–88.

8. John Finnis might withdraw some of his reservations (*Natural Law and Natural Rights*, [New York: Oxford University Press, 1980], 176–77) about this great intuition of Dostoevsky if he saw that, in Scheler's interpretation of it, Dostoevsky does not dissolve those bonds of responsibility that connect me with this person but not with that person, but rather leaves them all intact while giving expression to a different order of guilt and responsibility.

9. Scheler, *Der Formalismus in der Ethik und die materiale Wertethik* (Bern: Francke Verlag, 1966), trans. by Manfred Frings and Roger Funk as *Formalism in Ethics and Non-formal Ethics of Values* (Evanston: Northwestern University Press, 1973), 535–38. He recapitulates this analysis of transmitting good and bad in "Die Christliche Liebesidee und die Gegenwärtige Welt," in *Vom Ewigen im Menschen* (Bern: Francke Verlag, 1968), trans. by Bernard Noble as "Christian Love and the Twentieth Century," in *On the Eternal in Man* (Hamden, CT: Archon Books, 1972), 377–78.

responsible for the greater love that he would have shown throughout his life in all of his relations with innumerable others.

It is remarkable how Scheler's idea of moral solidarity, which for him can be understood in a properly philosophical way, finds expression in a recent papal teaching. In his 1984 Apostolic Exhortation, *Reconciliatio et paenitentia*, John Paul II says (para. 16):

> To speak of *social sin* means in the first place to recognize that, by virtue of a human solidarity which is as mysterious and intangible as it is real and concrete, each individual's sin in some way affects others. This is the other aspect of that solidarity which on the religious level is developed in the profound and magnificent mystery of the *Communion of Saints*, thanks to which it has been possible to say that "every soul that rises above itself, raises up the world." To this *law of ascent* there unfortunately corresponds the *law of descent*. Consequently, one can speak of a *communion of sin*, whereby a soul that lowers itself through sin drags down with itself the Church and, in some way, the whole world. In other words, there is no sin, not even the most intimate and secret one, the most strictly individual one, that exclusively concerns the person committing it. With greater or lesser violence, with greater or lesser harm, every sin has repercussions on the entire ecclesial body and the whole human body.

For a better understanding of Scheler and of the way he challenges a certain Western individualism, we have to bring into full relief a theme that is present in these texts of John Paul II, namely the reciprocity of guilt. Not only am I co-responsible for others, but they are commonly co-responsible for me; co-responsibilities interpenetrate. In one striking passage Scheler describes the experience of entering a home

> where filth, disorder, the low talk of the children, everything under our eyes, testifies to a *total* condition [*Gesamtzustand*] of moral putrefaction. Such a condition is indivisible—irrespective of how it arose, whose "fault" it is, whether the father's, the mother's, the great-grandfather's or anyone else's. Every human experience of a deeper kind teaches that such group-guilt [*Gruppen- und Gesamtschuld*] can never be wholly broken down into the guilt of individuals. Every attentively pondered experience teaches that the deeper we penetrate the moral interrelations of such a family, the more the *unfathomable reciprocity* of guilt is brought to light (my italics in this last sentence).[10]

---

[10]. "Christian Love and the Twentieth Century," 361. But we will directly below encounter a case of co-responsibility that lacks the full reciprocity of which Scheler speaks here.

With this "unfathomable reciprocity of guilt" in mind let us cast a glance back to our point of departure in the right and wrong of abortion. The responsibility for abortions is not limited to the women who have them or to the doctors who provide them or to the politicians and judges who legalize them. Scheler would challenge even those actively committed to resisting abortion to consider that their own moral failings have contributed to the moral milieu in which easy abortion is taken for granted. If Scheler were still alive and we were to ask him about the guilt for the "culture of death" in which we live, we can be sure that he would answer, not only by accusing Justice Blackmun, or President Clinton, but also by saying, "You who ask the question—you are in a way guilty, too. You of the pro-life movement, beware of the idea that the crimes of abortion are taking place completely apart from you. It is not enough to establish the fact that you did not commit the crimes, and in fact did not even instigate them, and have even officially disapproved of them. If you lived more just lives, if you were a less eager participant in the patterns of consumerism, it would be that much less possible for such a 'culture of death' to have taken root. And in accord with the 'unfathomable reciprocity' of guilt I must also tell you that you have been adversely affected by the culture of death—demoralized by it, desensitized by it—far more than you think."

I should add right away that Scheler would have been quick to reject the "quietistic" consequences that one sometimes tries to draw from his idea of solidarity. He would not say that it is hypocritical for us to condemn and to fight against the providers of abortion. He would not try to level all moral differences between those who support and those who condemn abortion, just as he did not try to abolish, as we saw, the difference between the guilty and the innocent states involved in the First World War. He would not do this, because he never intended that his *Gemeinschuld* should substitute for the other levels of political guilt where guilt is really more localizable. And yet it is true that those of us who fight abortion will be preserved from a certain pharisaism by remaining mindful that at a certain level of guilt even we may have some co-responsibility for the culture of death, and also remaining mindful that even we are liable to be morally desensitized by living in the culture of death.

But this is not yet the most important implication of Scheler's social philosophy for the question of abortion; we shall discuss at the end another implication of it.

For Scheler our solidarity shows itself not only in the guilt in which we are involved but also in the repentance to which we are called. Consider this from his great essay, "Repentance and Rebirth:"

> And so Repentance is as fundamentally concerned with our share in all guilt as with our individual culpability ... with collective [*Gesamtschuld*] and hereditary guilt of communities, families, peoples and all humanity as with individual guilt ... it is very superficial to say that one should rest content with "not judging" the guilt of others but rather be mindful of one's own individual guilt ... one should not only be mindful of one's own guilt but feel oneself genuinely implicated in this guilt of others and in the collective guilt [*Gesamtschuld*] of one's age; one should therefore regard such guilt as one's "own," and share in the repenting of it. That is the true sense of the *mea culpa, mea culpa, mea maxima culpa*.[11]

In this essay Scheler explains that just as an individual can be weighed down with his or her unrepented guilt, so a whole community can be weighed down with its unrepented *Gesamtschuld*. And just as an individual who repents can break his moral solidarity with this guilt and free himself from its oppressive weight, so in the same way an entire community that repents can perform the work of freeing itself from the encumbrance of its *Gesamtschuld*. This recovery of an encumbered freedom is just what John Paul II intended with the great ecclesial self-examination in which he led the Church in preparation for the celebration of the Jubilee year, 2000. He intended a "purification of memories" by acknowledging the wrong that was done in the past in the name of the Church and by leading the Church in acts of repentance. He thought that only through such collective repentance could the Church disentangle herself from the grasp of past sins and summon up all of her spiritual energy for facing the challenges of the third millennium. This audacious deed of the pope confronts us with exactly the guilt and repentance of which Scheler wants to say that it is collective rather than strictly individual in character. This is repentance of just the kind that Scheler longed to see in Europe in the wake of World War I.

11. Scheler, "Repentance and Rebirth," in *On the Eternal in Man* (Hamden, CT: Archon Books, 1972), 58. Translated by Bernard Noble. "Reue und Wiedergeburt," in *Vom Ewigen im Menschen* (Bern: Francke Verlag, 1968).

Scheler on Solidarity of Persons

2.

In editing the quotation just given I left out: repentance "is as fundamentally concerned with the tragic guilt to which we blamelessly fall prey as with the guilt which we freely incur." I left it out because it introduces an entirely new kind of common guilt as well as a new kind of repentance. A guilt that we fall prey to "blamelessly" is something altogether different from the guilt of others for which we are co-responsible. It is at first difficult to make anything of a guilt blamelessly contracted, although on closer reflection it becomes clear that original sin in Christian doctrine can be said to be just such a thing, since it is blamelessly contracted by each child of Adam. Perhaps there is even something in our experience that lets us grasp a guilt so different from the individual guilt that we bring upon ourselves. Consider certain "national apologies" that have recently been made by the leaders of Japan and Germany. They apologized on behalf of their entire nations for crimes committed against other nations during the last world war. Now if they apologize, then they must believe that they and the people of the present generation have some kind of share in those crimes. They had of course no personal hand in them, but they evidently feel some solidarity with those who committed them. But if they really do have this solidarity with their fathers that they presuppose in apologizing, then must they not have had it from birth? For from their birth until now they have surely done nothing to acquire it; they have only awakened to it. Here, then, is a kind of hereditary guilt into which we can be blamelessly born. Of course, this is guilt in a fundamentally different sense. The Germans and the Japanese who committed the crimes are the primary bearers of guilt; their grandchildren who are now apologizing for these crimes do not have the same kind of guilt, that is, they do not have the guilt of an accomplice. On the other hand, they must share *in some sense* in the guilt of their fathers. And it is not enough simply to say that the children are suffering from *the effects of* their fathers' crimes, for then it would remain unintelligible how it is that only they are in a moral position to apologize, since many others besides themselves, and most of all the victims, have suffered the effects of the crimes.

So it seems that we need to distinguish more clearly than Scheler does between two kinds of guilt and two kinds of repentance. There is the co-responsibility that we have for the guilt of others, along with the repentance for our complicity in their guilt; and there is the blameless sharing in the guilt of others, along with a certain repenting of this guilt. In the first case, the guilt originates in us; in the second, we are blamelessly infected with the guilt of others. In both cases, the moral solidarity of human beings is expressed. By the way, both kinds of guilt and repentance are at stake in the ecclesial repentance inaugurated by John Paul II. We can find both of them in a particularly significant sermon preached by John Paul on the "Day of Pardon" in the Jubilee Year, March 12, 2000. "Let us confess . . . our responsibilities as Christians for the evils of today. We must ask ourselves what our responsibilities are regarding atheism, religious indifference, secularism, ethical relativism, the violations of the right to life, disregard for the poor in many countries." Here he invites us to repent of the wrong for which we are co-responsible. But in another place in the same sermon he invites us to repent of the guilt in which we somehow share but without being co-responsible for it: "Because of the bond which unites us to one another in the Mystical Body, all of us, though not personally responsible . . . bear the burden of the errors and faults of those who have gone before us."

But we should not exaggerate the distinction between the two cases. The grandchildren of the Nazis labor under a moral liability; the guilt that they blamelessly contract is a moral burden to them, depressing rather than elevating their moral level. If they do wrong in their time, their evil ancestors are likely to be co-responsible for them. Thus we find here some co-responsibility situated within the blameless contracting of guilt. But this co-responsibility lacks the reciprocity of common guilt, since the children of the present generation can hardly be co-responsible for the crimes of their Nazi grandparents; the only co-responsibility is the co-responsibility of the previous generation for the present one.

I would say that most of Scheler's thought about *Gemeinschuld*, and certainly his deepest thought about it, concerns guilt in the first sense, the guilt that comes from us being co-responsible for the guilt of others and from others being co-responsible for our guilt. It is this guilt of which we shall speak in the following, unless we indicate otherwise.

Scheler is well aware that the very idea of sharing with others in guilt and in repentance has become almost incomprehensible to us and to our contemporaries. He held that one moral root of our incomprehension is the *ressentiment* that inclines us to the following principle of moral valuation: "Moral value pertains only to those qualities, actions, etc., which the individual has acquired by his own strength and labor."[12] Morally mediocre people feel *ressentiment* towards morally superior people and so they carry out what Nietzsche called a kind of slave revolt in morality. They devalue all the special callings, gifts, graces found in morally noble men and women; they declare that moral worth comes exclusively from something that is entirely available even to them, the mediocre, namely from their own moral efforts. Scheler says that this *ressentiment*-laden mentality will also resist any responsibility beyond that which one explicitly assumes. He says that "it is a sign of 'slave morality' ... to *limit* responsibility as much as possible, to reject all guilt for the acts of 'others,' and at the same time to 'accept no presents' in this respect." Just above on the same page he had said, appropriating Nietzsche for his own theory of *Gemeinschuld*, "when a morality springs from those who are certain of their value, who accept and affirm their deepest self and being, who live in the fullness of their wealth, it always tends to *extend* 'responsibility' as far as possible beyond the limits of the individual person—especially to all those whose lives are in some way dependent on this person's life."[13] The loss of this moral nobility and highmindedness, and the spread of the slave revolt in morality, goes far, according to Scheler, towards explaining our individualistic scruples about *Gemeinschuld*.

3.

But readers of Scheler who are free from any slave-like *ressentiment* may still suspect something depersonalizing about his *Gemeinschuld*, suspect that it interferes with the full truth about individual responsibility. The question is whether Scheler, in his teaching on the social dimension of guilt and repentance, sacrifices the individual to the community.

We might respond according to the mind of Scheler as follows. *Gemeinschuld* has its origin in individual persons who are co-responsible for their fellows in community, and it is nothing apart from such indi-

---

12. Scheler, *Ressentiment*, trans. by Lewis Coser and William Holdheim (Milwaukee: Marquette University Press, 1994), 111. German: *Das Ressentiment im Aufbau der Moralen*, in *Vom Umsturz der Werte* (Bern: Francke Verlag, 1955).

13. Ibid., 115.

vidual persons. Scheler is so far from denying individual responsibility that he extends the range of it, so that it includes not only responsibility for oneself but also co-responsibility for others. It is true that, according to the logic of Schelerian co-responsibility, I am not the only one who is responsible for myself but that others are co-responsible for me, and that, as a result, my responsibility for myself is somewhat modified. But for Scheler these others never prevent me from also being responsible for myself, nor from being really co-responsible for all of them.

If one thinks of *Gemeinschuld* in the other sense of a guilt that one can blamelessly inherit, then one can say the following. Only if it were meant by Scheler as replacing the guilt for which we are responsible, would the recognition of it be depersonalizing; but as long as it is only one level of guilt, sharply distinguished from the guilt for which we are responsible, it can be fully recognized without giving up anything that we want to affirm about individual guilt and responsibility.

But the concern that some may feel for the integrity of the individual person merits further discussion. Let us examine Scheler's understanding of the individual person and how it imparts a personalistic character to his philosophy of solidarity.[14]

Hans Urs von Balthasar helpfully explains Scheler's personalism[15] in terms of his struggle to overcome two philosophical positions of his time, as we saw in the previous chapter.[16] First, he wanted to overcome the *Lebensphilosophie* of Nietzsche and Bergson. He wanted to show that the spirit or person in man is not different just by degree from his vital powers but is rather the eruption of an utterly new principle, radically different in kind from all vital energy.[17] Thus in his ethics he strove to show that above the "vital values" there are the essentially higher "spiritual" and "religious" values.

Second, Scheler wanted to overcome German Idealism insofar as it dissolved the individual into a mere instance of the universal. He teaches that the recognition of "the infinite worth of the *individual* soul" is "the

14. In what follows I survey briefly some themes in Scheler's philosophy of the individual person that I have discussed much more thoroughly in the previous paper in this collection.

15. As we use this term personalism for the first time in this paper, it is worthwhile to recall the subtitle of Scheler's major work, *Formalism in Ethics:* "A New Attempt Towards the Foundation of an Ethical Personalism."

16. Von Balthasar, *op. cit.*, 85–89.

17. See, for example, *Formalism in Ethics*, "The Relativity of Values to Life," 275–95.

magna carta of Europe."[18] In the same place he "categorically denies that the individual person is a mere 'modus' of some generality—the State, say, or society, or 'world-reason' or an impersonal . . . historical process. . . ."[19] A most striking expression of his personalist individualism, as one could call it, is his teaching concerning *the individual value-essence* of each human person.[20] He teaches that each person not only instantiates the general essence of man, but also has an essence incommunicably his own, as we saw above in the previous paper. The ethical consequence is that each person not only has to act on maxims that are universal laws for all persons, but also on maxims that bind him alone and no one else. The universal laws constitute only an ethical minimum for each person, Scheler says; the fullness of a moral existence is only achieved in responding to all the special personal requirements and callings that are grounded in the individual value-essence. This teaching has an obvious polemical edge against the moral philosophy of Kant.

It follows, then, that Scheler's solidarity is the solidarity not of a mass or crowd, but of concrete-individual persons. His sense of solidarity does not interfere with the recognition of persons but is rather specified by this recognition as a properly personalist solidarity. Von Balthasar sees this clearly and has also well expressed a related point: the various forms of solidarity take on much greater significance and dignity when they are understood as presupposing the individual person in the sense of Scheler:

> Only on the basis of Scheler's personalism, which takes the person not only as a valuable individuality but also as a spirit transcending the vital, can issues regarding the social, the national . . . take up a definitive place among "the ultimate things." Previously they were always, as Scheler forcefully brings out, swallowed up either in the colorless generality of idealistic "reason" or in the anonymous flow of life as understood by *Lebensphilosophie*. Only when uniquely structured individuality as such has taken on a positive spiritual meaning, does the togetherness of human beings become an ultimate, irreducible reality. . . .[21]

In other words, collectivistic philosophies undermine the dignity even of the community by the very fact that they undermine the dignity of the individual persons who belong to it.

---

18. "Christian Love and the Twentieth Century," 384.
19. Ibid.
20. *Formalism in Ethics*, "Person and Individual," 489–94.
21. Von Balthasar, *op. cit.*, 88. The German text that I translated reads as follows: "Erst von dem Personalismus Schelers aus, welcher die Person sowohl wertvolle Individualität

On the basis of his deep understanding for the individual person Scheler can make telling criticisms of certain forms of social solidarity. Thus, for example, he objects as follows to the ideal of the *polis* that we find in Plato and Aristotle:

> ... they were ignorant of the independent, Stateless, God-created, spiritual and immortal soul, superior in its inmost being to any possible State, possessing an inner world of religion and morality.... Man they confined, to the very roots of his being, in the State, which meant in effect a restriction to things of this earth.[22]

One sees, then, that Scheler is perfectly capable of identifying some forms of solidarity as depersonalizing. His own philosophy of solidarity is expressed in strictly personalist terms.

But it is not enough just to juxtapose Scheler's affirmation of solidarity and his affirmation of the individual person. They are not just juxtaposed in his thought and so we do not do justice to him until we also understand their internal connection. On this subject I know of no more significant passage than the following:

> ... it is inherent in the *eternal, ideal nature* of a rational person that all its existence and activity as a spirit is from the very beginning just as much a conscious co-responsible, communal reality as a self-conscious, self-responsible, individual reality. The being of a man is just as originally a matter of being, living and acting "one with another" as it is a matter of existing for oneself.[23]

And in another place:

---

als auch überlebendigen Geist sein lässt, erhalten die Problemkreise des Sozialen, des Nationalen.... eine endgültige Stelle in den 'letzten Dingen.' Bisher waren sie stets, wie Scheler selbst scharf herausstellt, verschlungen, entweder in die farblose Allgemeinheit der idealistischen 'Vernunft' oder in den namenlosen Strom des lebensphilosophischen Allebens. Erst wenn das geprägte, einmalig gestalthafte Individuelle als solches einen positiven, geistigen Sinn hat, wird ein Miteinander zu einer letzten, unrückführbaren Angelegenheit...." Cf. also this in Von Balthasar, 187: "Wherever life was thought to be the highest value there could indeed be a instinctive sense of belonging based on pleasure and pain, guilt and atonement, but not an eternal and responsible being-there-for-one-another where each person is irreplaceable."

22. Ibid., 383.

23. Ibid., 373. Since I have amended the translation in several places, I give the German original of this particularly important text of Scheler: "Es gehört vielmehr zum *ewigen ideellen Wesen* einer vernünftigen Person, dass ihr ganzes geistiges Sein und Tun ebenso ursprünglich eine selbstbewusste, eine selbstverantwortliche individuelle Wirklichkeit ist, als auch bewusste mitverantwortliche Gliedwirklichkeit in einer Gemeinschaft. Sein des

... each individual is not responsible solely for his own character and conduct, responsible through his conscience before his Lord and creator, but each individual ... is, in its capacity as "member" of communities, also responsible to God—as fundamentally as for self—for all that bears spiritually and morally upon the condition and the activity of its communities.[24]

Just as the irreducible selfhood of each person is essential to each, so also is the existing towards others, existing with them, being co-responsible for them. This relation to the other belongs to our personhood no less than our selfhood belongs to it.

One sees why Scheler insists so often that it is the very essence of the human person, and not just the changeable historical circumstances of our being thrown together with others, which underlies the immeasurable co-responsibility in which we stand. Scheler does not think that we could just as well have nothing to do with each other, exercising no influence on each other, and that it is only the fact that our lot happens to be cast with others that occasions the vast mutual influence which we know from experience. No, he thinks that this mutual influence expresses something deeper in man, something metaphysical; the very essence of man as person is working itself out when persons become co-responsible for each other beyond any possibility of keeping track of the influence.

It is this image of the person as both self-responsible and co-responsible for others that underlies something else in Scheler—his rejection not only of collectivistic forms of solidarity but also of individualistic ways of dissolving solidarity. He fights in particular against any and every social philosophy that sees the highpoint of social life in *Gesellschaft*, or society, which for Scheler means that form of living together in which all bonds with others, and all responsibilities for others, arise only through persons, understood as complete in themselves, explicitly assuming responsibility for others.[25] He rejects the idea that the individual person arbitrarily

---

Menschen ist ebenso ursprünglich Fürsichsein als auch Miteinandersein, Miteinandererleben und Miteinanderwirken." "Die christliche Liebesidee und die gegenwärtige Welt," 371.

24. Ibid., 376. The polarity which Scheler recognizes in the human person—existing in oneself and existing for others—was also affirmed by Vatican II in *Gaudium et spes*, 24: " ... man, who is the only creature on earth that God has willed for its own sake, can fully discover his true self only in a sincere giving of himself."

25. Scheler's fullest discussion of *Gesellschaft* and its relation to other social formations, especially to *Lebensgemeinschaft* and *Gesamtperson*, is found in *Formalism in Ethics*, 526–41.

posits all the social relations in which he lives, and that before he acts to posit them he simply stands next to other persons in a kind of social vacuum, complete in himself and lacking any bond with them. What Scheler affirms, by contrast, is the idea that persons are bound to each other, and are thus co-responsible for each other, as a result of their very being as persons and in advance of any conscious acting (of course, he does not deny that there is also such a thing as an obligation that is freely assumed). We can even say that for Scheler individual persons are from the very beginning comprehended in a fundamental human community;[26] they do not create it, but awaken to it; their social existence unfolds within this community, and finds in it a basic norm.

It is because we are by our very nature as persons established one with another in a fundamental human solidarity and so have to do with each other even before assuming any particular responsibility—it is because of this that we dwell in an interpersonal space in which "there is no moral gesture so trivial that it does not radiate, like the splashing stone, an infinity of ripples—circles soon lost to the naked eye,"[27] a space in which "all is flowing and blending; a touch in one place sets up movement at the other end of the earth."[28] From the point of view of *Gesellschaft* the moral condition of each individual remains shut up in the individual until he turns to someone who consciously receives his act. But from the point of view of what Scheler calls "the principle of moral and religious reciprocity or moral solidarity," the moral substance of the individual person essentially tends to fill the already existing interpersonal space and so to affect for better or worse the spiritual atmosphere which the others breathe. In this way each individual person becomes co-responsible for the moral state of more of his fellow human beings than he can possibly count: and more of them than he can count become co-responsible for him.[29]

We can perhaps recapitulate by saying that just as Scheler's teaching on

---

26. On this fundamental community of mankind see Dietrich von Hildebrand, *Metaphysik der Gemeinschaft* (Regensburg: Josef Habbel Verlag, 1955), 226–30, to mention just one significant passage. Von Hildebrand develops here a philosophical sociology that is in some ways indebted to and in many ways akin to Scheler's.

27. "Christian Love and the Twentieth Century," 377.

28. Dostoevsky, *The Brothers Karamazov* (New York: The Modern Library, 1950), 383–84.

29. Now that we have studied Scheler's thought on solidarity we might think back to the paper in this volume that concerns empathy and in particular to my claim that empathetic understanding is possible only on the basis of some experienced solidarity. If we

solidarity has nothing to do with a collectivistic compromise of the individuality of persons, so his teaching on the individuality of persons has nothing to do with the individualism of the *Gesellschaft*, which undermines all deeper forms of solidarity. His personalism is something altogether different from bourgeois individualism as a result of being organically completed by his teaching on co-responsibility.

4.

It must, however, be said that Scheler's teaching on co-responsibility can be interpreted in an untenable sense that he does not consistently exclude. He sometimes seems to mean that I am just as responsible for others as for myself—not that my co-responsibility is just as essential a part of my personal being as my self-responsibility, but that the two dimensions of responsibility are, in respect of responsibility, entirely on a level with each other. This seems to obscure the fact that I am handed over to myself in an absolutely unique way, a way in which no other person can be entrusted to me. We could perhaps say it like this: just as I am present to myself with a subjective intimacy with which I can never be present to another and with which another can never be present to me,[30] so I have a responsibility for myself which I can have for no other and which no other can have for me.

It is also necessary to mention here another thesis of Scheler's about solidarity that somewhat compromises his personalism. He distinguishes between individual persons *(Einzelpersonen)* and collective persons *(Gesamtpersonen)* and holds that the latter, typified in a state and even more in a nation or in the Church, *are as truly and authentically persons as individual persons.*[31] He thinks that the highpoint of solidarity is achieved when we individual persons live fully in a *Gesamtperson* like a nation. Scheler undoubtedly has a deep understanding for the unity, the properly personal unity, formed by a community such as a nation. In his great work on sympathy he explores in the most original way the co-

---

put this paper together with that one, does it not follow that those who experience Scheler's moral solidarity are thereby capable of empathy with others on the grounds that others are fellow human beings?

30. On this subject see the first pages of my paper on empathy at the beginning of this volume.

31. Scheler, *Formalism in Ethics*, 519–60, esp. 519–25 and 543–48.

performance *(Miteinandervollzug)* of which certain acts are capable. Thus, he says, parents grieving at the funeral of a beloved child do not just grieve each for himself or herself, as if they were united only in having the same motive for their grief; no, they are also united in the subjectivity of their grieving, that is, they co-grieve, grieving one with another, uniting almost to form a common subject of grief.[32] This co-experiencing can run through an entire community, as when an entire people grieves over some national humiliation or over the death of a beloved leader. This helps us to see how a community can sometimes have a unified consciousness, or collective subjectivity, of its own, and thus take on a quasi-personal character. And yet we cannot go all the way with Scheler; we have also to affirm that such a community is not a person in the same proper sense in which an individual person is a person. When we speak of a community in terms of subjectivity, grieving, rejoicing, having rights, etc., we speak of these things in a very derived sense.[33] Here is one way of showing that it is derived: a collective person exists in a fundamental dependency-on-others that has no counterpart in an individual person. For a collective person presupposes individual persons and exists only in and through them and apart from them is nothing at all (though of course it is more than the sum of them). But an individual person does not in the same way exist in collective persons or in anything else; much as he may owe them for the fullness of his life, he does not exist *in* them in the way in which they exist in individual persons: as individual person he exists in himself.[34]

But Scheler's tendency to exaggerate the ontological status of the *Gesamtperson*, though it is a real weakness of his personalism, is no necessary part of his teaching on co-responsibility and solidarity; we can repudiate this tendency of his even while we affirm his principle of moral

---

32. Scheler, *The Nature of Sympathy* (Hamden, CT: Archon Books, 1973), Part I, ch. 2, especially 12–13. Translated by Bernard Noble. *Wesen und Formen der Sympathie* (Bern, 1973).

33. Throughout her treatise "Individuum und *Gemeinschaft*," Edith Stein makes various criticisms of Scheler's excesses regarding the *Gesamtperson (Jahrbuch für Philosophie und phänomenologische Forschung* 5 [1922], 116–283).

34. We ought at least to mention another criticism of Scheler raised by von Balthasar (*op. cit.*, 187–92), who speaks of "the fundamental ambiguity of his concept of the person as being both world-bound and worldless [seines welthaft-weltlosen Personbegriffs]" (186). As I understand him, he means that Scheler falls prey to a certain spiritualistic

Scheler on Solidarity of Persons

and religious solidarity. It is not as if we have to lapse back into bourgeois individualism if we do not accept all that Scheler says about *Gesamtpersonen*.

5.

We conclude by returning to our point of departure. Important as it is, indispensable as it is, to affirm that in every abortion a right is violated, this has to be completed by another affirmation. If our stance in this central moral question of our time is not to suffer a certain individualistic distortion, then we must also appeal to the moral solidarity of all human beings, to the fundamental responsibility for one another in which we are established. Then it becomes evident that abortion is not only the violation of a right, but also the betrayal of a brother or a sister. It not only violates the rights of the aborted person, but also the fundamental solidarity in which we stand with him or her.

Let us recall the well-known article of Judith Thomson that appeared in a philosophy journal some years ago with the title, "A Defense of Abortion." It was very widely read and exercised no little influence. For the sake of her argument she assumed that the human embryo that is aborted is a person. She argued as follows. It is indeed very generous if a woman lets the child live which she has conceived, but the burdens of pregnancy are such that she usually has no obligation to keep it; in most cases the mother who keeps it is a Good Samaritan who goes beyond the call of duty. Abortion is justified from this point of view, not on the grounds that the embryo is not a *human* being, but rather on the grounds that it is not a *fellow* human being. Thomson seems to think that such "fellowship" as we have with others exists only as a result of our con-

---

excess in the way he affirms that human persons "proceed from the creative hand of God without any connection with nature" (191). He thinks that Scheler fails to do justice to the human nature common to all human persons and thus undermines his own insights into solidarity and co-responsibility: "The possibility of a solidary guilt of all human beings certainly rests on the potential, 'natural' ... sphere of a human nature...." (192) In contemporary terms von Balthasar wants to say that Scheler in his anthropology sacrifices the pole of "nature" to the pole of "person," to the detriment of his philosophy of solidarity. It would require another study—a study that needs to be undertaken—to test the validity of von Balthasar's critique.

sciously creating it. Indeed, she writes, exactly in the spirit of Scheler's *Gesellschaft*, "Surely we do not have any such 'special responsibility' for a person unless we have assumed it, explicitly or implicitly."[35] This point of view is challenged precisely by Scheler's principle of solidarity and of the co-responsibility for others in which we are established *even before we do anything in their regard*.

Perhaps we could even take a step beyond Scheler and say that there are also levels of responsibility for others that lie beyond the level based on our common humanity. The child that the woman carries is not only a fellow human being to her, but is entrusted to her in a more particular way, being flesh of her flesh. If she aborts her child she betrays this maternal trust, in addition to violating a right. People like Judith Thomson will say that the relation of mother to child is at first a merely "biological" relation, and that only some "assumption" of responsibility by the mother lets an authentic interpersonal relation arise between them. This is exactly the point we ought to contest. There are in reality all kinds of ways in which we are made responsible for one another "by nature," prior to all the responsibility that we freely contract. The mother-child relation is "by nature" a morally charged relation. It is a false body-soul dualism to declare the relation "merely biological;" from the beginning it involves body and soul, and thus morally binds the mother to her child even before she assumes any responsibility towards the child. Once we have understood with Scheler the basic human solidarity in which we are established with all other human beings, we can proceed to understand some of these more particular forms of solidarity in which we are established with certain others. In coming to understand better these various levels of solidarity, we will overcome that individualism which is one main impediment to thinking rightly about an issue like abortion.

Everyone knows the magnificent final chorus of the Ninth Symphony of Beethoven. The text of Schiller and the music of Beethoven celebrate a fundamental solidarity of all human beings, which is a source of profound joy for them. Dostoevsky has given expression to this solidarity in *The Brothers Karamazov*. Now Max Scheler has explored it philosophical-

---

35. Judith Jarvis Thomson, "A Defense of Abortion," originally in *Philosophy and Public Affairs* 1.1 (1971), 47–56; reprinted in Abelson and Friquegnon, eds., *Ethics for Modern Life* (New York: St. Martin's Press, 1987), 137.

ly in his elaboration of "the principle of moral and religious solidarity," which has a central place in his personalist philosophy. It has lost none of its timeliness since Dostoevsky and Scheler first formulated it, indeed it answers today more than ever to the deepest aspirations of human persons.

CHAPTER 9

Dietrich von Hildebrand on the Fundamental Freedom of Persons

How is it possible knowingly and deliberately to do wrong? With a view to answering this question I will turn to the German phenomenologist, Dietrich von Hildebrand (1889–1977) and will call attention to a highly original contribution of his and will try to retrieve it from the state of neglect in which it presently lies. I conclude by articulating the fundamental freedom of human persons that emerges from von Hildebrand's account of deliberate wrongdoing.

1.

I take my point of departure from the undeniable fact that we human persons are entirely capable of doing some wrong *in the full awareness that it is wrong.* Socrates, of course, is well known for denying this, but with his denial he flies in the face of the most evident moral facts, as already Aristotle said in criticizing him. Surely St. Paul speaks for all of us when he says: "The good that I will to do, I do not do; but the evil I will not to do, that I practice" (*Romans*, 7:15). Consider St. Augustine's theft of the pears, as related at the end of *Confessions* II. He says that he was not only aware of the wrongness of his theft, but that he took a particular

---

* An earlier version of this paper appeared under the title, "How Is It Possible Knowingly to Do Wrong?" in the *Proceedings of the American Catholic Philosophical Association* 74 (2000), 325–33. The present text represents a thorough revision and considerable expansion of that article.

delight in this wrongness. We read that he threw the stolen pears away and "ate from them only the evil, which I enjoyed and delighted in."[1] He asks rhetorically "whether it was possible to act against the law." And again, also rhetorically: "Was it possible to desire what was not allowed, and to desire it not for the sake of something else, but precisely because it was not allowed?"[2] He means that he stole for the very reason that it was not allowed to steal. He surmises that he wanted thereby to ape the divine omnipotence (". . . bearing an obscure resemblance to omnipotence by doing with impunity what was not allowed."[3]) Augustine's famous self-examination requires us to affirm the very thing that Socrates thought impossible: Augustine did wrong knowingly.

The theft of Augustine also makes us go beyond the teaching of Aristotle on doing wrong knowingly. This is at first surprising, since Aristotle, as was just mentioned, rejects the Socratic teaching and insists that we do sometimes do wrong knowingly. But Aristotle limits the wrong we knowingly perform to what he called *akrasia*, or incontinent acting, or what we might more freely render as doing wrong out of weakness, as in regretfully yielding to certain powerful urges even while never losing the awareness that it is wrong to yield. Augustine presents his theft as too malicious and too defiant to qualify as akratic behavior, nor does he anywhere mention the note of weakness that belongs to akratic behavior. Furthermore, in acting akratically, the doing of wrong is not the point of our acting; the point is usually to possess some good, and the wrongdoer wishes it were possible to possess the good without doing any wrong. But Augustine stole precisely in order to *"facere contra legem."* Thus we can say: akratic behavior represents one of the more harmless kinds of knowingly doing wrong; there are also darker, more obstinate kinds of it. These were not noticed by Aristotle, but the theft of Augustine forces us to recognize them. But of course the theft of Augustine is a modest piece of malicious wrongdoing, as malicious wrongdoing goes.

The task that results for moral philosophy is to explain how such deliberate wrongdoing is possible. The task would not be so difficult if we

---

1. St. Augustine, *Confessions*, II, 6, 12: "epulatus inde solam iniquitatem, qua laetabar fruens."
2. Ibid., II, 6, 14: "an libuit facere contra legem?" "Potuitne libere quod non licebat, non ob aliud, nisi quia non licebat?"
3. Ibid.: "faciendo inpune quod non liceret tenebrosa omnipotentiae similitudine."

were at liberty to say: the human person can recognize the wrong of some action and perform the action for the very sake of the wrong, as if the will were capable of recognizing the good and willing that, but just as capable of recognizing the bad and willing that. But we are not at liberty to say this because of a thesis about the will that has been rightly maintained by almost everyone within the *philosophia perennis:* the will has for its object the good *(bonum)*, so that it desires whatever it desires under the aspect of good and cannot desire anything under the aspect of bad. The will does not stand indifferently between good and bad, equally open to each; the will belongs to the good, and the good to the will.

And so moral philosophy seems to face a dilemma. The will of the person who does wrong deliberately departs from that which is objectively good. We cannot say that it departs from the good because of an error about the good, for the wrongdoing is a *deliberate* wrongdoing. But we also cannot say that it departs from the good as a result of embracing what is bad under the aspect of it being bad. Neither of these positions is available to us; the first one—the intellectualist position of Socrates—makes the will too dependent on the recognized good, and the second one makes the will too independent of the recognized good. How, then, do we fashion the correct position?

2.

One might object that on closer inspection we can after all discern some fundamental goods that even the rebellious young Augustine was pursuing. This means that it is not really so difficult to verify in him the connection between the will and the good that the *philosophia perennis* has affirmed. This in turn means that the dilemma just mentioned is not so difficult to escape.

The objector will point out that Augustine, though he sometimes says that he stole for the very reason that stealing was forbidden, also mentions certain goods he hoped to share in by doing what was forbidden. He mentions a certain liberty ("mancam libertatem") that he strove for by flouting the moral law with impunity. We saw that he also speaks of a likeness to divine omnipotence ("similitudo omnipotentiae") that made the theft attractive for him. Towards the end of the passage he says that he would have never committed the theft acting alone, implying that he hoped to cement a certain bond with his companions by stealing with them. If the theft of Augustine had no connection at all with these goods of liberty, sovereignty, and solidarity, or no connection with any other such goods, then we would be inclined to say that the theft as described was impossible, that it could have hardly been committed by a human person. Thus the axiom of the will being moved by the good and only by the good is easily verified in the case of Augustine.

In what, then, consists the disorder of Augustine's will? How do we explain this disorder without lapsing back into the Socratic intellectualism? We explain it, according to this point of view, by saying that a person like Augustine prefers lesser goods to greater goods. This is an answer particularly welcome to the defenders of the privation theory of evil, for the answer says that the evil in a will like that of the young Augustine consists in a lack of due order. Even such a will is moved by goods, one says, but the will lacks the ordinate relation to goods that it ought to have.

I proceed to show why we can hardly be satisfied with this answer, which shows only that goods form part of the motive of a morally bad will like that of Augustine but not that they form the whole of it.

Let us return to the freedom that Augustine says he was seeking in his lawless behavior. Now there are various goods for man that go by the name of freedom, and I grant for the sake of argument that some of these goods were confusedly present to Augustine when he decided to steal and that they in part explain his decision to steal. The question I want to put is: how serious is he about these goods? Is there perhaps something else moving his will besides them and even more than they do?

Suppose that we had been able to approach the young Augustine and explain to him that the deepest freedom of which he is capable is based not on lawless but on lawful behavior—that to serve is to reign—that lawless behavior will in the end enslave him to his passions—that he will eventually cry out that he ceased to be the captain of his soul and will admit to the whole world in his *Confessions* that the freedom he has gained by lawless living amounts to a "mancam libertatem," a maimed freedom, which is more servitude than freedom. If Augustine is really serious about freedom, then once he understands the truth of what we tell him, he must renounce his plan to steal the pears and indeed renounce all such lawless action; he must resolve to seek his freedom by living under the moral law instead of flouting it. "He who wills the end wills the means"; if he wills the end of freedom, and now knows what alone leads to that end—or better, now knows in what freedom alone consists—how can he fail to choose this?

And yet it is quite conceivable, given all we know about Augustine's state of mind and soul at age sixteen, that he would have insisted on pursuing lawless freedom, *even though he would not deny anything we had told him, even though he would have no reason to doubt the truth of what we had said about freedom and law.* It does not matter, of course, what Augustine would have really done; the crucial point for our discussion is that a person who at some level of himself knows that there is no real freedom in lawless living, may nevertheless pursue freedom lawlessly. It is not difficult to understand such a person; at times we are ourselves such a person. And at these times we seem to be pursuing something in addition to the good of freedom, something that we want more than this good; for we know what leads us to this good and what leads us away from it, and we still choose the latter. We do not want to forfeit this good simply for the sake of forfeiting it—we have already agreed that this is not a possible way of being motivated—but we forfeit it for the sake of something else, something that has not yet been acknowledged and thematized in the traditional analysis of the morally disordered will.

This "something in addition to the good of freedom" also presses upon our attention if we think of cases where wrongdoing seems to be based on some error. For example, there are those who erroneously see the specter of heteronomy rising from lawful behavior; who think that lawful behavior, and the moral law on which it is based, constitute some kind of foreign principle that can only deprive us of our true freedom. We might say that they err in thinking this, and that their error is the basis for pursuing freedom through lawless living. But surely we cannot stop with assuming some such error; we have to face the question: how is such an error possible? It would seem to be hardly possible at all, for the moral law is not a foreign law but the law of our own being; it is the basis not of heteronomy but of autonomy. How is it possible that something can be taken for the opposite of what it really is? Such an error seems all the more unlikely if one recalls that many plain men and women, and children too, have effortlessly understood (if only in a pre-philosophical way) that our freedom is a finite, created freedom that thrives as freedom only when we respect the moral law. There is no great intellectual problem here at all (something that Kierkegaard understood so profoundly). At issue is a kind of knowledge that unfolds in so interior a way that in a certain sense it can never be forgotten. If a person is really turned to the good, and hence to the good of authentic freedom, he does not have to lose a lot of time puzzling over whether this good is to be attained by lawless or by lawful behavior. If he does puzzle over it, or if he mistakes for heteronomy that lawfulness which is the heart and soul of authentic freedom, then, again, we can only assume *that he is turned to something besides the good and besides goods such as authentic freedom.*

Here is an analogy. Suppose that someone facing a number of job offers is said to be exclusively concerned with salary. And suppose that we wonder whether this is true. If we observe that he takes one of the lower paid positions, or even that he just considers one of them seriously, or that he fails to find out about the highest paid position when he could have easily found out about it, then we know that it is not true that he is concerned only with salary; we know that he must be concerned with other aspects of the job offers. And so with the man who refuses to do the good he recognizes as having a claim on him, or who fails to know the good he could easily come to know: he must be interested in something besides good. Do not say: he desires a lower good that he chooses in place of a good that he recognizes as higher. In saying this you just describe the fact to be explained but you do nothing to explain it. For the question remains: how is it possible for a will, ordered by its nature to good, to choose the lower over the acknowledged higher good? This choice makes no more sense than does the choice of the lower paying job in our example. And so I say that there must be something else besides good that moves the will of the one who prefers the lower to the higher. But how can anything but good move the will?

3.

One could say in response that knowingly choosing the lower over the higher good is after all not a fact that requires us to abandon the ancient teaching on the will and good, and for this reason. One could say that the appeal of a good depends not only on its recognized hierarchical rank, but also on the relation of the good to the present and the future. In other words, a good that can be realized only in the far distant future will have less motivational power than a good of the same value or even of lesser value that can be realized today. For example, the present advantage of using fossil fuels can objectively not compare with the disadvantage of destroying the ozone layer 10,000 years from now, but the fact that the advantage is present whereas the disadvantage is far distant may leave the advantage with the greater motivational power—even for those who acknowledge that, objectively, the disadvantage is far too high a price to pay for the present advantage. One might then say that if the lower good that you knowingly though wrongly prefer to some higher one can be immediately achieved, whereas the higher good can only be brought about much later, the choice is easily understandable without departing in any way from the traditional teaching on the will and the good; it is explainable simply through the fact that the futurity of a good understandably takes the edge off of its appeal for us.

I respond as follows. The futurity of a good may indeed weaken its appeal for me and make understandable how I might be willing to squander it for the sake of getting a lesser good in the present. But this factor of time seems to have no application to the wayward will of the young Augustine, and thus to be only a partial explanation of deliberate wrongdoing. For authentic freedom, based on respect for the moral law, is not a good achievable by Augustine only in the distant future; he could achieve something of it right now by behaving lawfully. This freedom does not come later, long after lawful behavior, like a reward that comes only in the next life; it is the inner resonance of such behavior and is experienced together with the behavior. When then Augustine acts to undermine his own authentic freedom we cannot infer that he really wants this good but is just too impatient to wait for it; for he could have it right now. He does not really want it, for he knowingly chooses that which squanders it. And so our question remains how a will ordered to good could knowingly squander such a present good for the sake of a good that admittedly cannot compare with it.

We can no longer suppress our suspicion that the will of Augustine is moved by something other than good. With this I come to the new proposal made by Dietrich von Hildebrand.[4]

---

4. Dietrich von Hildebrand, *Ethics* (Chicago: Franciscan Herald Press, 1972), chs. 1–3, 30–35. But the most important single chapter is ch. 3.

4.

This neglected philosopher says with the entire *philosophia perennis* that the human person can approach reality asking the question: "What is really good? What has a claim on my service? What merits my love and respect?" Approaching the world in this way the human person grasps many things that are really good for man, or perfective of him, and not only that, but also many things that are intrinsically splendid or worthy, which latter von Hildebrand calls things of value. And the human person not only grasps them, but approaches them in the readiness to share in them, to be made happy by them, and to give them their due. This fundamental attitude of reverence is the way we ought to approach the world; only in this way can we fully become ourselves as persons. However, von Hildebrand continues, we persons can depart from our real vocation as persons and can approach the world differently. We can live in what he calls the attitude of pride and/or concupiscence, approach the world looking for what cools our "unbitted lusts," for what gratifies our vanity and what inflates our pride, and simply ignore all that has no bearing on the satisfaction of our pride and concupiscence.

Now this may not yet sound like any very original contribution. But as soon as one avoids trying to capture the idea in certain traditional categories, it begins to appear in its originality. What one must above all avoid saying is that in the attitude of pride and concupiscence our grasp of *bonum* is distorted in such a way that we are left with a *bonum apparens*. One must avoid this, because von Hildebrand means that the *ratio boni*, the aspect of what is really, objectively good, though still present in the *bonum apparens*, is in fact in this attitude entirely abandoned. *Swollen with pride and itching with concupiscence one finds all kinds of things to be attractive and desirable even though one quite realizes that none of them is really perfective of one's nature or is intrinsically splendid or worthy.* One can, like the dissolute young Augustine, enjoy trampling on law and right, not just because one mistakenly thinks that one will thereby share in some *bonum*, but because one is elated by a sense of absolute sovereignty. Do not say that sharing in such sovereignty is sought as a *bonum*; the person arrogating it to himself will say, and he will mean, that he does not care what is really perfective of his nature or what is intrinsically splendid or worthy; he will admit that he abandons all such concerns in wanting to enjoy the illusion of absolute sovereignty. Of course, such a person must have some understanding, however distorted, of the value or dignity of divine sovereignty; he would not grasp for it as he does if he did not have some such understanding. To that extent his acting still has a connection with *bonum*. But he does not want to give the right response to this *bonum*, as by venerating it, or perfecting himself through sharing in it; he wants to steal it for his own glory. Imagine such a person caring about what perfects his real self and lets him become more truly what he really is! If he cared anything about this he would quickly see that an exclusively divine attribute such as the divine sovereignty cannot possibly belong to the perfection of a creature. He can try to reach for this attribute only because he is driven by something over and above an appetite for apprehended *bonum*—only because his pride makes certain things attractive to him with an attractiveness that falls altogether outside of *bonum*.

C. S. Lewis expressed this alternative to *bonum* when in his admirable little essay, *The Abolition of Man*, he said: "When all that says 'it is good' has been debunked, what says 'I want' remains."[5] The traditional view has been that there is no way to say "I want" apart from something at least apprehended as good; Lewis rightly sees that there is in fact a wanting of which we are capable where the thing wanted does not even have the aspect of good.

But neither Lewis nor von Hildebrand mean that the thing wanted has only the aspect of bad and is wanted as bad. Under what aspect is it then wanted? To understand von Hildebrand's answer we have to get acquainted with his concept of *importance*. He defines importance as that which can move the will or affect the heart of a person. On this definition importance immediately divides into *positive* and *negative* according as a thing attracts or repels a person. In what follows we will limit ourselves to positive importance. Now for von Hildebrand there are two fundamental ways in which a thing can become important; he speaks of two fundamental categories or kinds of importance. There is the importance that being reveals to those who live in the attitude of reverent openness to being: this is the importance of that which is intrinsically worthy and splendid; it includes the importance of that which is really perfective of

---

5. C. S. Lewis, *The Abolition of Man* (New York: Macmillan, 1968), 77–78.

us human beings. But there is also the importance that things take on in relation to the attitude of proud glorification of self and/or concupiscent indulgence of self, which he calls "the importance of the merely subjectively satisfying." Now recall Augustine's statement that he took pleasure in the wrong he did. Von Hildebrand does not think that the doing of wrong was delightful for Augustine under the aspect of being wrong; he thinks that it was delightful under the aspect of being subjectively satisfying for him. The wrongdoing had positive importance for him, but not the positive importance of *bonum*, of the objectively good and worthy, rather it had the positive importance of the merely subjectively satisfying. We acknowledged above that there may have been some elements of *bonum* in the motives of Augustine; but these elements were "supplemented" and distorted by the positive importance relative to his pride and arrogance. His motivation is unintelligible without taking account of this "supplement" and this distortion. It is in this sense that the motivation of the destructive young Augustine included elements of importance falling outside of the *ratio boni*.

I find in a study by Grisez, Boyle, and Finnis, a remarkable acknowledgement of this truth. We read: "Whenever one makes *any choice*, one's will, insofar as it is a rational appetite, must be specified by some intelligible good.... [And] that specifying good either is or is reducible to the instantiation of one or more of the basic human goods" (my italics). This, of course, is the restriction of the will to *bonum* that I have been criticizing. But they continue:

Until we completed the manuscript of this article, we assumed that what is true in many cases is true in all cases. However, as this article is about to appear, we are having a second thought on this point. It may be that the intelligibility which specifies the will in making certain immoral choices merely is to use effective means to satisfy desires, hostile feelings, or other emotions, *whose precise objects are not reducible to any of the basic human goods. If so, the basic human goods are not reasons for such immoral choices, but only serve to rationalize them.*[6] (my italics)

With this they glimpse what von Hildebrand has developed in considerable detail: the turning of the person towards *bonum* is a choice, for there is an alternative; one can hanker after that which agrees with one's pride

---

6. Germain Grisez, Joseph M. Boyle, and John Finnis, "Practical Principles, Moral Truth, and Ultimate Ends," *American Journal of Jurisprudence* (1987), 147–48.

and concupiscence and which lacks any aspect of *bonum* for the one desiring it.

One sees how fruitful this broadened understanding of the object of the will is for our question of how it is possible knowingly to do wrong. Philosophers have shown a chronic temptation to restore some kind of error-theory of wrongdoing. It is well known how Aristotle, though he wanted to break with the Socratic-Platonic teaching that no one knowingly does wrong, ends up practically restoring this teaching in the very passage in which he disputes it (*Nicomachean Ethics*, VII, 1–3). This intellectualist error would seem to be inescapable as long as one thinks that the will responds only to *bonum*. The invaluable distinctions of von Hildebrand enable us to understand how I can recognize an action as good and right and yet take no interest in performing it on the grounds that it offers nothing to my pride and concupiscence. Of particular significance is the fact that the two kinds of positive importance are radically incommensurable;[7] this is why it is possible to choose that which gratifies my pride in the full awareness that I am departing from that which is really good. Von Hildebrand's teaching on the incommensurability of the two kinds of importance also enables us to understand how we can recognize something as wrong and yet be eager to do it; how we may, like Augustine stealing the pears, want to do it because it offers much to our pride and concupiscence. In fact, with his stress on this incommensurability von Hildebrand is enabled to vindicate the very thing that is lost in all the intellectualist theories of wrongdoing: he can do justice to the fact that wrongdoing represents a deficiency not of the intellect but of the will.[8]

Von Hildebrand's new understanding of the objects of the will also

---

7. But not so incommensurable as to prevent us from saying that, when the requirements of the objectively good and worthy conflict with the pull of the merely subjectively satisfying, the former ought to be chosen over the latter.

8. Affirming as we do here the connection between freedom of choice and the incommensurability of the goods chosen, we again converge with a teaching of the Grisez school. But von Hildebrand recognizes this freedom-enabling incommensurability not only at the level at which Grisez has recognized it, namely at the level of the basic human goods that are incommensurable one with another, but also at the more fundamental level at which good in all its forms is incommensurable with the importance of that which gratifies my concupiscence or inflates my pride. Only at this fundamental level does incommensurability throw light on the mystery of deliberate wrongdoing.

enables us to understand how we can fail to apprehend many a good that was within easy reach of our apprehension. It is all too understandable that we should repress the knowledge of many a good whose demands would interfere with the satisfaction of our pride and concupiscence. We end indeed in blindness and error about these goods, but such error in no way explains wrongdoing or renders von Hildebrand's account of the will irrelevant to explaining wrongdoing; just the contrary, it is an error that only his philosophy of the will and its object can explain.

At the same time, we can preserve much that the tradition has wanted to say about the will and the good belonging to each other. We quite agree that the human person cannot will what is bad under the very aspect of it being bad; only if the bad takes on a certain positive importance in relation to our pride and concupiscence does it become a possible object of the will. And we would have no difficulty admitting that the worst will can never break entirely away from any and every element of good—that the worst will always retains some residual connection with some good. We are also ready to recognize that almost all wrongdoing—but not absolutely all of it—is "rationalized" by the wrongdoer, that is, insincerely presented in terms of right and good, to which the wrongdoer thus pays his tribute even when he is not in fact primarily motivated by these. Above all: we entirely affirm with the tradition that persons can live and thrive only by living for the good; though they are free to depart knowingly from the good, they are not free to be happy in thus departing.

5.

At this point one might raise the following serious objection to the proposal of von Hildebrand on deliberate wrongdoing. The objection is epitomized in the saying of Chesterton that a young man knocking at the door of a brothel is really searching for God. The objection can also be stated as a certain interpretation of the youthful Augustine. When Augustine looks back on his morally most dissolute days, one will say, he discerns a restless searching and striving that was in some way aiming at God; at the time of writing the *Confessions* he thinks that in finding God he has found the fulfillment of all that he had been searching for earlier. Since God is the supreme *bonum*, all those things that he sought as a dissolute youth must have been *bona*, otherwise the search for them could not have found its fulfillment in God. This means that I was wrong to claim above that there is something in the motivation of Augustine that lacks the *ratio boni*. It also means that there is no need to depart from the traditional teaching about *bonum* being the object of the will.

I respond, or rather prepare my response, by distinguishing two phases in the spiritual development of Augustine. After his conversion to a life of philosophy at the age of eighteen, under the influence of Cicero's *Hortensius*, Augustine was searching for the truth about God. He himself says of himself as he was at this time, "I had begun that journey upwards by which I was to return to You."[9] And so we can say that what he sought in vain among the Manicheans he finally found in Christianity. When he broke through to Christian faith he reached the fulfillment of all that he had sought in his wanderings as a Manichean. Here the later commitment is rightly taken as the fulfillment of the earlier confused commitments. And we can rightly infer, from the supreme *bonum* that he found as a fulfillment, the fact that the earlier commitments were made under the aspect of *bonum*. But this analysis does not hold for Augustine as he describes himself at the time of the theft of the pears. He could not possibly say of this theft, "I had begun that journey upwards by which I was to return to you." We cannot say that what he sought in destroying his neighbor's property for the fun of destroying it was fulfilled when years later he found the God of Christianity. There is no relation of fulfillment between the youthful recklessness and the later conversion. In fact, the very concept of *conversion* suggests almost the opposite of fulfillment; it suggests reversal, turning around, in contrast to the continuity of fulfillment. Precisely the fact that the importance that moved the young Augustine was incommensurable with the importance that later moved him, precisely the fact that the *ratio boni*, so prominent in his later searching, was missing in his earlier lusts, is well suited to explaining the "break" that went with his conversion.

Perhaps one will try to save this objection by saying that Augustine sought a kind of freedom in committing his theft and that he found a spiritual freedom in Christ. But the sense of freedom is in each case utterly different, so that the incommensurability of importance that the objector is trying to escape recurs here as an incommensurability of freedoms.

---

9. St. Augustine, *op. cit.*, III, 4.

The later Christian freedom can hardly be taken as the fulfillment of the youthful license of Augustine.

It is true that Augustine, like all human persons, was made for *bonum* and for the supreme *bonum* and that he was bound to suffer when he turned away from it and to pay tribute to it in the very act of resisting it. Everyone knows the famous passage in the *Confessions* where Augustine talks about the restlessness that comes from being made for God while living for the world. We can readily discern in the thieving, carousing young Augustine various symptoms of his existing as *capax Dei*. But from these symptoms we cannot infer that the young Augustine sought what he sought under the aspect of God, or of the good that is in God, or sought it with some implicit religious passion. From the fact that the restlessness that he felt in his youth was to some extent taken away as a result of turning to God, we cannot infer that his youthful striving was fulfilled, or completed by turning to God. No, as a wayward boy he sought things in a way that had to be abandoned before he could come to God, he did not seek them in a way that was fulfilled in coming to God.

6.

Let us call attention to the fact that von Hildebrand not only throws new light on the freedom exercised in doing evil, but also on the freedom exercised in doing good. Since the will is not by its very nature tethered to *bonum*, as if it could be drawn to nothing but *bonum*—it has, as we have seen, an alternative to *bonum*—it is not just living out its nature in turning to *bonum*; it is rather the case that a person exercises a fundamental freedom in turning with his will to *bonum*. For St. Thomas and others a person is not praiseworthy for being attracted to things always only under the aspect of *bonum*; for von Hildebrand a person is praiseworthy for this.

There is, then, a certain fundamental freedom in von Hildebrand that has no counterpart in thinkers like St. Thomas. It can be expressed in terms of the two loves of which St. Augustine speaks in *De civitate Dei* (XIV.28): the *amor sui usque ad contemptum Dei* (loving oneself to the point of holding God in contempt) and the *amor Dei usque ad contemptum sui* (loving God to the point of holding oneself in contempt). The most fundamental freedom we can exercise in our moral existence is to choose which of these loves will predominate in ourselves. The reason why this freedom is far more fundamental in von Hildebrand than in St. Thomas is that he differs from St. Thomas on the relation of love to good *(bonum)*. St. Thomas thinks that even the person dominated by self-love is moved by good; this person wills the good of himself in a wildly disordered way, but it is nevertheless a good that he wills. This person differs from the one who is dominated by the love of God in this, that his love of good is disordered whereas the other's love of good is well ordered. Von Hildebrand holds, by contrast, that the person dominated by self-love wills something besides good; to the extent that he lives for the merely subjectively satisfying his will is directed to a positive importance that lacks any aspect of good. If he undergoes a conversion and gives up the *amor sui* and embraces the *amor Dei*, then he turns away from the merely subjectively satisfying and towards good, value, and the truly beneficial. With this he does not just achieve the right order among goods, but he does the more fundamental thing of turning towards them and for the first time letting them be central in his motivation.[10]

7.

Here at the end we ask in what respect von Hildebrand's contribution is a distinctly personalist contribution.

1. As we saw in chapter 5, Wojtyla defines "personalist" in contrast to "cosmological."[11] In the cosmological view of man one looks at man from without, as one being among others; in the personalist view one looks at man from within, as he experiences himself from within himself, and at other beings in relation to man. In the former view man is conceived in the categories of the Aristotelian philosophy of nature, such as matter, form, substance; in the latter view he is conceived in terms of interiority and subjectivity. Of course, Wojtyla thinks that the full truth about man requires both the personalist and the cosmological approach. Now on this

---

10. For a fuller study of the bearing of von Hildebrand's contribution on the thought of St. Thomas see the doctoral dissertation of my student, Jules van Schaijik, "Dietrich von Hildebrand on Deliberate Wrongdoing," International Academy of Philosophy, Principality of Liechtenstein, 2001. Van Schaijik takes St. Thomas as his main interlocutor in his work of unfolding von Hildebrand's contribution.

11. Karol Wojtyla, "Subjectivity and the Irreducible in the Human Being," trans. by Theresa Sandok, *Person and Community: Selected Essays* (New York: Peter Lang, 1993).

understanding of cosmological and personalist, the traditional view criticized by von Hildebrand has some clearly cosmological markings on it. One sees this especially in the way this view is commonly defended. One starts with an observation belonging to the philosophy of nature, namely with an observation about the teleology proper to all living beings: they all naturally incline to achieve the fullness of their being. Man is one of these living beings naturally inclining to the fullness of his being. One tries to capture what is distinctive about man by saying that in him the natural striving for perfection becomes conscious; it is based on knowing and carried out by willing. But because the discussion of human striving is from the beginning cosmologically situated, one assumes that this striving can only be motivated by the perfection of man. Every striving being in nature aims at its own perfection; surely man in his striving aims at his own perfection; the new factors of consciousness, knowledge, deliberation, and choosing surely do not put this end into question but just specify the way in which it is pursued. Since the will is understood from the outset in the light of the natural striving for perfection, it seems almost self-evident that the object of the will, its only possible object, should be perfection, or *bonum*.

But if one sets aside this cosmological framework and begins from within, with the way we experience ourselves being attracted or repelled, one notices that it is entirely possible to want something while remaining indifferent to whether the thing is really beneficial, really excellent, really worthy. One notices that those new factors of consciousness, knowledge, deliberation, and choosing, which announce the person, open the possibility of a new kind of striving, otherwise unknown in nature, a striving detached from any concern with what is really beneficial and good. There is something distinctly personalist about the way von Hildebrand discovers this new kind of striving by exploring the subjectivity of motivation.

2. In the setting of personalist philosophy one commonly works with a contrast between "person" and "nature." For our present purposes I define "nature" as meaning all that is "given" in man, all that is established in him without any cooperation of his freedom, whereas "person" means freedom, it means all that is wrought in man by him acting through himself. Now in this sense of the terms we can say that as we move from the traditional view of the will to von Hildebrand's view of the will and its fundamental freedom, there is a shift in the relation between person and

nature: person increases, nature decreases. More exactly, person takes over a certain work that had traditionally been assigned to nature. For the will was traditionally thought to be tied by nature to *bonum;* the turning to *bonum* was not thought to be an achievement of the person but a given of nature. Thus von Hildebrand, by teaching that it is through our fundamental freedom that we become turned to *bonum* and capable of being motivated by it, claims for person what had traditionally been left to nature. He shows that the freedom of persons had been underestimated; one thought that we human beings were being borne along by nature where in fact we are challenged to the most fundamental choosing of which we are capable. He awakens us from our cosmological slumber.

3. Personalist philosophy aims at doing full justice to the freedom of persons. This freedom can be obscured by the way in which one relates person and nature, as we just saw. But it can also be obscured by a certain intellectualism, by which I mean any philosophy that overrates the knowledge of good, to the detriment of our freedom in choosing the good, or overrates error in explaining moral evil. As long as one thinks that the will has *bonum* for its only possible object, one cannot escape intellectualism of some kind or other, as we have already remarked. Philosophers will continue to go the way of Aristotle, who unwittingly restores ethical intellectualism in the very passage (*Nicomachean Ethics*, VII, 1–3) in which he wants to combat it. One will be inescapably driven to make too much of error in explaining moral evil; deliberate wrongdoing will remain a scandal for moral philosophy. Only von Hildebrand's idea of incommensurably different kinds of importance, of which *bonum* is only one, will let us make sense of the persons who, as St. Paul says of himself *(Romans, 7)*, do the evil that they know they should not do. Or let us say it like this: no one can overcome the ethical intellectualism of Plato and vindicate the moral freedom of persons in as theoretically satisfying a way as von Hildebrand can.

APPENDIX. *On the Platonic Intellectualism*

I said in this paper that attempts at understanding the fundamental freedom of persons have from the beginning of Western philosophy been blocked by a certain intellectualism, according to which we can depart from the good only by mistaking what is bad for some good. I propose in this appendix to study this intellectualism as it exists in Plato and as it stands in relation to my claims about the fundamental freedom of persons.

In *Republic* VII Plato speaks of a "conversion" of a man to the world of eternal being and to the Idea of the Good. Those in the darkness of the cave need to turn to the light, and this turning is a conversion. But whereas for our ears conversion includes a distinct moral component, a turning of the will, as we see it for instance in the final conversion of St. Augustine (*Confessions*, VII), the Platonic conversion is an almost exclusively intellectual turning. The intellect has to turn from becoming to being, from shadows to reality; it is in this way, through knowledge, that a man comes to be purified in his soul and attuned to the supreme reality of the Ideas. Thus Reale speaks here of a Platonic intellectualism;[12] the soul is purified when the intellect is turned to its proper object, that is, to eternal being. Plato does not seem to acknowledge, even implicitly, any distinct task of freedom in converting to eternal being, no collaboration of intellect and what we call free will, but the turning is almost exclusively a turning of the intellect to its natural object.

Now I propose to examine here a particular aspect of this intellectualism: I mean the thesis, at once Socratic and Platonic, that no one knowingly does wrong, that a wrongdoer always acts in ignorance of the wrong that he does and of the moral harm that he inflicts on himself, and that whoever knows what is right, unfailingly does the right that he knows. This thesis, or cluster of theses, can be found throughout the dialogues, from early ones such as the *Gorgias* and the *Protagoras*, through the latest ones, including the *Timaeus* and the *Laws*.

---

* First published under the title, "Does Plato in *Republic* IV Surpass His Intellectualism?" in Reale and Scolnicov (eds.), *New Images of Plato* (Sankt Augustin: Academia Verlag, 2002), 347–55. The text as first published here has been slightly enlarged for the purpose of serving as an appendix to my paper on fundamental freedom.

12. Reale, *Plato and Aristotle* (Albany: State University of New York, 1990), 166–67.

1.

It is a hard saying, which finds few defenders. It seems obvious to most of us that we often enough knowingly do wrong. We have only to recall the account that St. Augustine gives us in the *Confessions* II of his youthful theft of his neighbor's pears; he makes it abundantly clear that he knew the wrong he was doing even as he did it, taking particular delight, as we saw, in the wrongness of his theft. We understand St. Augustine, we can identify with him; we sometimes act just as maliciously. And surely St. Paul speaks for all of us when he says: "The good that I will to do, I do not do; but the evil I will not to do, that I practice" (*Romans*, 7:15). We understand him perfectly when he refers his bad behavior not to a darkened intellect but to a wayward will. How could Plato have denied the possibility of what St. Augustine and St. Paul relate of themselves and of what we know in ourselves?

Let us begin by trying to retrieve certain elements of truth in this intellectualist teaching of Plato. And first of all it is true that we have to know the good that we do and cannot do the good in the absence of any knowledge of it. But this is only to say that some knowledge of the good is a *necessary* condition for doing good; it is not to say with Plato that knowledge of the good is a *sufficient* condition for doing it.

Secondly, it is perhaps true that there is a knowledge of the good that is so intimately lived that we cannot possibly fail to do the good that we know. In other words, if our knowledge of the good has certain perfections, if we do not just know abstractly about it but concretely feel it in all its dignity, then our knowledge may well become a sufficient condition for doing the good that we know. The phenomenologist Max Scheler was so taken by the power of *such* moral knowledge to determine the will, that he spoke of a "Restitution des sokratischen Satzes."[13] But Scheler knew that this was only a partial reinstatement of the Socratic/Platonic teaching, for neither Socrates nor Plato had limited and qualified the knowledge that determines the will, nor had they contrasted it with other, more abstract knowledge of the good that fails to determine the will.

Moreover, the limited concession made here to the Socratic/Platonic teaching is further reduced by considering just why we unfailingly act in accordance with a certain kind of intimate knowledge. It would not be

---

13. Scheler, *Der Formalismus in der Ethik und die materiale Wertethik* (Bern: Francke Verlag, 1966), 87–88. Von Hildebrand follows Scheler in his interpretation of Socrates: *Die Idee der sittlichen Handlung* (Darmstadt: Wissenschaftliche Buchgesellschaft, 1969), 83–85.

Appendix: On the Platonic Intellectualism 213

quite right to say that this intimate knowledge irresistibly determines the will. Such knowledge is not the whole reason for the unfailing adherence of the will to the good known. It seems rather to be the case that a person must first be deeply committed to the good before it can fully show its face to him. When then a person unfailingly does the good that he knows in this intimate way, his unfailing adherence to the good comes in part from the commitment that he brings to the good. It is not only the attractive power of the good intimately revealed to him but also his prior commitment to this good, that determines the unfailing adherence of his will. This adherence is, then, not so purely intellectual an activity as Plato thinks. It follows that the second element of truth that we here acknowledge in the Socratic/Platonic thesis is far from letting us declare the thesis to be simply true.

Perhaps we can distinguish a third element of truth connected with the thesis. There is indeed some connection between wrongdoing and ignorance of the good, and to that extent the thesis has some basis in reality. We human beings have a tendency to push out of consciousness our knowledge of good whenever we act against it. We cannot bear to face the truth about good when we act against it. Perhaps this third element of truth follows from the second. We repress our moral knowledge, or at least render it as abstract as possible, because we know that, if it remains in us at full strength, we will hardly be able to act against it.

But this element of truth by no means suffices to make the whole Socratic/Platonic teaching true. For according to that teaching, ignorance of the good is a *cause* of a wayward will, whereas here we are saying that ignorance of the good is a *result* of a wayward will.

It seems, then, that however we try to look for elements of truth in and around the famous thesis of Plato, in the end we just cannot make it entirely our own. Whether we look at the way in which morally good action presupposes knowledge of the good, or at the particularly perfect kind of knowledge of the good from which we cannot depart in our acting, or at the way in which the lawless will wants to be ignorant, we are still left wondering how the incomparably wise Plato could have really thought that no one knowingly does wrong.

2.

I want now to look more closely at the way Plato presents this teaching of his in the *Protagoras*. Then I will look at his teaching in *Republic* IV on the soul and its three levels, and argue that he is here on the threshold of breaking out of his intellectualist doctrine. In other words I will try to employ Plato in order to surpass Plato.

But before turning to these two dialogues, I want to point out one passage—certainly not the only passage—in which Plato seems clearly to acknowledge deliberate wrongdoing as a fact. Unfortunately he does not let this fact challenge his theory, but the acknowledgment is significant. I refer to the passage at the end of the *Symposium* where the drunken Alcibiades expresses his profound veneration of Socrates. He says that the teaching of Socrates, when he hears it again, comes to him like some mystic music and cuts him to the quick, convicting him of leading a disordered life. Alcibiades says, "He makes me admit that while I'm spending my time on politics I am neglecting all the things that are crying for attention in myself" (216 a; translation by Michael Joyce). Alcibiades does not just mean that Socrates shows him that his *past* involvement in politics led him to neglect the much greater good of his soul. If this is all Alcibiades meant, then Plato could always say that Alcibiades was ignorant of these greater goods at the time he neglected them. But it is clear from the whole speech of Alcibiades that he knows right now, even as he speaks, that Socrates is right and that he should be tending to the good of his soul, and it is clear that he has no intention of giving up politics and tending to his soul. He does not choose the good that he acknowledges; he turns away from it even as he acknowledges it. Socrates has so great a power of convincing him of the good he ought to pursue that he cannot fail to continue to know in some way of this good even when he betrays it in his action. When, then, Alcibiades committed shameful deeds in Athens, he was not acting in the ignorance required by the Platonic teaching; he had fallen too deeply under the influence of Socrates ever to act again in such ignorance. If Plato had made room on the level of his philosophy for the deliberate wrongdoing that he acknowledges in Alcibiades, then, so it seems to me, he would have had to abandon his thesis that no one knowingly does wrong.

It should be admitted that some of the truth connected with the Platonic teaching is also expressed in this Alcibiades passage. Consider this:

there's no getting away from it, I know I ought to do the things he tells me to and yet the moment I'm out of his sight I don't care what I do to keep in with the mob. So I dash off like a runaway slave, and keep out of his way as long as I can, and then next time I meet him I remember all that I had to admit the time before, and naturally I feel ashamed. (216 b)

Appendix: On the Platonic Intellectualism

Alcibiades seems to say that if he were to let the teaching of Socrates about the goods of one's soul make its full impression on him, he would not be able to continue his dissolute life but would have to convert to the way of Socrates. Here we see the second and third elements of truth in the Platonic teaching that we discussed above. There is a certain intuitive fullness of moral knowledge that Alcibiades would not be able to act against and that he represses. Of course, the question for Plato remains: if Alcibiades knows that Socrates teaches the truth about good, and if he flees from Socrates for this very reason, is he not in some significant sense knowingly opposing the good?

3.

It is now time to carry out our plan to turn to the *Protagoras* for a closer look at the way Socrates defends this thesis about deliberate wrongdoing. I choose this dialogue, because Plato deals here more than anywhere else with a view directly opposed to his own, namely with the view that the craving for pleasure can lead us to act against the good that we acknowledge as good.

Every student of the *Protagoras* puzzles over the fact that Plato here assumes an entirely uncharacteristic hedonism for the sake of establishing his thesis that no one knowingly does wrong. Perhaps, as A. E. Taylor suggests, he is simply assuming the hedonistic point of view because he thinks that it is held by the many who also say that the love of pleasure leads us knowingly to do wrong. If these many equate good with pleasurable, and if Socrates wants to dispute their claim that one can knowingly do wrong, he would understandably want to make the *ad hominem* argument that their hedonism in fact implies that one can do wrong only by making a mistake. In any case, it seems to me that Socrates makes just this *ad hominem* argument very convincingly. The craving for pleasure cannot betray you into knowingly acting against some higher good, he says, because from the point of view of hedonism there is no good higher than pleasure. The higher good that you ought to have respected is also a pleasurable good. To call it higher is simply to say that its pleasure-index is greater than the good you chose. But it is not possible from a hedonist perspective knowingly to destroy the more pleasurable good for the sake of getting the less pleasurable one. Whoever sacrifices the more to the less in this irrational way can only be the victim of an error. The only criticism we can make of his action is that it contains some error. If only he knew where the greater pleasurable good lay, he would unfailingly choose it. This Platonic intellectualist conclusion certainly follows necessarily from the hedonistic point of departure.

Let us consider how this hedonism might be modified so that it would no longer lend support to this Platonic conclusion. Suppose that some pleasures were fundamentally different in kind from others; suppose, for example, that the pleasures experienced when one is spiritually awakened were so different in kind from the pleasures experienced when one lives in the body, as to be incommensurable with them. We might still say that the spiritual pleasures rank higher, and always have the stronger claim on us in the event of a conflict between them and bodily pleasures, but they would not be related to the bodily pleasures in the sense of a quantitative more. Given this incommensurability of pleasures it becomes somewhat understandable that one could live so immersed in the body that, though one knew some bodily pleasure was not the right pleasure to choose, one nevertheless chose it. Plato may have been aware of this way of explaining why people can knowingly do wrong, for he eliminates all such incommensurability of pleasures from the hedonism that he takes as implying his intellectualist teaching on wrongdoing. He speaks in that passage at the end of the *Protagoras* of our need for some "metric" of pleasure and pain, some rule for quantifying particular pleasures and pains and then determining in a given situation whether on balance pleasure or pain predominates, and by how much. In the frame of this quantitative, arithmetical hedonism, Plato's conclusion about the impossibility of knowingly doing wrong seems to be secure.

From this we can learn something about what it will take to overcome this Platonic teaching. One must first get beyond a univocal understanding of the good that allows only a quantitative more and less of good; one has to make sense of goods that are fundamentally incommensurable with each other. Since we are trying to overcome Plato by means of Plato, let us look in the dialogues for this incommensurability of good. I think that we can find it in *Republic* IV.

4.

Consider the passage where Plato distinguishes three levels in the human soul, and especially the part of that passage where he shows that there are indeed three and not just two or one. Here is the way he distinguishes the rational from the appetitive part of the soul:

Then if anything draws it [the soul] back when thirsty, that must be something different in it from that which thirsts and drives it like a beast to drink. For it

Appendix: On the Platonic Intellectualism

cannot be, we say, that the same thing with the same part of itself at the same time acts in opposite ways about the same thing. (439 b; translation by Paul Shorey)

The same drink of water that seems attractive to my appetitive nature may not meet the approval of my reason; I may, for example, be fasting for religious reasons and so refuse to drink, though I am very thirsty. This conflict indicates to Plato that my appetitive nature is distinct from my rational nature, and in fact that they represent two different levels of the soul. Note well that Plato does not mean that the rational power of the soul is just an instrument for maximizing the satisfaction of the appetitive, as if the conflict of which he here speaks were merely the conflict between prudently calculated long-term appetitive satisfaction, for which the deliberation of reason is necessary, and short-sighted instant appetitive satisfaction, which requires no such use of reason. If this were all he meant, then he would have reverted back to the position of the *Protagoras*. He rather means that *a new order of goods and evils presents itself to reason and that it is incommensurable with the order of goods and evils presenting itself to our appetitive nature.*

See what follows for our question. Here we have the incommensurable goods we are looking for, deriving from incommensurable levels in the soul. The difference between these goods is not just a difference in quantitative degree, any more than the difference between the appetitive and the rational levels in the soul is a difference in quantitative degree. It now becomes clear that though in a given situation I am aware of the judgment of reason concerning the drink of water, I may insist on living in my appetitive nature, of remaining in the appetitive point of view. In this case I may drink the water even as I am conscious of the prohibition issued by my reason: and so I knowingly do wrong.

While Plato does not draw this conclusion, he lays the foundation for it. He advances here beyond the concept of good presupposed at the end of the *Protagoras*, namely beyond an undifferentiated pleasure. Now the soul has different levels and, corresponding to the point of view of each, incommensurably different pleasures. Incommensurable aspects of good can now be found in one and the same thing. Having reached this point Plato seems to be not far from understanding that we may be well aware of the good that has a rational claim on us even while we cling to the appetitive point of view and pursue some appetitive good at the expense of fulfilling that claim.[14]

14. Christopher Rowe, the translator and student of Plato, told me once in conversation that in his opinion Plato here in *Republic* IV in fact completely abandons his teach-

5.

But for all the progress made in *Republic* IV towards a principled understanding of deliberate wrongdoing, there is still something in the thought of Plato in the *Republic* that interferes with this progress. The differences between the levels or parts of the soul are so strongly stressed by Plato that the unity of the soul, or the oneness of the soul that has these levels, tends to get neglected. It is not always clear whether a human soul is in the end one or three. The analogy that Plato draws between the three parts of the soul and the three classes of society encourages this neglect. The image of the soul that appears at the end of IX (588 b to 589 b) encourages this neglect even more. One will recall that Plato represents the soul as a many-headed creature that has the head of a man and the head of a lion along with the heads of the many tame and wild beasts. The head of the man represents the rational part of the soul, the head of the lion the spirited part, and the many heads of the beasts the appetitive part. Just as it is not clear how many animals there are in this creature, so it is not clear how many souls there are in a human soul. That a human soul is really one soul is just as unclear as that this creature is really one animal.

The problem for a theory of wrongdoing is this. Let us suppose that reason and appetite conflict with each other in myself and that reason yields to appetite. If I identify myself with reason and if the appetite that diverts me from reason is felt to come from outside of me, then the yielding to appetite has to be described as a kind of interference with the exercise of my reason. In this case my falling away from reason can hardly be called an act of wrongdoing. It would be more a matter of suffering injustice than of committing it, to speak Platonically. If I am going to be able to do wrong, then the I that makes a judgment of reason must be identical with the I that feels the pull of an appetite. It must be one and the same person who thinks rationally and desires appetitively. It must be a question of one person morally torn between different levels within himself and not a question of two souls one of which interferes with the other.

But once we see this deficiency in Plato, we can set about repairing it. We can affirm, more forcefully than he ever did, the unity of one person that underlies the multiplicity of rational, spirited, and appetitive levels of the soul.

---

ing that no one knowingly does wrong. Rowe thinks that only the early Plato held this Socratic teaching but that by the time of the *Republic* he had abandoned it. I hope Rowe is right, for then the criticism that I have been venturing to make of Plato by means of Plato, exists in fact already in Plato himself as self-criticism.

Appendix: On the Platonic Intellectualism

See what then follows from our analysis for the problem of intellectualism. When Alcibiades lives out of his rational soul, he understands that he ought to care for nothing so much as for his growth in justice; but when the same Alcibiades lives out of a lower level in himself, he cares above all for the glamour and power of political life. The existence of these fundamentally different points of view in the same person opens up a task of freedom for Alcibiades that went unnoticed in the Platonic intellectualism. Alcibiades can choose the level in his soul at which he will dwell. The demands of reason do not unfailingly determine his will; they determine it only to the extent that he wills to live from the point of view of reason. But he can depart from this point of view, abandoning himself to an appetitive point of view. Then the demands of reason, while still in some way known to Alcibiades, lose their power over him, and he lives instead for appetitive goods. When he does wrong by violating the demands of reason, he does so not because of simple ignorance of these demands, but because he has consciously turned away from them. He cannot quite forget them even when he violates them.

And though Plato never arrived at this teaching, we can arrive there by poring over his inexhaustibly rich writings, learning from his mistakes and developing his insights.

6.

Though we can find much more in the *Republic* than might have been expected for the problem of deliberate wrongdoing, we can by no means find all that we need, and there is one respect in which we have to go completely beyond Plato. As I have tried to show in my paper on fundamental freedom, we have to acknowledge in ourselves an antagonism to reason that cannot be identified with the appetitive level of the soul intruding upon the rational level. I am thinking of the two loves of St. Augustine, the *amor sui usque ad contemptum Dei* and the *amor Dei usque ad contemptum sui*. If a person chooses to live by the first love and to reject the second, he is not necessarily yielding to bodily appetites. A disembodied spirit who knows no such thing as bodily appetite could conceivably face this fundamental choice of ultimate loves. In fact, Christians believe of devils that their choice of the *amor sui* over the *amor Dei* had nothing to do with yielding to bodily appetites, just as they believe of angels that their choice of the *amor Dei* over the *amor sui* had nothing to do with the mastering of bodily appetites. One might respond that at least in us human beings the *amor sui* always takes the form of choosing bodily gratification over the goods of a higher kind of love. But this is at odds with the experience we have of ourselves. While there is indeed the moral disorder known as concupiscence, which we really can characterize as giving ourselves over to bodily gratification, there is also the deeper and darker thing in us that is known by such names as pride, arrogance, playing God, and this moral disorder does not in the first place result from the intrusion of our appetitive nature into our life of reason. And so we can say that even within the rational principle itself we find in man an incommensurability of loves and of goods that makes deliberate wrongdoing understandable. Thanks to this incommensurability we can will to live by the *amor sui* even in the awareness that the *amor Dei* is the only right way to live. We do not have to set the rational principle at odds with an appetitive principle in order to find such incommensurability.

As I say, this further step in the analysis of the possibility of deliberate wrongdoing takes us entirely beyond Plato, who thinks that the whole source of moral disorder in our acting is the body intruding with its appetites and cravings; he thinks that once liberated from the body the soul will effortlessly turn towards the good. The idea that there is some brokenness *in the rational soul itself* that impedes the turn towards the good, is foreign to Plato; it is an idea proposed to the human mind for the first time by Christianity.

By the way, many of Plato's descriptions of reprobate people (like Alcibiades) and of reprobate types of people (as in *Republic* IX) "contain" the distinction between pride and concupiscence, that is, it would not be difficult to show that the moral evil masterfully portrayed by Plato in these descriptions is in fact irreducible to concupiscence, is a more "spiritual" evil than Plato's anthropology allows, and requires, if full theoretical justice is to be done to the pride and arrogance present in these descriptions, that we acknowledge, in addition to Plato's distinction between rational and appetitive levels of the soul, also some distinction of levels (or points of view) *within* the rational soul. So even here, where we surpass Plato entirely, it will be possible to make some use of Plato.

In any case, I have tried to draw these distinctions in the paper to which this appendix is attached, and so to deal with the intellectualism that we inherit from Plato, and to vindicate the freedom of persons that is obscured by the intellectualism.[15]

15. Many thanks to Christopher Rowe, Jonathan Sanford, and Fulvio di Blasi for their helpful reactions to earlier versions of this paper on Plato.

CHAPTER 10

John Henry Newman on Personal Influence

In the course of explaining the origins of the Oxford Movement in his *Apologia Pro Vita Sua* (1864), John Henry Newman (1801–90) complains of his friend, Palmer, an ally in the Oxford Movement:

> ... nor had he any insight into the force of personal influence and congeniality of thought in carrying out a religious theory... [For Palmer the] *beau ideal* in ecclesiastical action was a board of safe, sound, sensible men.... I, on the other hand, had out of my own head begun the Tracts; and these, as representing the antagonist principle of personality, were looked upon by Mr. Palmer's friends with considerable alarm.[1]

We cannot even begin to understand Newman and to receive his rich legacy if we do not understand his "principle of personality" and in particular his teaching on personal influence. It has been well said that Newman "stands at the threshold of the new age as a Christian Socrates, the pioneer of a new philosophy of the Individual Person and Personal Life."[2]

1.

In an early sermon, "Personal Influence, the Means of Propagating the Truth," Newman asks how revealed truth has made its way and held its

---

* This paper was first published under the title "Newman on the Personal" in *First Things* no. 125 (August/September 2002), 43–49. It has been somewhat expanded.

1. John Henry Newman, *Apologia Pro Vita Sua* (New York: America Press, 1942), 65.
2. Edward Sillem, *The Philosophical Notebook*, I (Louvain: Nauwelaerts Publishing House, 1969), 250.

ground in the world. He answers that it has certainly not been by rational arguments, and in fact he goes surprisingly far in granting the advantages that unbelievers have over believers on the level of "garrulous Reason." Then he gives what he takes to be the true answer: revelation "has been upheld in the world not as a system, not by books, not by arguments, nor by temporal power, but by the personal influence of such men as have already been described, who are at once the teachers and the patterns of it."[3] And he explains: "Men persuade themselves, with little difficulty, to scoff at principles, to ridicule books, to make sport of the names of good men; but they cannot bear their presence: it is holiness embodied in personal form which they cannot steadily confront and bear down."[4]

Years later he had occasion to apply this idea in a particular historical moment. It was 1850, and Newman was dealing with an outburst of anti-Catholic agitation set off by the act of Pope Pius IX restoring the Catholic hierarchy in England. In one lecture Newman was discussing with a Catholic audience in Birmingham the many absurd stereotypes that controlled the thinking of English Protestants about Catholics, and was advising his fellow Catholics on how to deal with these stereotypes. Citing his earlier sermon he distinguished between "metropolitan opinion" about Catholics, centered in London, and "local opinion" about Catholics, centered in the neighborhoods where they live. He admonished his listeners to forget about the former, and give great care about the latter.

> You cannot make an impression on such an ocean of units; it [metropolitan opinion] has no disposition, no connexion of parts. The great instrument of propagating moral truth is personal knowledge. A man finds himself in a definite place; he grows up in it and into it; he draws persons around him; they know him, he knows them; thus it is that ideas are born which are to live, that works begin which are to last. It is this personal knowledge of each other which is true public opinion; local opinion is real public opinion; but there is not, there cannot be, such in London.[5]

There immediately follows in this lecture a piece of vintage Newmanian satire. He imagines the division of mind that is bound to arise in Pro-

---

3. John Henry Newman, *Oxford University Sermons* (Westminster, MD: Christian Classics, 1966), 91–92.
4. Ibid., 92.
5. John Henry Newman, *The Present Position of Catholics in England* (London: Longmans, Green, and Co., 1908), 381.

testants who have become personally acquainted with individual Catholics but who have not yet given up their anti-Catholic stereotypes.

... the Birmingham people will say, "Catholics are, doubtless, an infamous set, and not to be trusted, for the *Times* says so, and Exeter Hall, and the Prime Minister, and the Bishops of the Establishment; and such good authorities cannot be wrong; but somehow an exception must certainly be made for the Catholics of Birmingham.... Priests in general are perfect monsters; but here they are certainly unblemished in their lives, and take great pains with their people. Bishops are tyrants, and, as Maria Monk says, cut-throats, always excepting the Bishop of Birmingham, who affects no state or pomp, is simple and unassuming, and always in his work."[6]

Newman takes his satire to another level when he proceeds to imagine what the Protestants of Manchester will say:

"Oh, certainly, Popery is horrible, and must be kept down. Still, let us give the devil his due, they are a remarkably excellent body of men here, and we will take care no one does them any harm. It is very different at Birmingham; there they have a Bishop, and that makes all the difference; he is a Wolsey all over; and the priests, too, in Birmingham are at least one in twelve infidels. We do not recollect who ascertained this, but...."[7]

Of course, Newman hopes that the personal influence exercised by Catholics will eliminate this comical situation by destroying altogether the Protestant stereotypes; then the dividedness of the Protestant mind would give way to an understanding of Catholicism based entirely on the personal influence of individual Catholics.

Newman himself exercised powerfully the personal influence of which he speaks. He did more than anyone in England in his time to dismantle Protestant prejudices by the force of his own personal influence. At his death in 1890 the *Times* of London said, speaking in the vein in which so many Protestant voices spoke at the death of Newman, "Of one thing we may be sure, that the memory of his pure and noble life, untouched by worldliness, unsoured by any trace of fanaticism, will endure, and that whether Rome canonizes him or not he will be canonized in the thoughts of pious people of many creeds in England."[8] The writer of these lines is

6. Ibid., 387.
7. Ibid.
8. Quoted by Philip Boyce, O.C.D., in "Newman as Seen by His Contemporaries at the Time of His Death," in Strolz and Binder (eds.), *John Henry Newman: Lover of Truth* (Rome: Urbaniana University Press, 1991), 113.

remembering not Newman's arguments, not his accomplishments, not the things he founded, but rather the purity of his personality, which is the main thing that undermines the writer's anti-Catholic prejudices. One might object that the *Times* was expressing not local opinion but metropolitan opinion. But when the one exercising personal influence is a personality of Newman's proportions, metropolitan opinion and local opinion coincide; Newman's neighborhood had become the whole nation.

2.

Newman's writings on education show us another aspect of his teaching on personal influence. They also show us personal influence as it exists among friends and not, as above, as it overcomes enemies. I quote here from a paper called "What is a University?" which Newman published in the *University Gazette*, a paper he founded in the course of setting up his Catholic university in Dublin in the early 1850s. Newman begins by discussing the *litera scripta*, or written word, which has become available in his time, he says, in an unheard-of abundance. He acknowledges that "the inestimable benefit of the *litera scripta* is that of being a record of truth, and an authority of appeal and an instrument of teaching in the hands of a teacher." And then he continues, "but . . . if we wish to become exact and fully furnished in any branch of knowledge which is diversified and complicated, we must consult the living man and listen to his living voice." He says that people really serious about education "avail themselves . . . of the rival method [rival to reading the printed word], the ancient method, of oral instruction, of present communication between man and man . . . of the personal influence of a master, and the humble initiation of a disciple."[9]

In fact, real education is possible without the support of books at all. In his paper, "Athens," Newman says, "I doubt whether Athens had a library till the reign of Hadrian. It was what the student gazed on, what he heard, what he caught by the magic of sympathy, not what he read, which was the education furnished by Athens."[10]

9. John Henry Newman, *Historical Sketches* III (London: Longman, Green, and Co., 1903), 8.
10. Ibid., 40.

Newman on Personal Influence

Newman asks why it is that this ancient method of oral instruction plays so large a role in all real education, and he answers tentatively:

... perhaps we may suggest, that no books can get through the number of minute questions which it is possible to ask on any extended subject, or can hit upon the very difficulties which are severally felt by each reader in succession. Or again, that no book can convey the special spirit and delicate peculiarities of its subject with that rapidity and certainty which attend on the sympathy of mind with mind, through the eyes, the look, the accent, and the manner, in casual expressions thrown off at the moment, and the unstudied turns of familiar conversation.[11]

This coheres entirely with Newman's teaching in the *Grammar of Assent*, where he says that in our reasonings in concrete matters our minds work with far more strands of thought than can be formulated in propositions. He goes so far as to say that the most exact propositions we can formulate are little more than specimens or symbols of the innumerable reasonings that coalesce in our minds and incline them in the direction of some conclusion. Thus the inner life of a mind is vastly richer than all that can be rendered in propositions. In the passage just quoted Newman seems to suggest that much of this inner richness, though it escapes propositional formulation, can be expressed in non-propositional ways—"through the eyes, the look, the accent, and the manner." Here, then, is something that the living teacher can bring to education: a medium for expressing thought that is more subtle and more versatile than the *litera scripta*.

We might think that when Newman comes to religious education, he would make more of the *litera scripta*, which for him is nothing less than the Bible. But consider what he says of religious education:

its great instrument, or rather organ, has ever been that which nature prescribes in all education, the personal presence of a teacher, or, in theological language, Oral Tradition. It is the living voice, the breathing form, the expressive countenance, which preaches, which catechises. Truth, a subtle, invisible, manifold spirit, is poured into the mind of the scholar by his eyes and ears, through his affections, imagination, and reason ... by propounding and repeating it, by questioning and re-questioning, by correcting and explaining, by progressing and then recurring to first principles. . . .[12]

11. Ibid., 8–9.
12. Ibid., 14–15.

This is said by someone who lived deeply immersed in the scriptures and whose sermons are full of deep and original meditations on scripture.

Newman contrasts his ideal of personal influence, not only with the written word and the reading of books, but also with the organization and juridical structure of a university. In another paper in his *Gazette*, "Discipline and Influence," he constructs a dialogue with a critic who says, "I cannot help thinking that your *Gazette* makes more of *persons* than is just, and does not lay stress enough upon order, system, and rule, in conducting a University."[13] In response Newman acknowledges that order, system, and rule are indeed indispensable for the *integrity* of a university, but he says that teaching and learning by way of personal influence constitute the *essence* of the life of a university, and in this way he asserts the primacy of personal influence. "I say, then, that the personal influence of the teacher is able in some sort to dispense with an academical system, but that the system cannot in any sort dispense with personal influence. With influence there is life, without it there is none."[14]

Some years ago I became embroiled in a debate at my university about a proposal to offer university degrees by means of "distance education." Courses were to be put on audiotape, and some limited email contact between teacher and student was envisioned. It was only when I went back to these papers of Newman that I realized why I was so strenuously opposed to it. Distance education in the form proposed would largely block the flow of personal influence. The living presence of a teacher as well as the interpersonal medium constituted by a community of learners would be filtered out; little more than information would pass from the teacher to the student through the audiotapes. The electronically facilitated transmission of information is not education, at least not in the same sense in which teaching and learning on the basis of personal influence is education; it can never enable influence to flow between persons as it does when teachers and learners see each other in the flesh and live in community with each other. Newman would have deplored the proposal on the grounds that it makes for de-personalized, disembodied education.

---

13. Ibid., 70.
14. Ibid., 74.

3.

After being received into the Catholic Church in 1845 Newman surveyed the various religious communities in the Church, looking for the one in which he would be at home. He eventually joined the Oratory of St. Philip Neri, and in fact brought the Oratory to England for the first time. In talks given to his brother Oratorians Newman tried to articulate the genius of religious community as lived in the spirit of St. Philip. In one of these Newman goes back to the funeral oration of Pericles, as reported in Thucydides, and in particular to the famous passage in which Pericles contrasts the Athenian and the Spartan. Newman wants to say that the genius of Athens, once it is baptized and made the principle of a religious community, yields the spirit of the Oratory. "The point of the Orator's [Pericles'] praise of the Athenians is this, that they, unlike the Spartans, have no need of laws, but perform from the force of inward character those great actions which others do from compulsion. Here the Oratorian stands for the Athenian, and the Spartan for the Jesuit."[15]

This means for Newman that in the Oratory, as in Athens, personal influence has a natural home. "Obedience to the official Superior is the prominent principle of the Jesuit; personal influence is that of the Oratorian."[16] And again: "Jesuit Fathers are part of a whole, but each Oratorian stands by himself and is a whole, promoting and effecting by his own proper acts the well-being of the community."[17] Newman explains what he means by "his own proper acts": "It is the common sense, the delicacy, the sharp observation, the tact of each which keeps the whole in harmony. It is a living principle, call it (in human language) judgment or wisdom or discretion or sense of propriety or moral perception, which takes the place of formal enactment"[18] and of commands and prohibitions. Newman returns here again to the contrast with the Jesuit, who is of course deliberately made into a stereotype for the sake of sharpening the contrast: "An Oratorian as I have said is in a great measure a law to himself, and is almost the reverse of a regular, for instance a Jesuit."[19]

15. Placid Murray, O.S.B. (ed), *Newman the Oratorian: His Unpublished Oratory Papers* (Dublin: Gill and Macmillan Ltd., 1969), 210.
16. Ibid., 211–12.
17. Ibid., 210.
18. Ibid., 208.
19. Ibid.

We find everywhere in Newman this aversion to the Spartan spirit, as found in those who slavishly follow and apply rules that remain external to them, and everywhere this admiration for the Athenian spirit, as found in those who have so internalized rules and laws as to be eminently free in living by them and imaginative and resourceful in connecting them with concrete situations. These latter are alive as persons, they engage others as persons, they give and receive personal influence, while the former act in a passive and mechanical way.

4.

In his great work in religious epistemology, *The Grammar of Assent*, Newman contrasts (above all in ch. 8, sections 1 and 2) formal inference, as found in a demonstration in geometry, with informal inference, as found in discerning the upshot of a complex body of concrete evidence. As an example of the latter he mentions the way in which someone who really knows the Latin classics and the culture out of which they grew, also knows that they could not have been forgeries of the medieval monks who copied them. No demonstration *more geometrico* is available to this person; he cannot force his reasoning on some willful colleague who insists on the hypothesis of forgeries; he cannot prove deductively the absolute impossibility of a medieval monk composing the *Aeneid*. And yet he reasons no less than the geometrician does, and no less successfully, even if he does so in his own non-deductive, informal way.

What particularly fascinates Newman about the master of informal reasoning is the highly personal way in which the master reasons. In reasoning formally I tend to disappear behind some paradigm of argument, which even has a certain existence outside of my reasoning and which in a way does the work of reasoning for me, whereas in reasoning informally it is preeminently I who reason. I take responsibility for my informal reasoning in a way that is not necessary when I rely on forms of deductive proof. Reasoning informally "is a personal gift, and not a mere method or calculus."[20] "It is seated in the mind of the individual, who is thus his own law, his own teacher, and his own judge in those special cases of duty which are personal to him."[21] It follows that "the personality of

20. John Henry Newman, *A Grammar of Assent* (London: Longmans, 1898), 316.
21. Ibid., 354.

the parties reasoning is an important element in proving propositions in concrete matter."[22] What Newman is defending is simply the Athenian principle of spontaneity as transferred from the conduct of social life to the activity of reasoning. What he is objecting to is the Spartan principle of compulsion that appears in the intellectual life as an over-reliance on formal demonstration.

Consider how the master of informal inference will address others. I who reason in this personal way also challenge my interlocutor to the same personal engagement. If the other is going to agree with me, he will not "indolently be carried along into"[23] the conclusion that I argue for, he will not be effortlessly transported to the conclusion *ex opere operato;* no, he will have to stir up all the resourcefulness in himself of which he is capable and make the same investment of himself in my reasons that I have made. Shortly after Newman entered the Catholic Church he was asked by someone to give a brief account of his reasons for taking this step; he responded in a memorable letter with well-founded impatience:

I do not know how to do justice to my reasons for becoming a Catholic in ever so many words—but if I attempted to do so in few, and that in print, I should wantonly expose myself and my cause to the hasty and prejudiced criticisms of opponents. This I will not do. People shall not say, "We have now got his reasons, and know their worth." No, you have not got them, you cannot get them, except at the cost of some portion of the trouble I have been at myself. You cannot buy them for a crown piece. . . . You must consent to *think*. . . . Moral proofs are grown into, not learnt by heart.[24]

Newman is challenging his critics to exert themselves as persons and not to hide behind a show of reasons and arguments that is really an escape from thinking. He says that he wants to "lead them on by their own independent action, not by any syllogistic compulsion."[25] Those who rise to Newman's challenge and really think with him about the Catholic claims are liable not only to contract an intellectual debt to him but also to be personally influenced by him.

---

22. Ibid., 320.
23. Ibid., 305.
24. Letter of February 8, 1846, in *The Letters and Diaries of John Henry Newman* XI (London: Thomas Nelson and Sons, 1961), 110.
25. *A Grammar of Assent*, 309.

5.

Informal reasoning is so connected with the individual person that each person will do it differently, even as each is a different person. In this remarkable passage Newman is striving to harmonize the universal validity of all truth with the highly personal path to truth that persons take when they reason informally:

> I begin with expressing a sentiment, which is habitually in my thoughts, whenever they are turned to the subject of mental or moral science . . . viz. that in these provinces of inquiry egotism is true modesty. In religious inquiry each of us can speak only for himself, and for himself he has a right to speak. His own experiences are enough for himself, but he cannot speak for others: he cannot lay down the law. . . .

He proceeds to acknowledge the unicity and universality of truth, saying, "He knows what has satisfied and satisfies himself; if it satisfies him, it is likely to satisfy others; if, as he believes and is sure, it is true, it will approve itself to others also, for there is but one truth." But then he resumes defending the paradox, "egotism in true modesty":

> it causes no uneasiness to any one who honestly attempts to set down his own view of the Evidences of Religion, that at first sight he seems to be but one among many who are all in opposition to each other. But, however that may be, he brings together his reasons, and relies on them, because they are his own, and this is his primary evidence; and he has a second ground of evidence, in the testimony of those who agree with him. But his best evidence is the former, which is derived from his own thoughts; . . . and therefore his true sobriety and modesty consists, not in claiming for his conclusions an acceptance or a scientific approval which is not to be found anywhere, but in stating what are personally his own grounds for his belief. . . .

Newman turns again to the universality of truth, finishing this sentence by saying, ". . . grounds which he holds to be so sufficient, that he thinks that others do hold them implicitly or in substance, or would hold them, if they inquired fairly. . . ." But he does not conclude until he reaffirms his professed "egotism": "However, his own business is to speak for himself."[26]

Newman's practice illustrates his personalist ideal of modesty. He never claimed to provide strict demonstration for his teachings, but he is always telling us how he personally came to them and why he holds them.

26. Ibid., 384–86.

This is part of the reason why Newman is so personally present in all that he writes. Our natural interest in the personal and the autobiographical makes us take a particular interest in his writings. Of course, it is not that Newman thinks his teachings are mere opinions, or that they are only "true for him"; nor is it that he is content to let mere autobiography substitute for real arguments. No, he thinks that every right-thinking person will agree with him. But he does not want to coerce you into agreeing with him, he wants to draw you by personal influence. And in fact by his personal approach he achieves an amazing universality. Once you begin to drink deeply at the well of Newman and to be influenced by him, you are aware of being drawn, not into the idiosyncratic views of an eccentric genius, but into the one truth.

6.

Let us examine more closely Newman's power of making himself present in his writings. Whoever reads Newman with sympathy and understanding cannot fail to be fascinated by the way he lives in his writings and speaks to his readers through them. If we think of St. Thomas Aquinas we right away notice the contrast to Newman. St. Thomas remains hidden behind the issues of which he treats; he practices a sober objectivity whereby he keeps his person out of his discourse; he wants to yield entirely to the truth that he serves and to let it speak for itself after he has presented it. But Newman serves the truth in a different way; in addition to uttering the objective truth, Newman is also present in his words, not only explaining how he personally came to the truth, but also giving witness to the truth. Yes, there is in all his religious writings this passion of a witness. The reader not only finds penetrating arguments and telling rebuttals, he also finds Newman solemnly bearing witness.

Some of the Oxford undergraduates who fell under Newman's influence scandalized people by saying, "Credo in Newmanum." This was not adolescent hype, not religious *Schwärmerei*, this just expresses what all of us who are deeply indebted to Newman are willing to say. We have not only been convinced by Newman's teaching, but also convicted by his witness. He has appealed to our intellect, and he has appealed to our imagination. Mind has spoken to mind, and heart has spoken to heart. His influence on us has been intellectual, and it has been personal.

In trying to understand Newman's presence in his writings and the personal influence that he exercises through them we are led to his almost preternatural capacity for sympathy with other persons. I will first let a contemporary of Newman who heard him preach describe this power:

A sermon of Mr. Newman's enters into all our feelings, ideas, modes of viewing things. He wonderfully realises a state of mind, enters into a difficulty, a temptation, a disappointment, a grief.... To take the first instance that happens to occur to us ... we have often been struck by the keen way in which he enters into a regular tradesman's vice—avarice.... This is not a temper to which we can imagine Mr. Newman ever having felt in his own mind even the temptation; but he understands it, and the temptation to it, as perfectly as any merchant could. No man of business could express it more naturally, more pungently.... Nay, he enters deeply into what even scepticism has to say for itself; he puts himself into the infidel's state of mind, in which the world, as a great fact, seems to give the lie to all religions ... and he goes down into that lowest abyss and bottom of things, at which the intellect undercuts spiritual truth altogether. He enters into the ordinary common states of mind just in the same way. He is most consoling, most sympathetic. He sets before persons their own feelings with such truth of detail, such natural expressive touches, that they seem not to be ordinary states of mind which everybody has, but very peculiar ones; for he and the reader seem to be the only two persons in the world that have them in common.

This is extremely well said; those of us who have not heard Newman preach but have immersed ourselves in the sermons have experienced just this power of sympathy. We agree with this contemporary of Newman when he concludes his remembrance saying, "Here is the point. Persons look into Mr. Newman's sermons and see their own thoughts in them."[27]

Perhaps we can explain this sympathetic power of Newman's like this. It is possible to write about avarice and infidelity in an "objective" way, characterizing the essence of these vices, bringing in their opposites for contrast, etc. When this objective approach is successful, the reader says, "yes, that's just the way it is with these vices, congratulations to the author for getting them right. Now I can think more clearly about them." But the reader feels no particular bond of sympathy between himself and such an author. But Newman's talk about the same vices is different; it has a "subjective" ring, for he is trying to understand these vices in himself, to understand how he himself has these vices, or vices similar to them, or at

---

27. Remembrance of James Mozley (1846), quoted by R. M. Church in his *The Oxford Movement* (Hamden, CT: Archon Books, 1966), 139–41.

least has the full potential for having them, and so understand what it is like to be subject to them. This is what creates the bond of sympathy with the readers who are struggling with these vices. They receive from Newman not only intellectual clarification about their sin but also the immeasurable personal benefit of being visited in their solitude by Newman, who shares with them his secret and thereby reveals to them their own secret.

In a sermon Newman ascribes to St. Paul just this "gift of sympathy." The sermon is unconsciously autobiographical. Newman says, "human nature, the common nature of the whole race of Adam, spoke in him, acted in him, with an energetical presence, with a sort of bodily fulness. . . . And the consequence is, that, having the nature of man so strong within him, he is able to enter into human nature, and to sympathize with it, with a gift peculiarly his own."[28] He goes on:

> . . . St. Paul felt all his neighbours, all the whole race of Adam, to be existing in himself. He knew himself to be possessed of a nature . . . which was capable of running into all the multiplicity of emotions, of devices, of purposes, and of sins, into which it had actually run in the . . . multitude of men; and in that sense he bore the sins of all men, and associated himself with them, and spoke of them and himself as one.[29]

This is just the way it is with Newman; for all the solitariness of his inner life, he also had the capacity to associate himself with others to the point of speaking of them and himself as one. This is what lets him achieve a deep solidarity with his readers; this is what lets him speak for them and reveal them to themselves.

Sometimes Newman directly acknowledged his gift of sympathy, as in the heart-rending sermon in which he took leave of the Church of England, "The Parting of Friends." Speaking of himself in the third person, he says, "if he has ever told you what you knew about yourselves, or what you did not know; has read to you your wants or feelings, and comforted you by the very reading . . . remember such a one in time to come."[30] He also acknowledged his gift of sympathy when he chose his motto as a cardinal: *cor ad cor loquitur*, heart speaks to heart.

28. John Henry Newman, *Sermons Preached on Various Occasions* (London: Longmans, Green, and Co., 1900), 95–96.
29. Ibid., 96.
30. John Henry Newman, *Sermons Bearing on Subjects of the Day* (London: Rivingtons, 1885), 409.

7.

We can enter more deeply into personal influence in the thought of Newman if we now consider his power of realizing the concrete and his power of awakening in others what he called a *real assent*. Newman loved the concrete individual and in fact he sometimes verges on extreme nominalism in his affirmation of the individual.[31] He is always warning against universals and their tendency to drain the concreteness out of things. He is always leading his readers and listeners beyond what he called mere notional assent, or purely intellectual assent, and towards real assent, which he also called imaginative assent, and sometimes also experiential assent; it is an assent born of the encounter with the world in all its concrete reality.

Take the fact that I will one day die: I can assent to this either notionally or really. If notionally, then I assent above all to the fact that everyone dies, and I include myself in the universal mortality of human beings. But if I give a real assent to my death, then I experience myself not just as a logical part of "everyone" but almost as if I were the only human being; I experience my death as something supremely concerning me personally. Then my assent shakes me to the roots of my being, raising my personal existence to an intense pitch, whereas the notional assent leaves me unmoved, almost as if I were just a spectator of my own future death.

Newman often thought about this difference as it shows itself in the

---

31. See the discussion at the end of ch. 8, section 1, of *A Grammar of Assent*, 279–84. Here, for example, he verges on nominalism: "Let units come first, and (so-called) universals second; let universals minister to units, not units be sacrificed to universals. John, Richard, and Robert are individual things, independent, incommunicable. We may find some kind of common measure between them, and we may give it the name of man, man as such, the typical man. . . . But we think we may go on to impose our definition on the whole race, and to every member of it, to the thousand Johns, Richards, and Roberts who are found in it. No; each of them is what he is, in spite of it" (279–80). "Each thing has its own nature and its own history. When the nature and the history of many things are similar, we say that they have the same nature; but there is no such thing as one and the same nature; they are each of them itself, not identical, but like. A law is not a fact, but a notion" (280). Of course, Newman never committed himself on principle to nominalism; these passages are a kind of nominalistic "outburst" that occurs in the course of showing the inability of formal logic to reach the concrete individual. In fact, in other places Newman takes universals very seriously, as when he shows in his essay on doctrinal development (in the first chapter) how certain of them hold together in history, or as when he studies, in another famous work, the *idea* of a university.

way the lives of the saints are told. There is an older style of hagiography in which a saint is presented in a highly idealized form; the ambiguities in his or her character, the unresolved struggles are left out and the saint is presented as if a mere instantiation of certain virtues. It is as if in writing the life of the saint the author were giving more attention to certain Platonic Forms than to the concrete reality of the saint. Such books about the saints are full of pious stereotypes. Newman intensely disliked this hagiography; he favored a greater realism, he favored presenting the full truth about the saint, including all the warts. For he thought that the stereotypical telling of the saint's life notionalizes the life, draining it of its concreteness and depriving it of its power to move us, whereas the same life, if only brought out in its concrete reality, has a power to arrest the imagination and to challenge the conscience.

One readily sees the pastoral reason that Newman had for this concern with real assent. It is almost the definition of merely conventional religion that believers give only a notional assent to the truths of religion. Their everyday lives remain little influenced by the religion they profess because their religious profession is only notional. Newman in England, like Kierkegaard in Denmark at the same time, was distressed at the hollowness of Christendom, and in fact his thinking on real and notional assent stands in a direct relation with this pastoral concern of his. Newman thought that the cure for this conventional hollowness was to convert notional assents into real assents, which is why we constantly find him in his sermons striving to effect this conversion. In a sermon dealing with the immortality of the soul he says, "every one of us is able fluently to speak of this doctrine. . . . And yet there seems scarcely room to doubt, that the greater number of those who are called Christians in no true sense realize it in their own minds at all."[32] And in another sermon on the same subject: "I am not attempting by such reflections to prove that there is a future state; let us take that for granted. I mean, over and above our positive belief in this great truth, we . . . attain a sort of sensible conviction of that life to come, a certainty striking home to our hearts and piercing them, by this imperfection in what is present."[33] Newman proceeds to try to lead his listeners beyond fluent speech about immortality that

---

32. John Henry Newman, *Parochial and Plain Sermons* I (Westminster, MD: Christian Classics, 1966), 17.

33. John Henry Newman, *Parochial and Plain Sermons* IV, 218.

remains purely notional; he spends most of the sermon trying to make them feel their immortality concretely and so to give a real assent to it. And so it goes throughout the sermons; Newman does not try to convince his listeners of truths they do not yet recognize, but rather to make them realize concretely truths that they have long recognized only notionally.

And why did Newman expect religious renewal from real assent? Because he held that we human persons are so constituted as to be moved to action much more through imagination than through intellectual abstraction. If our apprehension of the world is mediated too much by universals and general notions, we are left in the position of spectators; but the more we apprehend the world and other persons in all their concreteness, then the more personally engaged we become with them, the more capable of personally acting towards them. Thus in one well-known passage he says:

> ... deductions have no power of persuasion. The heart is commonly reached, not through the reason, but through the imagination, by means of direct impressions, by the testimony of facts and events, by history, by description. Persons influence us, voices melt us, looks subdue us, deeds inflame us. Many a man will live and die upon a dogma: no man will be a martyr for a conclusion.[34]

It was this love of the concrete and of real assent that kept Newman from ever warming to the God of the philosophers. He kept his distance to the traditional cosmological arguments for the existence of God. He did not deny their validity or their legitimate place in the Church, but he said that they "do not warm me and enlighten me; they do not take away the winter of my desolation, or make the buds unfold and the leaves grow within me, and my moral being rejoice."[35] He was instead at home with the God of religious men and women, the living God, the God who calls you and me by name, who reveals Himself, who acts unpredictably. And the reason is clear; the living God affected Newman's imagination and touched His heart and in this way elicited from him a profound real assent, whereas the God of rational theology only touched his intellect and only elicited a notional assent. The metaphysical necessities of the natural theologian tend to block the view of the living, personal God, who

---

34. John Henry Newman, "The Tamworth Reading Room," in *Discussions and Arguments* (London: Longmans, Green, and Co., 1899), 293.

35. John Henry Newman, *Apologia Pro Vita Sua*, 279.

reveals Himself not just in what He necessarily is but also in what He unpredictably does. In one early sermon Newman exults in the fact that Christianity discloses to us not a divine principle but a Divine Agent. "Here, then, Revelation meets us with simple and distinct *facts* and *actions*, not with painful inductions from existing phenomena, not with generalized laws or metaphysical conjectures, but with *Jesus and the Resurrection*."[36] These are just the kind of facts and actions that awaken a real assent and affect the imagination. By eliciting the sight and sound of them in us readers Newman can do what he could never do with rational proofs, namely take away the winter of our desolation and make our moral being rejoice.[37]

We have here another reason for Newman's uncanny power of exercising personal influence in his writings. If he had spoken more abstractly and had aimed mainly at mediating universal knowledge, he would disappear from his words, and his influence on us would be only intellectual, not personal. In fact, his influence is highly personal because he has this rare gift of reaching the heart by evoking in us a sense of the concrete reality of God and the soul. And it is not only Newman's practice of exercising personal influence in this way that interests us, it is also his teaching that whoever awakens real assents in others engages them more personally than when he or she just transmits notional assents to them.

We are now in a position to understand better Newman's distinction, encountered at the beginning of this study, between metropolitan opinion and local opinion. The former is a creature of notional assent, being based on stereotypes, while the latter is a creature of real assent, being based on the personal acquaintance that English Protestants have with their Catholic neighbors. Newman thought that a lasting victory in the

---

36. John Henry Newman, *Oxford University Sermons*, 27. Cf. this in the same sermon, 30: "Such, then, is the Revealed system compared with the Natural—teaching religious truths historically, not by investigation; revealing the Divine Nature, not in works, but in action; not in His moral laws, but in His spoken commands...."

37. In one of his papers in which he discusses the personal element in education, "Influence and Law," Newman distinguishes two aspects that God presents to the human mind: "the Supreme Being is both, a living, individual Agent, as sovereign as if an Eternal Law were not; and a Rule of right and wrong, and an Order fixed and irreversible, as if He had no will, or supremacy, or characteristics of personality" (*Historical Sketches* III, 72). Newman was always drawn to encountering God under the first aspect, for it is in this way that God personally engages us and engenders in us a real religious assent, far more than when He is encountered under the second aspect.

arena of public opinion could only be gained at the level of local opinion, so great was his esteem for the social power of real assent.[38]

Put all these things together, then, and you begin to understand Newman on personal influence: local opinion as distinct from metropolitan opinion, the Athenian spirit of spontaneity and freedom, the personal responsibility for one's informal reasoning, a certain egotism that is really modesty, the ardor of the witness, the gift of sympathy, and the power of realizing the concrete and of awakening real assent. Of course, I not only ask the reader to put these things together but also to try to discern the whole of which they are parts.

8.

At this point some readers who had begun with some sympathy for Newman's personalism may run out of sympathy and raise an objection along these lines. "Newman is flirting with subjectivism, he is making too much of religious feeling and experience, and of feeling with others. We were put off when he committed himself to the principle, 'egotism is true modesty,' but we let it pass at the time. Now you see where it leads; Newman begins by putting himself into his discourse, by speaking only for himself, as he says, and declining to make strong universal claims, and he ends by being more concerned with religious experience than with the truth about God. The mischief began already with Newman's enthusiasm for the Athenian spirit and its anti-authoritarian animus. Education needs more law and order than Newman allows; so does religious life; and so does our activity of reasoning. Newman seems to assert the personal at the expense of organization, authority, objectivity, universality."

I will defend Newman like this: everything this objector is looking for is found, and found abundantly, in Newman. One can find in Newman as strong an argument for authority and objectivity in religion as for the principle of personality. In fact, the first thing I learned years ago from Newman was his opposition to religious subjectivism and to theological Liberalism; only much later did I begin to do justice to his principle of personality. There are to this day many admirers of Newman who think

---

38. Cf. this from *A Grammar of Assent* (88): "They [real assents] kindle sympathies between man and man, and knit together the innumerable units which constitute a race and a nation. They become the principle of its political existence; they impart to it homogeneity of thought and fellowship of purpose."

of him mainly in terms of his anti-Liberalism. Let us say something about this other side of Newman's mind.

Newman was passionately committed to what he called "the dogmatical principle." Here are some lines from the finest single passage in Newman that presents the dogmatical principle:

> That there is a truth then; that there is one truth; that religious error is in itself of an immoral nature; that its maintainers, unless involuntarily such, are guilty in maintaining it; that it is to be dreaded; that the search for truth is not the gratification of curiosity; that its attainment has nothing of the excitement of a discovery; that the mind is below truth, not above it, and is bound, not to descant upon it, but to venerate it; that truth and falsehood are set before us for the trial of our hearts; that our choice is an awful giving forth of lots on which salvation or rejection is inscribed . . . —this is the dogmatical principle, which has strength.[39]

Here Newman is concerned not with our imaginative grasp of truth, not with the barrenness of a merely notional grasp of it, but rather with the sovereignty of truth.

One cannot even begin to understand Newman without understanding the depth of his commitment to the dogmatical principle; it is absolutely central to all of his thought and to his whole life's work. Consider the place of it in his conversion, which he underwent at the age of fifteen. He tells us that he was drifting towards unbelief, when a powerful experience of God overcame him. He describes it like this in his *Apologia:* "When I was fifteen, (in the autumn of 1816) a great change of thought took place in me. I fell under the influences of a definite Creed, and received into my intellect impressions of dogma, which, through God's mercy, have never been effaced or obscured."[40] Newman almost describes his conversion as his discovery of the dogmatical principle.

Let us look in on Newman in his early thirties, when he begins to lead the great reform movement in the Church of England called the Oxford Movement. In the *Apologia*, in the course of explaining the three foundational commitments of the movement, he says, "First was the principle of dogma: my battle was with liberalism; by liberalism I meant the anti-dogmatic principle and its developments. This was the first point on which I

---

39. John Henry Newman, *An Essay on the Development of Christian Doctrine* (Notre Dame, IN: University of Notre Dame Press, 1989), 357.
40. John Henry Newman, *Apologia Pro Vita Sua*, 22.

was certain."[41] In another place he explains more fully the Liberalism that he so abominated. Liberalism teaches,

> ... that truth and falsehood in religion are but matter of opinion; that one doctrine is as good as another; that the Governor of the world does not intend that we should gain the truth; that there is no truth; that we are not more acceptable to God by believing this than by believing that; that no one is answerable for his opinions; that they are a matter of necessity or accident; that it is enough if we sincerely hold what we profess; that our merit lies in seeking, not in possessing....[42]

And when towards the end of his life he surveyed his life's work he sometimes explained the unity of it in terms of the defense of the dogmatical principle. In 1879 he said in Rome, on the occasion of his being elevated to the cardinalate: "For thirty, forty, fifty years I have resisted to the best of my powers the spirit of Liberalism in religion."[43]

Along with the dogmatical principle there are other principles of Newman's religion that protect him from subjectivism. From the beginning of the Oxford Movement he was wedded with his whole being to the idea of a visible church with its divinely ordained structures; he laid particular stress on the "sacramental system" and on "episcopal authority."[44] We can only mention these great themes in Newman. To see just how seriously Newman took them one only has to recall the years of intellectual and spiritual agony that preceded his reception into the Catholic Church. Newman never had anything to do with that religious inwardness that would escape from history and dwell alone with God. Nor was his love of the Athenian spirit ever developed in an anti-authoritarian way.

Thus the turn to the personal and the subjective in Newman, which we have been studying, was carried out by one who was in fact the great anti-Liberal of the nineteenth century. It is a turn to the subjective that has nothing to do with subjectivism; Newman's "principle of personality" coheres entirely with his "dogmatical principle." These two principles enrich and perfect each other in the thought of Newman. Recall what was said about Newman giving witness—how he gives witness by the way he

41. Ibid., 73.
42. John Henry Newman, *Essay on the Development of Christian Doctrine*, 357–58.
43. John Henry Newman, "The Great Apostasy: the Biglietto Speech," in Francis Connolly (ed.), *A Newman Reader* (New York: Doubleday and Co., Inc., 1964), 384.
44. See, for example, the *Apologia*, 74-76.

personally lives in his writings, by the way his Christian subjectivity gains a voice in them. This is the subjective side of Newman. But what is he witnessing to if not the dogmatical principle and the whole creed of the Church? And who among those who have received his witness has ever become a subjectivist? Recall also the way in which he leads us to realize concretely revealed truth; this too belongs to his subjective side. How is the sovereignty of revealed truth undermined by the fact that Newman wants to assent to it, not only in a purely intellectual way, but with a full engagement of the whole person? He seems to show only a greater respect for truth by cultivating this full-bodied assent to it.

9.

I have long thought that the mystery of Newman can in part be explained by the union of apparent opposites in his thought.[45] For example: immerse yourself first in Newman's Anglican sermons, where often in the most severe and somber tones he calls England to repentance, as in the sermon, "Jewish Zeal, a Pattern to Christians," and then immerse yourself in the writings of Newman the Christian humanist, such as *The Idea of a University*. The severity and zeal of Newman the preacher seems to leave no room for the high intellectual culture of Newman the educator. And yet these two sides of Newman convincingly cohere, and in fact they perfect each other, his zeal being protected against un-Christian excesses by the fact that it is the zeal of a great Christian humanist, and his humanism being protected against aestheticism by the fact that it is the humanism of one who knew how terrible it is to fall into the hands of the living God. The inexhaustible abundance of Newman, his perennial power to fascinate, comes just from this union of apparent opposites, which repeats itself at all levels of his thought.

And so it is with the two aspects of thought that have emerged in the present discussion. The principle of personality as Newman develops it may seem to exclude the dogmatical principle. This is why some of his critics think that Newman with his principle of personality is a forerunner of the theological modernism condemned by Pope Pius X. And it is why some of his defenders seize on the dogmatical principle and tend to

45. See my paper, "The *Coincidentia Oppositorum* in the Thought and in the Spirituality of John Henry Newman," in *Anthropotes* (1990/2), 187–212.

repress their awareness of the principle of personality. These defenders have as much difficulty grasping the unity of Newman's thought as those critics do. The truth is that the dogmatical principle and the principle of personality exist in Newman in a most fruitful tension, each protecting and enriching the other. The personalism in Newman is secured against subjectivism by the dogmatical principle, and the affirmation of dogma is never so winning, never so convincing as it is when set within Newman's personalism.

I close with the words about Newman with which I opened: he "stands at the threshold of the new age as a Christian Socrates, the pioneer of a new philosophy of the individual Person and Personal Life."[46]

46. Edward Sillem, *The Philosophical Notebook*, I, 250.

CHAPTER 11

Karol Wojtyla's Personalist Understanding of Man and Woman

Karol Wojtyla had a special affinity for the love between man and woman from the very beginning of his priestly ministry. In his *Crossing the Threshold of Hope*, he writes: "*As a young priest I learned to love human love* [by which he means the love between man and woman]. This has been one of the fundamental themes of my priesthood. If one loves human love, there naturally arises the need to commit oneself completely to the service of 'fair love,' because love is fair, it is beautiful."[1] And Wojtyla not only possessed this special affinity for the love between man and woman; early on he also showed an unusual ability to reflect on man and woman and the love between them. His first book, *Love and Responsibility*, born of his pastoral experience with young couples, is a deep and original study of "fair love." The most important of his six dramas, *The Jeweler's Shop*, deals with this subject. As bishop of Krakow he set up an institute for the study of marriage and family, as he did later in Rome in the first years of his pontificate. He had hardly been elected pope when he began his famous five-year cycle of Wednesday addresses on man and woman. He was indeed personally called to the celibate life of a priest, which required the sacrifice of renouncing "fair love" in his own life for the sake of the kingdom of God; but he was given a rare gift for

---

* This paper was published as "John Paul II's Vision of Sexuality and Marriage: The Mystery of 'Fair Love,'" in Gneuhs (ed.), *The Legacy of John Paul II: His Contribution to Catholic Thought* (New York: The Crossroad Publishing Co., 2000), 52–70. The paper has undergone extensive revision and has been in places completely rewritten.

1. John Paul II, *Crossing the Threshold of Hope* (New York: Alfred A. Knopf, 1994), 123.

understanding this love and for reflecting philosophically and theologically on it. I want now to present and interpret some of the leading ideas of this reflection. My goal is to show that the personalism that emerges from the papers in the first part of this collection is present in Wojtyla's thought on man and woman and is in fact fruitfully developed by him, especially with respect to the embodiment of persons.

In the following we will for the most part ascribe this teaching on man and woman to Karol Wojtyla, since it can be found almost in its entirety in his pre-papal writings, and since we mean to present it, not as an exercise of the papal magisterium, but on its own philosophical merits.

1. The personalism of Karol Wojtyla

This is the only possible point of departure for understanding his thought on man and woman. His personalism underlies and informs all his teaching on "fair love," as it underlies and informs all the other regions of his teaching. When Wojtyla speaks of the "anthropological basis" of his teachings, he is referring to this underlying personalism. Much that seems puzzling in his teaching on man and woman becomes intelligible as soon as it is traced back to its personalist foundations.

In one of his pre-papal studies[2] Wojtyla distinguishes between what he calls a predominantly cosmological understanding of man and a predominantly personalist understanding of him. In the former, man is considered "from without," in the latter he is considered "from within," that is, as he experiences himself in consciously living his being. Others can experience him from without, but only he can experience himself from within. We could as well say that in the former, man is experienced objectively, and in the latter, subjectively, or according to his subjectivity. Now Wojtyla teaches that in order to get at man as person we must stop looking at man only from without and come to see him as he reveals himself to us from within, that is, as he lives his own being from his own inner center. The thought of Wojtyla will become clearer to some if we say that this subjectivity that is so revealing of persons is nothing other than the "interiority" of man. So his claim is that only if we try to understand man

---

2. Karol Wojtyla, "Subjectivity and the Irreducible in the Human Being," *Person and Community: Selected Essays*, trans. by Theresa Sandok (New York: Peter Lang, 1993). This is one of the most significant and seminal papers written by Wojtyla.

through his interiority can we hope to find him as person. At the same time Wojtyla insists that the objective (external) view of man has its own truth; this means that an adequate understanding of the person emerges not from replacing the objective view by the subjective, but by completing the objective by the subjective. It is just by aiming at this unity of objective and subjective that Wojtyla keeps clear of subjectivism as he explores with new interest the subjectivity of persons. We will encounter below a striking example of Wojtyla preserving the unity of these two aspects of man.

We can render the "subjective turn" of his thought more concrete by connecting it with our present theme of man and woman. Considered cosmologically, the meaning of the marital act is primarily procreation; from this point of view one will be struck by its likeness to subhuman sexual union. Only if we enter into the subjectivity of the marital act do we notice something that has no counterpart in the subhuman animals, namely the enactment of spousal love. This love dimension of the marital act is not a cosmological fact but a personalist fact; it is found in the self-experience of spouses, in their spousal subjectivity, and it reveals the deep personalist significance of the two in one flesh. Even the procreative meaning of the marital act reveals new and specifically personal dimensions of itself when considered from the point of view of spousal subjectivity, as we shall see.

We find Wojtyla doing this again and again in his teaching on man and woman: he brings out the personal by consulting the evidence of subjectivity and intersubjectivity. Thus in his rich commentary on the *Genesis* accounts of the creation of man and woman, he notices that one of the two accounts in *Genesis* 2 is more "subjective" than the other, that is, it explains man and woman, for instance, in terms of the *solitude* of man before the creation of woman, or in terms of the *shame* they felt before each other after sinning.[3] Wojtyla centers his commentary primarily on this subjective account; he finds it more congenial to his personalist reading of man and woman. Below we will look at his analysis of depersonalized sexuality in terms of a certain kind of lustful looking; Wojtyla is here exploring the subjectivity of fallen sexuality as it expresses itself in this way of looking.

3. John Paul II, *The Theology of the Body* (Boston, MA: Pauline Books and Media, 1997), 29–32.

But what exactly is it for us human beings to exist as persons? What result does Wojtyla get when he tries to understand man from within as person? He finds a certain "polar" structure in each person, a structure that he thinks is formulated with the greatest possible conciseness in the following sentence from the Vatican Council's "Pastoral Constitution on the Church in the Modern World" (*Gaudium et spes*, 24): although man is "the only creature on earth that God has wanted for its own sake," it is nevertheless true that man "can fully discover his true self only in a sincere giving of himself." This passage recapitulates the truth about a fundamental polarity of self-possession and self-donation in the makeup of the human person.

On the one hand, God wills each human being for his own sake, which means that God recognizes each human person as a being of his own, as existing in self-possession, as one who lives out of his own center, who cannot exist as a mere part of some whole, or as a mere instrumental means for achieving some result. This is why God is the very last one who would use persons in a merely instrumental way, as we can see from the way in which He appeals to and respects our freedom. When we respect each other as persons, giving each other the "space" in which each can live out of his own center, and abstaining from all using in our relations to each other, then we are acknowledging this pole of selfhood in human persons.[4]

On the other hand, each human person is made for self-donation, for communion with other persons; this is why he can only find himself by making a sincere gift of himself. We are not only beings of our own, belonging to ourselves, as if we were in the end closed in upon ourselves like monads, but we are also beings for others, made to exist not only with but for others, as Wojtyla puts it. He thinks that Christians have a privileged access to this truth through their Trinitarian faith: since God exists as a community of three divine persons, He cannot create an image of Himself in a person who can thrive in solitude; He can only create persons who thrive living in the communion of love with one another.

Wojtyla adds that there is not simply an antithesis here but a genuine

---

4. Wojtyla explores in great detail and with originality this personal selfhood in his work, *The Acting Person*, Anna-Teresa Tymieniecka (ed.), translated by Andrzej Potocki. Vol. 10 of *Analecta Husserliana* (Dordrecht: D. Reidel, 1979), especially the first three chapters.

polarity: the self-possession of persons does not interfere with their vocation to interpersonal communion, but rather makes it possible. If persons did not belong to themselves, then their union would be subpersonal. Persons are empowered precisely by their self-posssession to give themselves to others. Not only that, but they are never so much themselves as when they share their lives by self-donation.[5]

In section 3 we will consider what follows for the ethics of man-woman relations from the first part of this Conciliar statement (dealing with selfhood), and in section 4 what follows for man-woman relations from the second part of it (dealing with self-donation).

2. The equality of man and woman

Now that I have introduced Wojtyla's understanding of person, I proceed to his teaching on man and woman. And I begin with the equality of man and woman, which follows directly from the fact that they are both persons. Aristotle and the Aristotelian tradition in philosophy had denied this equality, teaching that the standard case of a human being was the man, and that the woman was a "deformed male." Aristotle explained himself in terms of his metaphysics of matter and form, saying that at the conception of a man form dominates matter in the right way, whereas when matter interferes with the due dominance of form the deficient result is the conception of a woman. Wojtyla disagrees with Aristotle, not only because he knows more about the biology of conception than Aristotle could have known, but above all because he thinks of man and woman in terms of a category unknown to Aristotle, the category of the person. He says that man and woman are both equally persons;[6] the for-

---

5. This polarity in virtue of which apparent opposites in fact condition and perfect each other appears in the philosophical anthropology of Norris Clarke, S.J., as the "dyadic" structure of the human person. See Clarke, *Person and Being* (Milwaukee: Marquette University Press, 1993), 32–82. Clarke's concept of dyadic serves to express well exactly what Wojtyla wants to say about the way in which self-possession and interpersonal communion are related to each other.

6. In fact, Wojtyla has gone so far in this direction as to say that the relation of man and woman in marriage is one of "mutual submission." He has raised some eyebrows among his supporters by speaking not only of a submission performed by the wife towards her husband, but rather of a mutual submission of husband and wife to each other. Cf. the encyclical of John Paul II, *Mulieris dignitatem* (Boston: Pauline Books and Media, 1988), para. 24.

mula of the person used by the Council, which brings together self-possession and self-donation, applies no less to woman than to man. It has already been shown in the first two papers in this collection that personhood is a great equalizer, an idea that harmonizes entirely with the thought of Wojtyla on man and woman. It is obvious to all who invoke the personhood of human beings that personhood does not admit of degrees, as if one human being could be more of a person than another. The excellences proper to persons come of course in degrees, but not the very thing of existing as person. Even the humanity proper to all human persons can be thought of as coming in different degrees, as Aristotle's teaching on man and woman clearly shows; but whereas there may be a substandard human being—a "barbarian" in contrast to "Greeks"—it does not even make sense to speak of "substandard persons." This is because personhood does not express some essential quality or kind that can be variously instantiated in different beings, but expresses the individual subject who has qualities.

Some critics charge that Wojtyla, speaking and acting as John Paul II (in his Apostolic Letter, *Ordinatio sacerdotalis*, 1994), has betrayed the equality of man and woman by solemnly teaching that the Church has no authorization to ordain women to the priesthood. He responds that the reservation of the priesthood for men is in no way based on any supposed superiority of man over woman, as in Aristotle. We have here a diversity of roles, which does not imply an inequality of personhood. We might add that the fact that God entrusts the conceiving, gestating, and nurturing of a new human being to women rather than to men does not imply that men are inferior as persons. And so if He chooses to entrust a certain sacerdotal function to man rather than to woman, He does not thereby cast woman into a position of inferiority.

This truth about the equality of man and woman has to be balanced by the truth about the complementarity of man and woman. The very principle of their equality, namely their personhood, is decisively modified by their gender, so that we have masculine and feminine persons. Each gender has its own "genius." As a result, man and woman, for all their equality, are called to complete each other in a unique kind of unity. Nothing could be farther from the mind of Wojtyla than to affirm equality at the expense of this difference and the complementarity that is based on it. We return below to this complementarity.

3. Showing respect for man and woman as persons

Let us now apply to man and woman the first part of the Conciliar statement about the polar structure of the person, namely the idea that each person exists in a sense for his own sake and is therefore willed by God for his own sake. What violates this selfhood of the person is any and every instrumental using of persons. This is why Wojtyla formulates the following norm and takes it as the foundational norm for sexual morality: "whenever a person is the object of your activity, remember that you may not treat that person as only the means to an end, as an instrument, but must allow for the fact that he or she, too, has, or at least should have, distinct personal ends."[7] Whenever Wojtyla evaluates some kind of man-woman relation he does so by measuring it against this norm, asking whether the man is in any way using the woman, or the woman using the man, or whether there is some kind of mutual using in their relationship. One may recall the firestorm of ridicule leveled at John Paul II in the international press when he said in an address (October 8, 1980) that the "adultery in the heart" condemned by Christ can be committed *even within marriage*.[8] From the point of view of his personalism this is so obvious as to be hardly worth mentioning. The fact that a man and a woman are married to each other is no guarantee at all that in their marital intimacy the one will not use the other as a mere object of gratification. If one of them does use the other like this, then he or she violates the other as person; if their using is mutual then they violate each other. Their being married and even being open to children does not necessarily prevent this violation from occurring. Sexual intimacy is not personalized until in and through it each person affirms and loves the other for his or her own sake.

This much-reviled address of Karol Wojtyla is closely akin to his personalist rethinking of the old idea that one of the purposes of marriage is the *remedium concupiscentiae*, or the relief of concupiscence. This was all too often interpreted to mean that marriage provides the only setting in which selfish sexual concupiscence can be "legally" lived out and burned off and in this way "relieved." It is not too much to say that Wojtyla abhors any such interpretation. Given his personalism he cannot abide the idea

---

7. Karol Wojtyla, *Love and Responsbility* (New York: Collins, 1981), 28.
8. John Paul II, *The Theology of the Body*, 156–59.

that marriage exists in part to legalize lust. The true "relief of concupiscence," he says, is something altogether different. It is a work of love whereby the sexual energy of a man or woman *is deprived of its selfish sting and made to express and serve spousal love.* Only in this way is sexual love personalized, formed in such a way that man and woman do not offend against the respect due to each other as persons.

Even if a man and woman are looking not just for sexual gratification but for offspring, they might still come into conflict with the personalistic norm of Wojtyla. For if they put their sexual union in a mere instrumental relation to offspring, so that in their sexual intimacy they are using each other for getting a child, then their action is personalistically indefensible. The excellence of the end does not abolish the disorder that results when persons achieve the end by using each other. Though Wojtyla makes much of the necessity of remaining open to offspring (as in his rejection of contraception, of which we will speak below), he is aware that there is a way of practicing this openness that involves the violation of the spouses as persons.[9]

He is also able to detect forms of depersonalization between man and woman that easily escape our attention, that is, ways of treating others that, while they may not involve any gross using of others, yet involve some failure to show others the respect due to them as persons. In discussing the "sexual values" that attract man and woman to each other he gives particular attention to the values of masculinity and femininity. When a man is fascinated by a woman in virtue of her femininity he feels a reverence towards her and a readiness to serve her. He does not approach her as a sex object, an object of sexual consumption, for this approach is based on purely bodily "values" of sex, whereas the femininity that captivates him is a sexual value that seems almost "spiritual" and is in any case far more than bodily.[10] Now Wojtyla wants to say that if a man is drawn to a woman only by her femininity, or a woman to a man only by his masculinity, then they have not yet reached each other as persons. The worth and dignity of a person lies deeper than even these sexual values that have a spiritual cast. We might use the language of Scheler to interpret Wojtyla: these are "vital" values, not yet properly "personal"

---

9. See Wojtyla, *Love and Responsibility*, 57–60, 233–34.
10. On the important distinction between these two sexual values see *Love and Responsibility*, 104–14.

values. One sign of this not-yet-personal character is, according to Wojtyla, the tendency of the man to idealize the woman whose femininity draws him, and the tendency of the woman to idealize the man whose masculinity draws her. In any case, if man and woman fail to find each other as persons they will not respect each other as persons; if they see no more than vital sexual values in each other, they will not be able to fulfill the personalistic norm in their relations with each other.

Now one might say that it is easy to understand the violation of this norm that is bound to result when one is drawn to another with a purely physical attraction; one turns to the other with a using, consuming attitude that is in a way the opposite of showing respect for persons. But, one might ask, why is one bound to offend against the personalistic norm in being drawn to another as masculine or feminine? The reverence we just mentioned as belonging to this attraction seems to be akin to respect for persons. We can gather something very deep from Wojtyla for responding to this question. He says that respect for another person can only exist as a fully free act. Now sexual values, including the higher ones based on masculinity and femininity, have a tendency to interfere with our freedom, "to take possession of an individual's senses and emotions, and, so to speak, 'lay siege to' his will."[11] If we always only experienced values like these we would be dominated by them and would never live as free persons. But the value or dignity of a person is different. On the one hand, it is more hidden, it does not jump out at us like the sexual values do; on the other hand, it does not just attract us, but binds us, claiming something from us. Wojtyla thinks, if I might interpret him a little beyond the letter of his text, that it is this double aspect of the dignity of the person—its "reserve" and its power to say "ought" to us—that explains why dignity can awaken our freedom. Now it is only in freedom that we can show others the respect due to them, as I just said; if we are fascinated by them, captivated by their vital values and so "under their spell," then we are too little free really to show them respect. Thus it is psychologically possible to fulfill the personalistic norm towards them only if we experience them as persons and as having the dignity that goes with being a person.

To this we might add, entirely along the line and in the spirit of Wojtyla, that a woman who fascinates a man by her femininity is something of a specimen or instance of femininity for the man; he will move

11. Ibid., 136.

on to others as soon as he realizes how partially she instantiates femininity. But to take a woman as a specimen of some universal type is to lose sight of her as unrepeatable person and so to lose the capacity to give her her due as person.

But once I lose sight of another as person, I am sure eventually to go farther in my defection from the personalist norm, not just failing to show others the respect due to them as persons but even acting at odds with the demands of the personalistic norm, which is perhaps why Wojtyla remarks on the particular susceptibility of the men and women moved only by vital sexual values to lapse back into selfish sensuality with its characteristic view of the other as object of sexual consumption.

It is important to add that Wojtyla is not saying that the personalistic norm requires us to prescind entirely from sexual values in the other, as if these values only interfered with the experience of the other as person. For Wojtyla the ideal is for the sexual values to be incorporated into the value or dignity of the person, so that one composite value whole is formed, anchored in the dignity of the person. He insists that the sexual values provide a material and an energy for personal respect and love that cannot be derived from any other source and that therefore offer an irreplaceable enhancement and enrichment of this respect and love.

Much more might be said about how Wojtyla explains the rights and wrongs of sexual behavior in terms of the fact that each person exists in a sense for his or her own sake. But instead I turn to consider the other part of the Conciliar definition of the human person, the part dealing with our vocation to self-donation.

4. *The vocation of man and woman to self-donation*

Karol Wojtyla thinks that the call to self-donation, inscribed in our being as persons, is also expressed, and eminently expressed, in the fact that we are divided into man and woman. There is a complementarity of man and woman that predestines them to a unique kind of love—spousal or conjugal love. But before we can really understand Wojtyla's mind on these subjects we have to bring into the discussion a fundamental article of his personalism, namely his understanding of the embodiment of persons.

In his view the modern world is not only afflicted by the materialism that reduces man to the body, recognizing nothing else in man but the body; it is also afflicted by a certain aversion to the body—Wojtyla sometimes speaks of a widespread "neo-Manichaean culture"—that conceives of persons as estranged from their bodies, as merely using their bodies in an instrumental way. This may be a new idea for many Christians, who perhaps take it for granted that the only real enemy is materialism, but in his encyclical on moral theology, *Veritatis splendor*, John Paul traces much of the disorder in present-day moral theology back to the failure to do justice to the embodiment of persons.[12] Many of our contemporaries think of the body as raw material available for instrumental use and manipulation by persons. They think that we are at liberty to impose on the body, or abolish from it, whatever meaning we want. One can see what results when they apply this disparagement of the body to our subject of man and woman. They think of the male-female difference as only an evolutionary product which just happened to come out as it did; compared with the fact that all human beings are persons, the sexual differentiation of human beings sinks to the level of the accidental. We can then take the physical given's of male and female and can construct masculine and feminine any way we like, in fact making up as many genders as we like. Thus man and woman are properly studied in an empirical way by the natural and social sciences, so that all that can be known about man and woman is of a neutral factual nature; there is no metaphysical nature expressed in man and woman, nor any intrinsic value.

While no Christian thinker could accept such an account of man and woman, Karol Wojtyla is distinguished by the depth at which he has overcome it and by the originality with which he has unfolded the truth that our personhood is embodied, and embodied as man and woman, so that all kinds of personal meanings are prefigured in our sexuality. He has given a personalist elaboration of the truth that the body is not just something physical but something sacramental, that is, a visible expression of the invisible interiority of man and woman, and that from the beginning the body in all its masculinity and femininity is ordered to participating in the life of the person.

In his rich "theology of the body,"[13] presented in the first years of his

---

12. Cf. my discussion in the paper above, "The Estrangement of Persons from Their Bodies," where I show how Wojtyla avoids the perennial temptation of personalism to become a dualism of person and body.

13. All the addresses making up the theology of the body are collected in John Paul II, *The Theology of the Body, op. cit.*

pontificate (though written before his election and in its main outlines present already in his book, *Love and Responsibililty*), Wojtyla unfolds the idea that the vocation of persons to self-donation, discussed above, is expressed in the bodies of man and woman. That it is not good for us to be alone, that we can find ourselves only through a sincere gift of ourselves, has its fundamental bodily expression in our existing as man and woman, and, in fact, cannot really be understood apart from the difference and complementarity of the sexes. It is as man and woman that we are first raised out of our solitude, and ordered one to another, and called to self-donation. The capacity of the masculine body and of the feminine body to serve self-donation is called by Wojtyla the "nuptial meaning" of the human body, a concept that stands at the center of his theology of the body. Through this nuptial meaning the body is more than biological, more than an object of biological science; it is rather inserted with all its maleness and femaleness into the life of the person.

Karol Wojtyla grasps with precision the self-donation for which man and woman are made by the masculinity and femininity of their bodies. He says that this love, which he calls spousal or conjugal love, is distinguished from all other human love, including even maternal love, by the gesture of self-surrender that belongs to it. In spousal love self-donation takes the form of self-surrender, that is, of abandoning oneself in love to the other and willing to make oneself belong to the other.[14] Hence the exclusivity of spousal love; there is no room in the human heart for living this self-surrender towards more than one person at the same time. Wojtyla marvels at the fact that a person living this self-surrender towards another seems to act against his or her own selfhood.[15] For how can I, who as person am my own, existing in some sense for my own sake, having my own ends, how can I make myself belong to another? I seem to be divesting myself of myself, annulling my birthright as person. The seriousness of the difficulty that Wojtyla feels here shows just how far-reaching the self-surrender of which he speaks is. I discern two main thoughts that he offers on the difficulty. He says that the self-surrender presupposes the self-possession of persons; if persons were not handed over to themselves so as to belong to themselves, they would never be in a position to give themselves away in love. If we never find anything like self-

---

14. See Wojtyla, *Love and Responsbility*, 95–100.
15. Ibid., 96–98, 125–26.

surrender in animals it is because we never find anything in them like the personal self-possession that would empower them to self-surrender. And he also says: "What might be called the law of *ekstasis* seems to operate here: the lover 'goes outside' the self to find a fuller existence in another. In no other form of love does this law operate so conspicuously as it does in betrothed love."[16] With this he tries to present as paradoxical what at first may have seemed to be self-contradictory.

Now the nuptial meaning of the body stands in the service of this mutual self-surrender. It also stands in the service of non-spousal love, according to Wojtyla, conditioning as it does all interpersonal communion; but in a unique way it serves spousal love. For it is in their sexual intimacy that man and woman live and enact in an incomparable bodily way their spousal self-surrender. Indeed, one can hardly understand just what this self-surrender is without referring to the sexual union of man and woman. It is not that spousal self-surrender is nothing but its sexual enactment; Wojtyla makes a great point of saying that this self-surrender is first of all and in itself something properly personal.[17] It is performed in a non-bodily way in the act of marrying. But at the same time he also wants to say that a man and a woman enact and live this self-surrender in an irreplaceable way in and through their sexual intimacy. Man and woman can fully live their properly personal self-donation only if they live it through the body by becoming one flesh.[18]

Karol Wojtyla has not only explored the nuptial meaning of the body, but also, and with great realism, the way in which this meaning gets lost in man-woman relations. The body can, in its fallenness, so obscure the person that it becomes an impediment to interpersonal communion. With depth and originality Wojtyla analyzes the way in which a man looks lustfully at a woman, seeing her body and its sexual values without experiencing its nuptial meaning and without seeing the feminine person who should be revealed in it. The body of the woman ceases to be expressive of her as person and so ceases to provide a point of departure for

16. Ibid., 126.
17. Ibid., 99, 127.
18. It would be very interesting to compare Wojtyla with Scheler on the love between man and woman. I suspect that Wojtyla would find an excessively vitalistic conception of this love in Scheler. I do not see that Scheler inserts the vital sexuality of this love into the person, at least not in the way Wojtyla does by connecting sexuality with the eminent form of personal love that he characterizes in terms of self-surrender and self-donation.

love. In this lustful looking, men see women as objects of selfish consumption rather than as persons to be loved; their look violates the personal selfhood of the other[19] and ignores the fact that each other person is "an enclosed garden," "a fountain sealed" (expressions taken by Wojtyla from the *Song of Songs*, 4:12, and applied to men and women as persons).

Inspired by Max Scheler's study of shame,[20] Wojtyla goes on to show that there is a noble sexual shame that is a kind of "personalist instinct" whereby women protect themselves from the lustful concupiscent look of men. His idea is that when a woman realizes that she is an object of male lust, she naturally tries to subdue all that could be sexually provocative about her appearance, not because she fears or despises her sexuality, but because she wants to defuse the male concupiscence which she feels threatening her. With great sensitivity Wojtyla adds that the subduing of her sexual values does not amount to a neutering of herself as woman, for in concealing them she "conceals them only to a certain extent, so that in combination with the value of the person they can still be a point of origin for love."[21] She thinks that her sexual values, shamefully subdued, manifest her as person, so that the looking that they elicit in the man will cease to threaten her as person. Of course, the man can also feel shame in relation to the lust of woman, but for obvious reasons Wojtyla gives particular attention to the shame felt by the woman.

The same woman who knows how to feel this sexual shame, will have no such reserve about revealing herself to the man who loves her as her husband, for she can trust him to look at her so as to see her sexual values incorporated into her value or dignity as person. In this connection Wojtyla speaks of the "law of the absorption of shame by love."[22] He also explains how this absorption of shame has nothing to do with shamelessness.[23]

We might point out what seems to be a certain incompleteness of Wojtyla's analysis of concupiscent looking, shame, and chastity. I detect this lack in the following sentence: "Sensuality in itself is quite blind to the

---

19. There are remarkable convergences between the analysis of shame in Wojtyla and in Sartre (*Being and Nothingness*, Part III, ch. 1.1 and 1.4).

20. Max Scheler, "Über Scham und Schamgefühl," *Schriften aus dem Nachlass*, I (Bonn: Bouvier Verlag Herbert Grundmann, 1986), 65–153.

21. Wojtyla, *Love and Responsibility*, 187.

22. Ibid., 181–86.

23. Ibid., 186–91.

person, and oriented only towards the sexual value connected with 'the body.'"[24] Let us test this from the point of view of a woman who feels herself to be the object of a man's lustful sensuality. She knows that he does not ignore her altogether as person and does not see in her only an attractive female body, for she knows that what would really inflame his lust is some readiness on her part to be sexually available to him, and she knows that this would inflame him not just because it signals bodily gratification but above all because her readiness is an essential part of what attracts him. Thus there is a certain subjectivity that the lustful man looks for in the woman; this is why he does not objectify her to the point of bracketing out all subjective life in her. He does indeed objectify her to the point of no longer seeing a person worthy of love and respect, but not to the point of reducing her to a mere body with which he might gratify himself. Such reduction of the woman to her body certainly occurs in some sexual perversions but it does not occur in the typical case of a man looking concupiscently and lustfully at a woman.

In a more properly theological part of his teaching on man and woman Wojtyla goes back "to the beginning," that is, back to man and woman as they lived their bodily being before and after the fall. This leads him to his profound analyses of the "original innocence" and the "original nakedness" of man and woman. He supposes that the first man and woman did not experience any shame in their nakedness because each could see in the body of the other another person, and because the attraction of masculinity and femininity stood completely in the service of love. It is not just that they mastered this attraction by strong self-control and made a right use of it by their will; this would express for Wojtyla a too extrinsic dominion of soul over body. Rather, each person dwelt so intimately in the body that the body expressed to the other the worth and splendor of the person, and bodily sexuality was completely absorbed in the energy of spousal love.[25] But with the sin of our first parents a rupture appeared in

24. Ibid., 108.
25. Cf. this from *The Theology of the Body:* "it seems quite clear that the 'experience of the body,' such as it can be inferred from the ancient text of *Genesis* 2:23 and even more from *Genesis* 2:25 indicates a degree of 'spiritualization' of man different from that of which the same text speaks after original sin (*Genesis* 3) and which we know from the experience of 'historical' man. It is a different measure of 'spiritualization,' which involves another composition of the interior forces of man himself, almost another body-soul relationship, other inner proportions between sensitivity, spirituality and affectivity . . ." (73).

the body-soul unity; the body now acquired the capacity to obscure the person as well as to reveal him or her; it could now awaken the selfish desire to consume as well as the desire to give oneself spousally; the freedom of original nakedness gave way to the anxiety of feeling shame.

The "redemption of the body," about which Wojtyla has much to say in his theology of the body, refers to the restoration of the lost integrity of our being. It refers to the re-integration of bodily sexuality and personhood, that is, to the radical "personalization" of masculinity and femininity. The redemption of the body, though it will be consummated in eternity, begins already now in time. Man and woman as they existed in the beginning, and as they will exist in the end, constitute a fundamental norm for men and women now living in earthly time.

It would exceed the scope of this study to go on and examine Wojtyla's personalist understanding of marriage and to consider how the commitment of marriage serves to integrate the sexuality of man and woman, and especially their sexual intimacy, into themselves as persons.

These, then, are the main themes in Wojtyla's account of the vocation to self-donation that is as it were inscribed in our being as a result of our existing as man and woman. We are now in a position to understand a bold theological move that he is led to make. He sees the image of the triune God in the man-woman difference. He thinks that since God exists as a communion of love among divine persons, He is just the kind of God who might create embodied persons who are turned towards each other as man and woman. Previously theologians had looked for this image in the soul of each individual human being, commonly following St. Augustine in looking at various triads within each individual soul. It is an entirely new idea to look for the image of God in interpersonal relation, and not just in the most spiritual forms of interpersonal relation, but in the man-woman relation. For Wojtyla even the human body images the triune God, and does so through its nuptial meaning. As far as I know, no pope before John Paul II ever spoke of the image of God in this way: "Man becomes the image of God not so much in the moment of solitude as in the moment of communion,"[26] and especially, as he means to say in this passage, in the communion based on the complementarity of man and woman.[27]

---

26. John Paul II, *The Theology of the Body*, 46.
27. The fullest statement of this thought is to be found in John Paul II's encyclical,

5. Procreation and parenthood

I cannot omit giving special attention to Wojtyla's stance on the ethics of contraception, for he himself has given special attention to the issue, first as a young professor of ethics at the University of Lublin and then later as Pope.

For centuries Catholic teachers explained the meaning of the marital act almost exclusively in terms of procreation; only in this century did they begin to explain the marital act in terms of the enactment of spousal love as well. Pius XII was, as far as I can determine, the first pope who strongly affirmed the love dimension, or as Paul VI called it, the unitive dimension, of the marital act. Wojtyla has gone well beyond his predecessors by explaining how this dimension is grounded in the nuptial meaning of the body. As a result of this enlargement of perspective, it may seem as if the ancient prohibition on sterilizing the marital act has become untenable. It may seem that such sterilization can be taken to be intrinsically wrong only as long as one thinks that the only *raison d'être* of the marital act is procreation. On this view there is something distinctly unnatural about any active suppression of fertility. But once one acknowledges in addition to the procreative meaning also the love meaning of the act, then it seems that there is something to justify the act even when its fertility has been suppressed. Contracepted marital intercourse need not be unnatural if only the spouses enact their love for each other.

The novelty of Wojtyla's stance on this issue is this: the sexual consummation of spousal love, though in itself distinct from procreation, is intrinsically connected with openness to procreation and to parenthood. The fertility of man and woman is not merely biological; it too is situated in the realm of their personal love. The bodily expression of spousal love is so intimately united with possible procreation that whenever the marital act is deliberately sterilized *it suffers as an expression of spousal love*, and it begins to be replaced with selfish using. The original insight

---

Mulieris dignitatem, para. 7, where we find passages like this one: "The fact that man 'created as man and woman' is the image of God means not only that each of them individually is like God, as a rational and free being. It also means that man and woman, created as a 'unity of the two' in their common humanity, are called to live in a communion of love, and in this way to mirror in the world the communion of love that is in God, through which the three persons love each other in the intimate mystery of the one divine life."

of Wojtyla is that openness to new life is not only important for the sake of new life, it is also indispensable for the integrity of the spousal self-donation. Critics of the traditional teaching on contraception typically say that this teaching, when lived, cramps the expression of spousal self-surrender; Wojtyla meets them on their own personalist level by responding that this teaching in fact guarantees the personalist character of spousal self-surrender, which is compromised by contraception.[28]

Some who agree with him about contraception are suspicious of the recognition of not one but two meanings of the marital act. They say that if we must have two meanings of the marital act, then at the very least the procreative meaning must be clearly ranked above the unitive meaning, and they are very worried that Wojtyla does not even do this, that he simply speaks of them as two equally fundamental meanings. Wojtyla responds to their concern by saying that the newly recognized unitive meaning is so interrelated with the long recognized procreative meaning that marital intimacy is compromised if the spouses do not remain open to procreation; that spouses have to remain open to new life not only for the sake of new life but also for the sake of the integrity of their sexual union. Thus he does not need to rank the two meanings of the marital act; even without any ranking, his teaching on the enactment of love in the marital act does not undermine but rather throws new light on the moral disorder of contraception.

Let us go back to Wojtyla's distinction between the personalist and the cosmological image of man. We said that, although he is above all concerned with bringing out and developing the personalist image, he does not want to do this at the expense of the truth of the older cosmological image of man. The task as Wojtyla sees it is not to make a simple substitution of images but to enrich the cosmological with the personalist. We can in fact say that the whole "philosophical project" of Wojtyla is to do justice to man as person and at the same time to keep the human person situated within the order of nature. Now this project is uniquely recapitulated in his stance on procreation and parenthood, in which he argues that the order of persons and the order of nature are intrinsically connected in the marital intimacy of man and woman in the sense that the love between persons is compromised if the openness to procreation is thwarted.

---

28. See the early presentation of this argument in *Love and Responsibility*, 224–44.

Wojtyla thinks that people have such a hard time understanding this because, being so used to treating the body as raw material to be instrumentally manipulated for human purposes, they cannot help treating bodily fertility in the same way. If only they can recover a sense of their embodied personhood, and hence of their masculine and feminine personhood, and hence of their paternal and maternal personhood, they will learn to see their fertility in a new personalist light.

Wojtyla sometimes inserts his discussion of procreation and parenthood in a theological perspective, invoking the sovereignty of God as creator of persons and as lord of nature. Let us just raise the question whether his argument for the moral disorder of contraception requires some such theological perspective in order to be complete, or whether it is complete already on purely personalist grounds.

6. The "genius" of woman

Some years ago Karol Wojtyla began developing his personalist understanding of woman. He began this work in his encyclical *Mulieris dignitatem*, 1988, and continued it in 1995 in a series of addresses and letters that has been published under the title *The Genius of Woman*.[29] We want at least to make mention of Wojtyla's thought on the genius of woman and on the "new feminism" that he advocates.

He explains "the genius of woman" in personalist terms, just as we would expect. He says that woman is gifted with a special sense for the concrete person; she is less inclined than man to think of people in terms of stereotypes or of achievements; by nature she is more sensitive to the *being* rather than the *having* of persons. Wojtyla makes his own the idea that modern technological civilization is onesidedly masculine and needs nothing so much as the "genius of woman" to protect it from becoming ever more depersonalized. Wojtyla thinks that it is the maternal vocation of woman, whereby she can receive a new human being into herself, which disposes her to see the person in others.[30] He says that men need to learn from women this sensitivity to persons. He thinks that all the regions of human life, including the life of the Church, will be vastly

---

29. John Paul II, *The Genius of Woman* (Washington, D.C.: United States Catholic Conference, 1997).
30. Cf. John Paul II's encyclical, *Mulieris dignitatem*, para. 18.

enriched when the "genius of woman" makes itself much more strongly felt within them. This is why he encourages women to become more present with their femininity in society and in the Church. Of course he reminds women that their contributions to society and the Church should not be made at the expense of their vocation to maternity; and yet he brings something new out of his tradition by saying that this maternal vocation should not be lived at the expense of these contributions. He wants Christian women to be bearers of the "genius of woman" in the contemporary world.

John Paul has gone so far as to apologize to women for the complicity of many Catholics in the neglect and disparagement of the genius of woman over the centuries. In the great ecclesial self-examination that he initiated in preparation for the new millennium, he has found much to repent of in the way members of the Church have conducted themselves towards women. He thinks that people in the Church have to be converted from certain patterns of thinking and evaluating if they are going to do justice to the complementarity of man and woman and to the genius of woman. He speaks of the immeasurable gain that he expects for the Church from a greater presence of woman with her genius in the life of the Church.

With this analysis of woman Wojtyla reinforces his teaching, discussed above, on the equality of man and woman. We mentioned the Aristotelian idea, which is at the same time deeply rooted in almost all human thought about woman and not just in the Aristotelian tradition, that man is the standard case of a human being and that woman is a substandard case of a human being. In his thought on the genius of woman Wojtyla gives a new reason for resisting this conception; in addition to the point that woman is a person no less than man, which we made above, he now adds that woman has certain excellences proper to herself. And they are properly personal excellences, such as a special sensitivity to concrete persons. Indeed, Wojtyla seems to be saying that one of the defining traits of persons, namely the vocation to self-donation, is in some ways more fully developed in woman than in man.

In Wojtyla's thought on the genius of woman there is also something that reinforces his teaching on embodiment. For the genius of woman is rooted in her capacity to conceive and to carry a new human being in herself: "Motherhood involves a special communion with the mystery of life, as it develops in the woman's womb.... This unique contact with the new human being developing within her gives rise to an attitude toward human beings, not only toward her own child, but every human being, which profoundly marks the woman's personality."[31] Wojtyla thus acknowledges a bodily basis for the altogether personalist excellence that distinguishes woman.

We said in the earlier paper, "The Estrangement of Persons from Their Bodies," that a personalism divorced from an adequate philosophy of embodiment creates no end of mischief in ethics. What we find in Wojtyla is a personalism based on a profound and original philosophy of embodiment. Such a personalism bears much fruit for our understanding of man and woman and for many of the ethical issues of man-woman relations.[32]

31. Ibid.
32. My thanks to Patricia Donohue-White for her comments on the first draft of this paper.

Bibliography

Anscombe, Elisabeth. "Modern Moral Philosophy." In *Collected Philosophical Papers*, III. Minneapolis: University of Minnesota Press, 1981.

Aquinas, St. Thomas. *Summa Theologiae*, I, q. 29 and q. 30. Translated by Fathers of the English Domincan Province. 2nd edition. London: Burns, Oates, and Washbourne, Ltd., 1926.

Augustine, St. *Confessions*. Translated by F. J. Sheed. Indianapolis, IN: Hackett, 1993.

———. "De Trinitate." In *Oeuvres de Saint Augustin*, XV and XVI. Desclée de Brouwer, 1955.

Bolt, Robert. *A Man for All Seasons*. New York: Vintage Books, 1990.

Boyce, O.C.D., Philip. "Newman as Seen by His Contemporaries at the Time of His Death." In *John Henry Newman: Lover of Truth*, edited by Maria Katharina Strolz and Margarete Binder. Rome: Urbaniana University Press, 1991.

Church, R. M. *The Oxford Movement*. Hamden, CT: Archon Books, 1966.

Clarke, S.J., Norris. *Person and Being*. Milwaukee: Marquette University Press, 1993.

Crosby, John F. "Autonomy and Theonomy in Moral Obligation: Response to Tollefsen." *The New Scholasticism* 63.3 (1989), 358-70.

———. "The *Coincidentia Oppositorum* in the Thought and in the Spirituality of John Henry Newman." *Anthropotes* 6 (1990/2), 187–212.

———. "Evolutionism and the Ontology of the Human Person: Critique of the Marxist Theory of the Emergence of Man." *Review of Politics* 38.2 (1976), 208–43.

———. "Karol Wojtyla on the Objectivity and the Subjectivity of Moral Obligation." In *Christian Humanism*, edited by Jane Francis. New York: Peter Lang, 1995, 27–36.

———. *The Selfhood of the Human Person*. Washington, D.C.: The Catholic University of America Press, 1996.

de Tocqueville, Alexis. *Democracy in America*, II. Translated by H. Reeve. New York: Vintage Books, 1954.

Dostoevsky, Fyodor. *The Brothers Karamazov*. Translated by C. Garnett. New York: The Modern Library, 1950.

Dupré, Louis. *A Dubious Heritage*. New York: Paulist Press, 1977.

———. *Transcendent Selfhood*. New York: The Seabury Press, 1976.
Dworkin, Ronald. *Life's Dominion: An Argument about Abortion, Euthanasia, and Individual Freedom*. New York: Alfred Knopf, 1993.
Finkielkraut, Alain. *In the Name of Humanity*. New York: Columbia University Press, 2000.
Finnis, John. *Fundamentals of Ethics*. Washington, D.C.: Georgetown University Press, 1983.
———. *Natural Law and Natural Rights*. New York: Oxford University Press, 1980.
———. "The Natural Law, Objective Morality, and Vatican II." In *Principles of Catholic Moral Life*, edited by William May. Chicago: 1980.
Fletcher, Joseph. *Morals and Medicine*. Boston: Beacon Press, 1960.
Freud, Sigmund. *The Ego and the Id*, edited by James Strachey. Translated by Joan Riviere. New York: Norton, 1962.
Fromm, Erich. *Man for Himself: An Inquiry into the Psychology of Ethics*. New York: Rinehart, 1947.
Grabowski, John S., and Michael J. Naughton. "Catholic Social and Sexual Ethics: Inconsistent or Organic?" *The Thomist* 57.4 (1993), 555–78.
Gracia, Jorge. *Individuality*. Albany: State University of New York Press, 1988.
Grisez, Germain. *The Way of the Lord Jesus, vol. 1: Christian Moral Principles*. Chicago: Franciscan Herald Press, 1983.
Grisez, Germain, Joseph M. Boyle, and John Finnis. "Practical Principles, Moral Truth, and Ultimate Ends." *American Journal of Jurisprudence* (1987), 147–48.
James, William. "The Moral Philosopher and the Moral Life." *Pragmatism and Other Essays*. New York: Washington Square Press, Inc., 1963.
John Paul II. *Crossing the Threshold of Hope*. New York: Alfred A. Knopf, 1994.
———. *The Genius of Woman*. Washington, D.C.: United States Catholic Conference, 1997.
———. *Mulieris dignitatem*. Boston: Pauline Books and Media, 1988.
———. *The Theology of the Body*. Boston: Pauline Books and Media, 1997.
Kant, Immanuel. *Foundations of the Metaphysics of Morals and What Is Enlightenment?* Translated by Lewis White Beck. New York: Liberal Arts Press, 1959.
Küng, Hans. *Existiert Gott?* Zurich and Munich: 1978.
Levi-Strauss, Claude. *Structural Anthropology*, II. Translated by Monique Layton. Chicago: University of Chicago Press, 1983.
Lewis, C. S. *The Abolition of Man*. New York: Macmillan, 1968.
Locke, John. *An Essay Concerning Human Understanding*. New York: Dover Publications, 1959.
Lotz, J.-B. "Sein und Wert. Das Grundproblem der Wertphilosophie." *Zeitschrift für katholische Theologie* 57 (1933).
Maritain, Jacques. *Existence and the Existent*. Translated by Lewis Galantiere and Gerald Phelan. New York: Doubleday and Co., 1956.
———. *The Person and the Common Good*. New York: Charles Scribner's Sons, 1947.

May, William. "The Natural Law Doctrine of Suarez." *The New Scholasticism* 58.4 (1984), 409-23.
Mounier, Emmanuel. *Personalism*. Notre Dame, IN: University of Notre Dame Press, 2001.
Neuhaus, Richard John. "The Divided Soul of Liberalism." In *Life and Learning: Proceedings of the Third University Faculty for Life Conference*, edited by Joseph Koterski, S.J. Washington, D.C., 1993.
Newman, John Henry. *Apologia Pro Vita Sua*. New York: America Press, 1942.
———. *An Essay in Aid of a Grammar of Assent*. London: Longmans, Green, and Co., 1898.
———. *An Essay on the Development of Christian Doctrine*. Notre Dame, IN: University of Notre Dame Press, 1989.
———. "The Great Apostasy: The Biglietto Speech." In *A Newman Reader*, edited by Francis Connolly. New York: Doubleday and Co., Inc., 1964.
———. *Historical Sketches* III. London: Longmans, Green, and Co., 1903.
———. *The Letters and Diaries of John Henry Newman* XI. London: Thomas Nelson and Sons, 1961.
———. *Newman the Oratorian: His Unpublished Oratory Papers*, edited by Placid Murray, O.S.B. Dublin: Gill and Macmillan Ltd., 1969.
———. *Oxford University Sermons*. Westminster, MD: Christian Classics, 1966.
———. *Parochial and Plain Sermons* IV. London: Rivingtons, 1870.
———. *The Present Position of Catholics in England*. London: Longmans, Green, and Co., 1908.
———. *Sermons Bearing on Subjects of the Day*. London: Rivingtons, 1885.
———. *Sermons Preached on Various Occasions*. London: Longmans, Green, and Co., 1900.
———. "The Tamworth Reading Room." In *Discussions and Arguments*. London: Longmans, Green, and Co., 1899.
Nygren, Anders. *Agape and Eros*. New York: Harper and Row, 1969.
Otto, Rudolf. *Aufsätze zur Ethik*, "Wert, Würde und Recht." München: C. H. Beck Verlag, 1981.
Parfit, Derek. *Persons and Reasons*. Oxford: Clarendon Press, 1987.
Plato. "Symposium." Translated by Michael Joyce. In *Collected Dialogues of Plato*, edited by Hamilton and Cairns. New York: Bollingen Foundation, 1964.
Rahner, Karl. "On the Question of a Formal Existential Ethics." In *Theological Investigations* 2. Translated by Karl Kruger. Baltimore: Helicon, 1963. German: "Über die Frage einer formalen Existentialethik." In *Schriften zur Theologie* II. Einsiedeln: Benzinger Verlag, 1955.
Ramsey, Paul. "The Morality of Abortion." In *The Ethics of Abortion*, edited by Baird and Rosenbaum. Buffalo: Prometheus Books, 1989.
Reale, Giovanni. *Plato and Aristotle*. Translated by J. Caton. Albany: State University of New York, 1990.
Sartre, Jean-Paul. *Being and Nothingness*. Translated by Hazel Barnes. New York: Washington Square Press, 1966.

Scheler, Max. "Die christliche Liebesidee und die gegenwärtige Welt." In *Vom Ewigen im Menschen*. Bern: Francke Verlag, 1968. Translated by Bernard Noble as "Christian Love and the Twentieth Century." In *On the Eternal in Man*. Hamden, CT: Archon Books, 1972.

———. "Der Genius des Krieges und der Deutsche Krieg." In *Gesammelte Werke* IV. Bonn: Bouvier Verlag, 1982.

———. *Der Formalismus in der Ethik und die materiale Wertethik*. Bern: Francke Verlag, 1966. *Formalism in Ethics and Non-Formal Ethics of Values*. Translated by Manfred Frings and Roger Funk. Evanston: Northwestern University Press, 1973.

———. "Vom Wesen der Philosophie und der sittlichen Bedingung philosophischen Erkennens." In *Vom Ewigen im Menschen*. Bern: Francke Verlag, 1968. "The Nature of Philosophy and the Moral Preconditions of Philosophical Knowledge." In *On the Eternal in Man*. Translated by Bernard Noble. Hamden, CT: Archon Books, 1972.

———. "Ordo Amoris." In *Schriften aus dem Nachlass*, I. Bonn: Bouvier Verlag Herbert Grundmann, 1986.

———. *Das Ressentiment im Aufbau der Moralen*, in *Vom Umsturz der Werte*. Bern: Francke Verlag, 1955. *Ressentiment*. Translated by Lewis Coser and William Holdheim. Milwaukee: Marquette University Press, 1994.

———. "Reue und Wiedergeburt." In *Vom Ewigen im Menschen*. Bern: Francke Verlag, 1968. Translated by Bernard Noble as "Repentance and Rebirth." In *On the Eternal in Man*. Hamden, CT: Archon Books, 1972.

———. "Über Scham und Schamgefühl." In *Schriften aus dem Nachlass*, I. Bonn: Bouvier Verlag Herbert Grundmann, 1986.

———. "Vom kulturellen Wiederaufbau Europa." In *Vom Ewigen im Menschen*. Bern: Francke Verlag, 1968. Translated by Bernard Noble as "The Reconstruction of European Culture." In *On the Eternal in Man*. Hamden, CT: Archon Books, 1972.

———. *Wesen und Formen der Sympathie*. Bern and Munich: Francke Verlag, 1973. Translated by Peter Heath as *The Nature of Sympathy*. Hamden, CT: Archon Books, 1973.

———. "Zum Sinn der Frauenbewegung." In *Vom Umsturz der Werte*. Bern: Francke Verlag, 1955.

Schopenhauer, Arthur. "Preisschrift über die Grundlagen der Moral." In *Sämtliche Werke* IV. Wiesbaden: 1950. Translated by E. F. J. Payne as "On the Basis of Morality." Indianapolis: Bobbs-Merrill, 1981.

Seifert, Josef. *Was ist und was motiviert eine sittliche Handlung?* Salzburg: Anton Pustet Verlag, 1976.

———. *What Is Life?* Amsterdam/Atlanta: Rodopi, 1997.

Sillem, Edward. *The Philosophical Notebook*. Louvain: Nauwelaerts Publishing House, 1969.

Singer, Peter. *Practical Ethics*. Cambridge: Cambridge University Press, 1979.

Spader, Peter. *Scheler's Ethical Personalism*. New York: Fordham University Press, 2002.

Stith, Richard. "On Death and Dworkin: A Critique of His Theory of Inviolability." *Maryland Law Review* 56.2 (1997) 289–383.
Spaemann, Robert. *Personen*. Stuttgart: Klett-Cotta, 1996.
Stein, Edith, St. "Individuum und Gemeinschaft." *Jahrbuch für Philosophie und phänomenologishe Forschung* 5 (1922), 116–283.
Suarez, Francesco. *De legibus ac de Deo legislatore*. Coimbra, 1612. Translated by J. B. Scott in *The Classics of International Law* 20. Oxford: 1944.
Taylor, Charles. *The Ethics of Authenticity*. Cambridge, MA: Harvard University Press, 1991.
Thomson, Judith Jarvis. "A Defense of Abortion." In *Ethics for Modern Life*, edited by Raziel Abelson and Marie-Louise Friquegnon. New York: St. Martin's Press, 1987.
Tollefsen, Olaf. "Crosby on the Prescriptive Force of Moral Obligation." *The New Scholasticism* 61.4 (1987), 462–76.
van Schaijik, Jules. "Dietrich von Hildebrand on Deliberate Wrongdoing." Unpublished dissertation. International Academy of Philosophy, Principality of Liechtenstein, 2001.
von Balthasar, Hans Urs. *Apokalypse der deutschen Seele*, vol. 3. Salzburg: Anton Pustet Verlag, 1939.
———. "On the Concept of Person." *Communio* 13 (Spring 1986), 18–26.
von Hildebrand, Dietrich. *Das Wesen der Liebe*. Stuttgart: Kohlhamer Verlag, 1971.
———. *Die Idee der sittlichen Handlung*. Darmstadt: Wissen-Schaftliche Buchgesellschaft, 1969.
———. *Dietrich von Hildebrand: Memoiren und Aufätze gegen den Nationalsozialismus, 1933–1938*, edited by Ernst Wenisch. Mainz: Matthias Grünewald Verlag, 1994.
———. *Moralia*. Stuttgart: Kohlhammer Verlag, 1980.
———. *Ethics*. Chicago: Franciscan Herald Press, 1972.
———. *Metaphysik der Gemeinschaft*. Regensburg: Josef Habbel Verlag, 1955.
———. *Reinheit und Jungfräulichkeit*. St. Ottilien, 1981.
White, John. "Scheler's Tripartite Anthropology." *Proceedings of the American Catholic Philosophical Association* 75 (2001).
Wojtyla, Karol. *The Acting Person*, edited by Anna-Teresa Tymieniecka. Translated by Andrzej Potocki. Vol. 10 of *Analecta Husserliana*. Dordrecht: D. Reidel, 1979.
———. *Love and Responsibility*. Translated by H. T. Willetts. New York: Farrar, Straus, Giroux, 1981.
———. "Subjectivity and the Irreducible in the Human Being." In *Person and Community: Selected Essays*. Translated by Theresa Sandock, 209–17. New York: Peter Lang, 1993.
———. "Über die Möglichkeit, eine christliche Ethik in Anlehnung an Max Scheler zu schaffen." In *Primat des Geistes*. Stuttgart: Seewald Verlag, 1980.
Zagzebski, Linda. "The Uniqueness of Persons." *Journal of Religious Ethics* 29.3 (Fall 2001) 401–23.

Index

Alcibiades, 12n, 214–15, 219–20
Anscombe, Elizabeth, 110n
Aristotle, 6, 14, 22, 69n, 138, 157, 162n, 177, 186, 194–95, 204, 208, 210, 211, 247–48, 262
Augustine, St., 133n, 194–98, 200–201, 203–7, 211–12, 219, 258
Averroism, 36–37, 147, 157

Beethoven, Ludwig van, 62, 192
Bergson, Henri, 146, 184
body, 7, 51–52, 113–27, 249–63
  estrangement of person from, 113–14, 117–27, 253
  "nuptial meaning of the body," 48, 254–55, 258–59
  Wojtyla on embodiment, 113–17, 121, 244, 252–63
  See also dualism of person and body; personalism; Wojtyla, Karol
Bolt, Robert, 102

Chesterton, G. K., 205
Cicero, 206
Clarke, Norris, S.J., 247n
common guilt *(Gemeinschuld)*, 161, 168, 174–93
  two kinds of, 181–83
  See also co-responsibility; individualism; Scheler, Max; solidarity
common human nature, 6–11, 13, 15–18, 20–24, 27, 29, 48–50, 56, 62, 69, 79–80, 132, 148–49, 191n, 233
  and replaceability, 9–11
  unity with incommunicable person, 15–18

conscience, 64–92, 93–112
  as contrasted with superego, 93–112
  Fromm on, 101–4, 106–7
  Newman on, 70–71, 73, 75–76, 80, 102, 104, 105–6, 110, 112
  Rahner (and Maritain) on concrete moral tasks, 170–72
  Scheler on personal vocation, 164–72
  religious dimension of, 84–92, 110–12
  See also superego
consciousness and person (personhood)
  irreducibility of person to consciousness, 131–41
  Locke on consciousness and person, 128–31
  personhood of the human embryo, 124n, 128–29, 136–37, 140–41
co-responsibility, 62, 161, 168, 174–79, 181–84, 186–92. *See also* common guilt; individualism; solidarity; Scheler, Max
Crosby, John F., ix, 41n, 42n, 65n, 76n, 78, 107n, 124n, 130n, 133, 135n, 137n, 151n, 241n
Curran, Charles, 114n

de Tocqueville, Alexis, 57–58
dignity of persons, 3–32, 63, 75, 105, 250–52, 256
  and incommunicability (unrepeatability), 7–32
  distinct from rights, 4–5
  related to God, 3–4, 24–27
  See also common human nature; incommunicability; Zagzebski, Linda

271

Dostoevsky, Fyodor, 62, 177, 188n, 192–93.
    See also common guilt (co-responsibility); solidarity
dualism of person and body, 117–19, 192, 253, 263
    and consequentialism, 125–26
    and in vitro fertilization, 121–23
    distinction between person and biological humanity, 123–24
    Locke on, 129
    See also personalism
Dupré, Louis, 85n, 89n, 135n
Dworkin, Ronald, 21n, 29–32, 150n

empathy *(Nachfühlen)*, 33–63, 188n, 189n
    and solidarity, 57–63
    distinguished from non-empathetic understanding, 36–40, 54–55
    distinguished from sympathy *(Mitgefühl)*, 38
    Scheler on, 33, 38–56, 188n

Fichte, Johann Gottlieb, 147
Finkielkraut, Alain, 14n
Finnis, John, 64–66, 68–69, 71, 74–75, 77, 79–85, 87–88, 91–92, 177n, 203
Fletcher, Joseph, 117
Francis of Assisi, St., 159n
freedom, 6n, 15, 49, 83n, 88, 105, 109, 114–15, 125, 130–31, 134, 194, 197–200, 204n, 206–10, 211, 219–20, 246, 251 258.
    See also von Hildebrand, Dietrich
Freud, Sigmund, 93–94, 96–97, 100–101
Fromm, Erich, 98–104, 106–7, 112. *See also* superego

Gaudium et spes, 89n, 187n, 246
German Idealism, 84, 146–47
Grabowski, John S., 114n
Gracia, Jorge, 21n, 148–49, 151n, 152, 155–56, 157n
Greek philosophy, 6, 14–15, 149, 150n, 161, 167n
Gregory of Nyssa, St., 130
Grisez, Germain, 64–66, 71, 75, 77, 80–81, 84–85, 203, 204n

Hegel, Georg Wilhelm Friedrich, 147

Herbart, Johann Friedrich, 90
Hocking, W. E., 89n
human. *See* common human nature; person, distinct from human
Husserl, Edmund, 24, 172

"image of God"
    and unrepeatability, 27n
    and interpersonal relations, 258, 259n
incommunicability (unrepeatability), ix, 7–32, 42, 47, 49, 53, 58, 60, 63, 88, 148, 161–63, 172, 185, 234, 252
    distinguished from communicability, 6–14
    unity with common human nature, 15–18
    See also dignity of persons, individuality
individualism, 159–61, 169, 175–76, 178, 189, 191–92
individuality, 21n, 39n, 145–73, 159
    and person, 148
    principle of individuation, 18, 147, 155–59
    person as "absolute individual," 155
    See also incommunicability; person; Scheler, Max

James, William, 86–87, 111

Kafka, Franz, 98
Kant, Immanuel, 75–76, 78, 83, 84n, 90, 102, 105, 109, 146–47, 166, 170, 185
Kelsen, Hans, 90n
Kierkegaard, Søren, 199, 235
Küng, Hans, 74n

Levinas, Emmanuel, 14, 42, 169n
Levi-Strauss, Claude, 61–62
Lewis, C. S., 202
Locke, John, 128–41 *passim. See especially* 128–31

Maritain, Jacques, ix, 148, 170
May, William E., 64, 66, 92n
moral obligation, 64–92, 101–10
    categorical force, 105
    discrepancy between finite goods and obligation, 70–79

Index

grounded in finite goods and values, 75–76, 77, 80, 83
impact on person, 76–79, 87–88, 102–8
religious significance, 84–92, 110–12
See also conscience; superego
More, St. Thomas, 102–3, 106
Mounier, Emmanuel, 148, 168n
Moussorgsky, Modest, 103

Nagel, Thomas, 37
Neuhaus, Richard John, 174–75
Nietzsche, Friedrich, 100–101, 146, 183–84
Newman, John Henry, ix, 40, 76, 79–80, 136, 221–42
  empathy, 49–50, 231–33
  "infinite abyss of existence," 40, 46, 88–89, 112, 136, 140
  opposition to Liberalism, 238–42
  personal influence, 221–42
  personal reasoning, 228–29, 230–31
  real and notional assent, 234–38
  religious significance of conscience, 84–92, 110–12
  two meanings of conscience, 70–71, 73, 80, 92, 101–6
Nygren, Anders, 3n

Otto, Rudolf, 75n, 85, 105n

Parfit, Derek, 8n
Paul, St., 49–50, 108–9, 194, 210, 212, 233
person (personhood), *passim*
  and individuality, 145–73
  cosmological and personalist view of, 114–16, 208–9
  dignity of, 3–32, 63, 75, 105, 250–52, 256
  distinguished from human, 8, 123–24
  embodiment of, 113–27, 244, 249–63
  equality of persons, 22–23, 58–59, 247–48
  See also dignity of persons; dualism of person and body; empathy; incommunicability; individuality; Scheler, Max; subjectivity
personalism
  as opposed to individualism and collectivism, ix

"incarnational" and "spiritualistic" ("gnostic"), 118–27, 252–61
Petrarch, 17
Plato, 6, 12n, 14, 127n, 129n, 138, 172–73, 186, 210
Platonic intellectualism, 204, 211–20
Pope John Paul II, 113–14, 125–27, 130, 243n, 245n, 247n, 248–49, 253, 258, 261n, 262
  solidarity and repentance, 178, 180, 182
  See also Wojtyla, Karol
Pope Paul VI, 259
Pope Pius IX, 222
Pope Pius X, 241
Pope Pius XII, 259
Pushkin, Alexander, 103

Rahner, Karl, S.J., 170–72
Ramsey, Paul, 3, 25–26
Reale, Giovanni, 211
Rowe, Christopher, 217n

Sartre, Jean-Paul, 256n
Scheler, Max, ix, 15n, 21n, 28n, 33–35, 69n, 83, 90, 94–97, 100, 121n, 145–73, 174–93, 212, 250, 255n, 256
  Lebensphilosophie, antagonism to, 146, 153, 184–85
  collective person (*Gesamtperson*), 159, 187n, 189–91
  collective subjectivity (and co-experiencing), 35–36, 38–39, 60–61, 63, 190
  common guilt (*Gemeinschuld*)/ co-responsibility, 174–93
  compared with Rahner, 170–72
  critique of analogical reasoning theory, 51–53
  knowledge of personal individuality, 161–63
  empathy, 33, 38–56, 188n
  heteropathic identification, 95–97, 100–101, 107, 160
  individual value-essence, 163–69, 185
  personal vocation, 163–69, 170–72
  principle of personal individuation, 155–59
  ressentiment, 183
  solidarity and repentance, 62n, 174–93

Schiller, Friedrich, 192
Schopenhauer, Arthur, 39n, 84n, 147, 154
Seifert, Josef, 6n, 73n
Shylock, 58
Sillem, Edward, 221, 242
Singer, Peter, 9–11, 13, 18, 30
Socrates 137–38, 140, 194–96, 212–15. *See also* Plato
solidarity, 14n, 33, 36, 45, 49, 56, 161, 168–69, 174–93
   and empathy, 57–63
   See also Scheler, Max
Spader, Peter, 164
Spaemann, Robert, 8n
Stein, Edith, 190n
Stith, Richard, 21n, 29–32, 150n
Suarez, Francisco, 64–70, 79–80, 84, 90–91
   on moral obligation, 66–68
   two senses of moral law, 66, 70
subjectivity
   and conscience, 106–7
   as distinct from subjectivism, 116, 245
   first and third person perspective, 34, 36, 38, 39, 42
   hiddenness of, 34–37, 43
   moral subjectivity, 76–79
   Wojtyla's essay, "Subjectivity and the Irreducible in the Human Being," 114–17, 208, 244–47
   See also empathy; person
superego, 93–112 *passim*
   in contrast to conscience, 101–9
   Fromm on, 98–104
   See also conscience
sympathy *(Mitgefühl). See* empathy

Taylor, A. E., 215
Taylor, Charles, 168–69

Thomas Aquinas, St., 8, 15, 20–21, 126n, 157, 175, 207–8, 231
Thomson, Judith Jarvis, 191–93
Tollefsen, Olaf, 65n, 73n, 89–91

unrepeatability. *See* incommunicability

van Schaijik, Jules, 208n
Vatican Council II. *See Gaudium et spes*
von Balthasar, Hans Urs, 12n, 145–46, 148, 158–59, 167n, 175n, 177n, 184–86, 190n
von Hildebrand, Dietrich, ix, 73n, 100n, 119n, 194, 200–210, 212n
   community of mankind, 188n
   deliberate wrongdoing, 200–207
   experience of moral obligation, 106–8
   merely subjectively satisfying, 201–5
   personal vocation, 106–8, 165–66
   personalist contributions, 208–9
   value, 69n, 75n, 201

White, John R., 153n
Wojtyla, Karol (Pope John Paul II), ix, 76, 83n, 107n, 175, 243–263
   "genius of woman," 261–63
   "nuptial meaning of the body," 48, 254–55, 258–59
   on embodiment, 113–17, 121, 244, 252–63
   self-donation, 116, 246–48, 252–58, 262
   Wojtyla's essay, "Subjectivity and the Irreducible in the Human Being," 114–17, 208, 244–47
   theology of the body, 253–54, 257n, 258
   See also Pope John Paul II

Zagzebski, Linda, 14n, 27–29. *See also* dignity of persons

Personalist Papers was designed and composed in Minion by Kachergis Book Design of Pittsboro, North Carolina. It was printed on 60-pound Westminster Natural and bound by McNaughton & Gunn, Inc., of Saline, Michigan.

www.ingramcontent.com/pod-product-compliance
Lightning Source LLC
Chambersburg PA
CBHW032030290426
44110CB00012B/739